PROFIT OVER PRIVACY

PROFIT OVER PRIVACY

How Surveillance Advertising Conquered the Internet

MATTHEW CRAIN

University of Minnesota Press

Minneapolis

London

Published by the University of Minnesota Press
111 Third Avenue South, Suite 290
Minneapolis, MN 55401-2520
http://www.upress.umn.edu

ISBN 978-1-5179-0504-0 (hc)
ISBN 978-1-5179-0505-7 (pb)
Library of Congress record available at https://lccn.loc.gov/2021022890.

Printed in the United States of America on acid-free paper

The University of Minnesota is an equal-opportunity educator and employer.

UMP BmB 2021

FOR CORRINE

A book about advertising therefore becomes inevitably a critique of the society.

JAMES RORTY, *OUR MASTER'S VOICE*

CONTENTS

Introduction   1

1 The Revolution Will Be Commercialized   19

2 A Framework for Global Electronic Commerce   41

3 The Web Gets a Memory   57

4 The Dot-com Bubble   75

5 Surveillance Advertising Takes Shape   93

6 The Privacy Challenge   113

7 The Legacy of the Dot-com Era   135

Acknowledgments   149
Notes   151
Index   189

INTRODUCTION

THE RACE TO COMMERCIALIZE THE INTERNET IS OVER. Advertising is the big winner. This is excellent news if you are an executive or major shareholder of one of the handful of companies that dominates the $330 billion global digital advertising economy.[1] For almost everyone else, advertising's good fortunes have meant the erosion of privacy, autonomy, and security, as well as a weakening of the collective means to hold power accountable. This is because the industry's economic success is rooted in its virtually unrestrained monetization of consumer surveillance. Digital advertising technologies are widely distributed, but largely operate under the control of a few giant companies whose monopoly-like market power has, among other ills, unleashed a wave of manipulative communication and deepened a revenue crisis among the nation's most important journalism outlets. For the ownership class of Silicon Valley, digital advertising is a gold mine of epic proportions. For democratic society, it is gasoline on a fire.

This book is about how the race to commercialize the net was won two decades ago by the purveyors of what I call surveillance advertising, a business model based on persistent and invasive data collection. At its core, surveillance advertising uses data to try to find ever more effective ways to predict and influence people's behaviors and attitudes.[2] As your friendly neighborhood advertising historian will tell you, companies, politicians, and other groups have long been interested in knowing and influencing many kinds of publics. Surveillance advertising on the internet is not so much a new development as it is an acceleration of long-standing social trends at the intersection of technology, marketing, politics, and capitalism at large.

To unpack these dynamics, this book traces the historical construction of surveillance advertising to the 1990s, when the new technology of the World Wide Web was transformed from an outpost on the fringes of business to a central nervous system for commercial monitoring. To paraphrase Thomas Streeter, surveillance advertising is not something that happened; it is something that was done.[3] The massive data collection infrastructure that undergirds the internet today is the result of twenty-five years of technical and political economic engineering. Surveillance advertising was created by marketers, technology start-ups, investors, and politicians, a coalition bound by the desire to commercialize the web as quickly as possible. Through bouts of competition and collaboration, private and public sector interests steered digital networks toward maximizing their monitoring and influence capacities, tilling the soil for all manner of deceptive communication practices and wreaking havoc on less invasive media business models. The legacy of this period is the concentration of surveillance capacity in corporate hands and the normalization of consumer monitoring across all digital media platforms. Although certainly not the only way to write this history, this book is my attempt to give surveillance advertising an origin story.

The political and economic roots of surveillance advertising are important pieces of a larger conversation about internet companies and the power they wield in society. This conversation went mainstream in 2018 as journalists, tech workers, activists, and academics investigated and publicized a cascade of scandals coming from Silicon Valley. In what became known as the techlash, the world's biggest internet companies faced international public rebuke over controversies around gender discrimination, appalling labor conditions, lax data security, anticompetitive behavior, tax avoidance, addictive product design, algorithmic bias, and objectionable military contracts.[4] Public opinion cratered as pollsters reported that "few Americans trust major tech companies to consistently do what is right."[5]

Facebook was at the epicenter of the techlash.[6] Despite efforts by company leaders to avoid culpability and downplay the scope of problems, a public relations crisis erupted when two interrelated scandals spiraled out of the 2016 U.S. presidential election. In the first case, a seedy U.K.-based data broker firm, Cambridge Analytica, used Facebook's data collection tools to secretly harvest information from 87 million unwitting people in an attempt to build psychological profiles for political advertising operations.[7] The company was hired by Donald Trump's election campaign to, among other tactics, use Facebook's advertising platform to discourage highly specific groups of likely Democratic voters from going to the polls.

Shortly thereafter, Facebook admitted that operatives linked to the Russian government had used its ad system in attempts to spread misinformation, exacerbate political divisions, and influence electoral outcomes.[8] A federal investigation found evidence that Russia had spent millions of dollars on manipulative campaigns designed to aggravate racial tensions and other social frictions among different groups of U.S. citizens.[9] Although the frame of foreign election meddling received outsized attention, investigative journalists later revealed that Democratic Party operatives used similar strategies to try to depress Republican voter turnout in an Alabama Senate race.[10] Evidence continues to pile up that such techniques are used widely by a broad range of political actors. Young Mie Kim's groundbreaking research found that unidentifiable "dark money" groups used Facebook to purchase waves of divisive, microtargeted political advertising across key electoral battleground states.[11] As the scrutiny intensified, Facebook's founder and CEO, Mark Zuckerberg, was called to congressional hearings to testify about his company's information practices. Making his way up the steps of Capitol Hill, Zuckerberg passed demonstrators holding signs that said "Stop Corporate Spying."[12]

The vitriol levied at Facebook around the election reflected a deeper complaint: the pervasive consumer surveillance at the heart of the internet's advertising business model was out of control. The large reserves of public goodwill that Facebook, Google, and the like had enjoyed for much of their existence seemed to be running dry. Certainly these companies had faced criticism in the past—as one journalist put it, "Power breeds resentment"—but the techlash was different in that it fostered more than disconnected, one-off condemnations of this or that shameful incident.[13] A structural analysis began to take shape, particularly around the collective harms of business models based on surveillance advertising.[14] As Nathalie Maréchal argued, microtargeted advertising "drives company decision making in ways that are ultimately toxic to society."[15] It was becoming widely obvious that consumer data collection was not simply about providing "relevant" ad messages, as ad platforms often claimed. "Their business depends on manipulating behavior," wrote the *Financial Times'* Rana Foroohar. "It is a business model that causes endless collateral damage."[16] Even the creator of the World Wide Web weighed in. "We don't have a technology problem," said Tim Berners-Lee. "We have a social problem."[17]

In this sense, what is important about the techlash is not that it was propelled by a series of extraordinary scandals. It is the realization that these scandals were business as usual, outgrowths of a surveillance advertising system that most people had simply taken for granted as the way the internet works. In a telling observation, the *New York Times* noted that Cambridge Analytica did not need to "build everything from scratch" because "Mark Zuckerberg and others had already built the infrastructure" for them.[18] Facebook and other ad platforms framed the scandals as a matter of "bad actors" hijacking their systems, but this defense was a shallow attempt to obscure the fact that data-driven influence peddling is their industry's bread and butter.[19] Facebook had not been hijacked. Its platform had been used as intended. The same was true for disinformation operations, which simply plugged into the existing digital advertising apparatus to reach groups deemed most susceptible to political influence. Leveraging surveillance to strategically target vulnerable audiences is not some rogue use of digital advertising technology; it is its fundamental feature. Just months before becoming infamous in the election aftermath, Cambridge Analytica received a prestigious award from the Advertising Research Foundation trade group for its cutting-edge work in psychological profiling.[20] As Dipayan Ghosh and Ben Scott put it in their summary of the election scandals, this stuff is "digital marketing 101."[21]

The Business of Surveillance Advertising

Today more money is spent on digital advertising—meaning online and mobile formats—than on any other media channel in the United States.[22] Analysts estimate that more than half of global ad spending goes to digital platforms.[23] Consumer monitoring is now effectively ubiquitous under what Julia Angwin calls a "dragnet" of surveillance.[24] This system depends on an infrastructure of data collection and targeted messaging that undergirds nearly all modern digital media. Leading ad platforms like Google and Facebook operate vast networks of surveillance that extend well beyond their own sites and applications. A study of one million popular websites found that nearly 90 percent collect and exchange data with external third parties of which most users are unaware.[25] From period-tracker apps to porn sites, ad platforms scoop up all manner of sensitive personal information to power their "digital influence machine."[26] Privacy has been obliterated as surveillance advertisers have created numerous ways to link online and off-line information.[27] According to internet security expert Bruce Schneier, internet privacy is a lost cause: "There are simply too many ways to be tracked."[28]

Surveillance advertisers use data to build consumer profiles, sorting people into various categories and rating them against any number of predictive benchmarks such as creditworthiness, propensity to buy a luxury car, or risk for alcoholism. Facebook maintains profiles not only for its 2.7 billion users but also for people who have never signed up for any of the company's services.[29] Seemingly innocuous data can be used to make startling and intimate predictions. In a highly publicized 2013 study, researchers were able to divine a range of sensitive personal attributes using only Facebook "likes."[30] Personality traits, political and religious views, sexual orientation—all were predicted with high accuracy. A follow-up study found computational derivation of personality traits based on people's digital footprints to be more accurate than judgments made by friends and family members.[31] As one headline put it: "Facebook knows you better than your mom."[32]

The business objective of all of this data collection and profiling is to sell the capacity to influence people's actions and attitudes, what Shoshanna Zuboff calls the "means of behavioral modification."[33] Today, the cutting edge of this practice uses data signals to forecast and test people's vulnerability to different kinds of appeals.[34] Advertising that is designed to exploit emotions and personality traits has been found to be particularly promising.[35] Internal documents leaked in 2017 show that Facebook claimed its ad platform could predict the emotional states of teenage users to enable advertisers to reach those who feel "worthless" and "insecure" in real time.[36] The unspoken premise was that emotionally vulnerable consumers are more pliable to persuasion.

Yet there is good cause to be skeptical of claims about surveillance advertisers' persuasive power. As Cory Doctorow argues, microtargeted advertising is more a sales pitch aimed at marketers than a consumer mind-control ray.[37] Despite the proclamations of self-interested proponents and well-meaning critics, many studies find that internet advertising is not all that effective at modifying consumer behavior.[38] But, as Doctorow points out, focusing on the effectiveness of a given ad campaign misses the forest for the trees. Leading advertising platforms like Google and Facebook have created a global communications infrastructure grounded in covert surveillance and asymmetrical control over information. In building these kinds of systems, ad platforms encourage, naturalize, and profit from manipulative and discriminatory behaviors by their clients, rendering internet users as little more than marks to be sold to the highest bidder.

Surveillance advertising is a propulsive force in creating what Robert McChesney calls a "golden age of insincere communication."[39] This explains how it was business as usual when the British army used Facebook to run a recruitment campaign targeting sixteen-year-olds around the time that standardized test results were released, typically a moment of heightened anxiety about the future.[40] The ads suggested that students who were disappointed in their academic performance should pursue a career in the armed forces, rather than, say, aim to attend university. In 2015, antiabortion groups used mobile geofencing to send ads to women who visited reproductive health clinics across the United States. The emotionally charged messages were triggered via GPS location data and were sent to women up to thirty days after leaving the clinics.[41] Time and again, researchers have documented how the negative impacts of commercial surveillance disproportionately affect marginalized communities.[42]

The surveillance advertising industry is dominated by two ad platforms, Google and Facebook, which together control nearly three quarters of the U.S. internet advertising market.[43] These companies are the world's foremost purveyors of commercial surveillance and among the most valuable corporations in existence. Market power and political power are deeply intertwined. Google is not only the leading lobbyist in the tech sector. It is also the largest lobbyist in the United States, maintaining a "55,000 square foot office, roughly the size of the White House, less than a mile away from the Capitol Building."[44] In the wake of the techlash, surveillance advertisers mounted a lobbying offensive to stave off the threat of potential government regulation.[45] As the *Guardian* wrote in a headline: "Forget Wall Street, Silicon Valley is the new political power in Washington."[46]

One of the most troubling outgrowths of the Google/Facebook duopoly is that their market dominance has exacerbated a revenue crisis among U.S. news organizations. For over a decade, news outlets have been confronting a death spiral in which declining ad revenue prompts cutbacks and layoffs, which reduce the quantity and quality of news production, which further depresses revenue. Although the problem is multifaceted, the fact that 70 percent of online advertising spending in the United States goes to Google and Facebook means that news organizations must compete with every other ad-supported internet service for the scraps.[47]

Newspapers, still the most important source of original reporting, have suffered the worst. According to the Pew Research Center, the total number of newsroom employees in the newspaper sector was cut in half between

2006 and 2018.[48] As ad platforms have grown rich using consumer data to power targeted advertising, news organizations have shuttered their doors at an alarming rate. Paper closures have created a dramatic expansion of what Penelope Muse Abernathy calls "news deserts." Today, "half of the 3,143 counties in the country now have only one newspaper, usually a small weekly, attempting to cover its various communities."[49] The dismal outcome of this journalism crisis, writes Victor Pickard, is "a lack of public access to high-quality information, a loss of diverse voices and viewpoints, and the evisceration of public service journalism."[50]

The median annual salary for newspaper reporters is about $35,000.[51] In 2018, Mark Zuckerberg earned the same amount roughly every seventy-five seconds.[52] One of the richest people on earth, Zuckerberg owns estates and properties in Lake Tahoe, Hawaii, San Francisco, and Palo Alto. Shortly after purchasing the Palo Alto residence, Zuckerberg spent an additional $45 million to buy the houses of his four immediate neighbors—you know, for privacy.

It didn't have to be this way. No law of nature says that every new communications technology must be harnessed to the cause of advertising, let alone transformed into an engine of systemic consumer surveillance. Although there were strong social pressures to bring advertising to the internet, there was no guarantee such efforts would succeed, particularly not on the World Wide Web, which was released into the public domain by Tim Berners-Lee in the hopes that it might become a "universal medium for sharing information."[53] Early web technology was designed to be open-ended and flexible, but it was also anonymous and nonintuitive, hardly optimized to serve the marketing needs of business. So how exactly did we get here? One might look to Silicon Valley itself for some answers.

What's Politics Got to Do with It?

One of the more interesting ripples of the techlash has been a procession of Silicon Valley defectors taking to opinion pages and conference daises to lament the state of their industry.[54] Having more or less disembarked from the surveillance advertising money train, a handful of former executives and investors have newly emerged as conscientious objectors. Chamath Palihapitiya, who served as Facebook's vice president of growth, confessed that he felt "tremendous guilt" for his role in the company's global expansion, even though it made him extremely wealthy.[55] After condemning his former employer for "creating tools that are ripping apart the fabric of society," Palihapitiya added: "I don't use this shit and my kids are not allowed to use this shit."

Another prominent voice in this chorus belongs to venture capitalist Roger McNamee, an early Facebook funder and erstwhile mentor to Mark Zuckerberg. In a *New York Times* op-ed titled "A Brief History of How Your Privacy Was Stolen," McNamee decried the tech sector's embrace of "business models based on surveillance and manipulation."[56] According to McNamee, there are two major causes at play. One is that technological innovation has removed prior constraints on data gathering and processing, making it easier than ever to push the norms of decency in business. The other is a recent cultural shift in Silicon Valley, whereby company leaders and investors have moved away from ethical capitalism to pursue aggressive, greedy, and monopolistic business practices. As Google and Facebook raked in the profits, ethics were thrown out the window, and consumer surveillance began to flourish in more industries across the economy.

For McNamee, these shifts have "transformed capitalism"[57] to such an unpleasant degree that it is now necessary for the government to step in. Although he rightly calls attention to the growing harms of commercial surveillance, McNamee's account rests on the idea that the marriage between technology and capitalism has only recently become dysfunctional, and now that things have gone off the rails, external political forces must be marshaled to bring things back into proper alignment. In this telling, the techlash represents an aberration from a benevolent technocapitalism that normally functions largely outside of politics. The state enters into the picture only as a last resort, the bumbling sheriff summoned to rein in the excesses of power-hungry villains like Mark Zuckerberg, Peter Thiel, and the "PayPal mafia."[58]

This book makes a different case. Surveillance advertising has never existed outside of politics. On the contrary, like every other communications system in existence, the internet's prevailing economic structure has been heavily shaped by public policy. Perhaps the most important policies are those created by what Paul Starr calls "constitutive choices," the formative decisions that have structuring effects on subsequent media system development.[59] For example, various forms of legislation, regulation, and government subsidy were foundational to the establishment of U.S. commercial broadcasting in the 1920s and 1930s. It was the Federal Radio Commission, at the behest of Congress and the executive branch, that "cleared the dial" of many public and nonprofit broadcasters to give exclusive licenses (for free) to some of the nation's most powerful technology companies.[60] From that point forward, broadcasting proceeded almost entirely on advertising-supported basis.

In the absence of public activism, the state has reliably made media policy in service of private sector interests, but no political outcome is ever guaranteed. Commercial radio was highly contested, as evidenced not only by organized citizen opposition but also by the decisions of peer nations like Great Britain to reject advertising and establish alternative public models.[61] Ideally, democratic political institutions should provide countervailing levers of control over media development, though U.S. history shows a mixed track record in that regard.[62] Nevertheless, even in the face of strong structural inertia, there are always real political choices to be made, especially during a platform's formative years. The internet was no exception.

For surveillance advertising, two moments of policy making stand out as particularly important. The first was the overarching decision that the internet would be privatized and commercialized. Beginning in the late 1980s, federal policy makers worked closely with a range of commercial interests to establish what was framed as a "non-regulatory, market oriented" approach to internet policy.[63] The guiding principle was that the private sector would lead internet system development, and the government's primary role was to facilitate private profits. This left a regulatory vacuum around consumer data collection and gave the nascent online advertising industry free rein to build business models around hidden surveillance.

The latter moment occurred at the end of the 1990s, when the progenitors of today's surveillance advertising behemoths faced the very first public activism for internet privacy. Responding to increasingly invasive data collection practices, a coalition of advocacy groups mounted a campaign to convince legislators to reverse the government's laissez-faire approach to internet privacy. Despite the public concern, Congress and the White House prioritized the growth of the commercial internet over serious consideration of the ramifications of a surveillance-based digital economy. Though largely overshadowed by the web's mythos of friction-free markets and entrepreneurialism, the regulatory foundations of modern commercial internet surveillance were forged in this period through negotiations over privacy policies, user consent, data merging, and industry self-regulation.

McNamee's framing of Silicon Valley's moral failure hews closely to

Shoshanna Zuboff's influential theory of "surveillance capitalism."[64] Zuboff's premise is that the relationship between technology, business, and consumer data under surveillance capitalism represents a marked deviation from prior modes of economic production. For Zuboff, capitalism has gone "rogue."[65] Much like diagnoses that ignore the net's political foundations, this position disregards historical continuities to focus only on what is new.[66] Although the magnitude of contemporary commercial surveillance is certainly mind-bending, the system reflects enduring structural imperatives within a capitalist political economy dependent on perpetual growth.[67] As Douglas Rushkoff notes, when we point to "corruption" as the source of technology woes, "we are implying that something initially pure has been corrupted by some bad actors."[68] Concentrating on bad actors often means ignoring the political economic forces that have incentivized surveillance advertising and so fabulously rewarded its most successful practitioners.

Neil Postman once proposed that the first question to ask about a new technology must be: "What is the problem to which this technology is a solution?"[69] Adding another layer of inquiry, Raymond Williams argued that "the key question about a technological response to a need is less a question about the need itself than about its place in an existing social situation."[70] In other words, what matters is not only who shapes technology and for what purpose, but also the social position of both the shapers and the purposes. Surveillance advertising has been developed as a tool to help marketers understand, predict, and control consumer behavior. It is a technological response to a concrete business problem: how do we sell more stuff as efficiently as possible? But surveillance advertising also reflects a broader set of deeply rooted social needs within the capitalist political economy. To answer both Postman and Williams, the structural problem surveillance advertising is meant to address is the accumulation of capital, arguably among the most pressing needs of the most powerful people in our society for quite some time.

A Political Economy of Surveillance Advertising

Internet advertising was precipitated by a commercial mass media system that, over the course of the twentieth century, came to play a central role in the global economy. Rather than a break from the past, supercharged online surveillance is better understood as an acceleration of ongoing trends within what might be called the marketing complex. Although advertising is sometimes discussed as a single industry, it is really a nexus of business activity across many institutions and economic sectors. Companies of all kinds spend money on advertising to reach new and existing customers. They hire ad agencies, public relations firms, and many variations in between to create and execute strategic communication campaigns on their behalf. Most of this money flows through various kinds of media outlets, which earn revenue by selling access to their audiences. John Sinclair summarizes all of this as an "assemblage of interests we can think of as the manufacturing/marketing/media complex."[71]

Adapting Sinclair's phrase, I use the term "marketing complex" as a shorthand to describe the various private sector institutions that sought to mold the new interactive media of the 1990s into an efficient tool for advertising. My emphasis on marketers is deliberate because although advertising puts a lot of coins in a lot of pockets, the purse is largely controlled by companies looking for ways to drive consumption. Still, the marketing complex is a roomy concept that allows for internal divisions, disagreements, and competition among its participants, all of which are held together by a basic need to continuously enlarge the social canvas on which advertising takes place.

Writing in the 1930s, James Rorty delivered one of the first popular critiques of mass advertising. After working on Madison Avenue, Rorty became disillusioned with what he saw as a profession dedicated to producing vapid and depoliticizing propaganda for consumer capitalism. In a nod to the advertising industry's subservience to marketers, Rorty called his book *Our Master's Voice*.[72] Contemporary internet advertising seems a far cry from the days of sponsored radio broadcasts and print circulars, but there are important continuities in the ways that private sector communications technologies have repeatedly been molded to serve the needs of the marketing complex. Were he alive today, Rorty would no doubt be dismayed, but not surprised, to find that in the era of surveillance advertising, our master's voice has been augmented by our master's eyes and ears.

As its name suggests, the field of political economy of communications provides a useful lens to make sense of the overlapping layers of politics and economics at play in surveillance advertising's historical construction and its relationship to larger structures of social power.[73] This approach helps to foreground how and why particular surveillance technologies and practices were elevated or suppressed as the web congealed around business priorities. In other words, political economy tests the notion that, as Jonathan Hardy succinctly put it, "capitalism influenced the internet more than vice versa."[74]

Historical analysis is foundational to a political economy of surveillance advertising because it denaturalizes prevailing institutional arrangements and social relations, showing the structural forces and human political agency at work. The marketing complex began to coalesce in the late 1800s as the U.S. economy became increasingly organized around mass production and consumption.[75] Manufacturers, retailers, advertising agencies, and media outlets found common interest in building out national consumer markets. The need to rationalize and professionalize the creation of consumer demand within an increasingly productive and centralized corporate capitalism precipitated what Daniel Pope calls "the making of modern advertising."[76] In increasingly concentrated markets, brand advertising became a way for big companies to compete with each other without lowering prices and to erect barriers to keep out potential new competitors.[77]

Although modern ad campaigns took a variety of forms, mass marketing became the prevailing strategy, in alignment with the affordances of industrial printing and broadcasting technologies. Mass-produced goods in the same product category were often more or less equivalent, so advertising was used to create product differentiation, or what Thorstein Veblen called the "production of saleable appearances."[78] Over time, the tone of advertisements shifted from the descriptive nature of early print ads to the more affective character of brand marketing, but the core component of mass media advertising was its reach. Beginning with turn-of-the-century large-circulation newspapers and magazines, and intensifying during the network broadcasting era, "scale was king."[79]

Some degree of market segmentation entered the picture with commercial radio and specialty magazines, but only according to rough estimates of consumer demographics. Gathering and processing detailed information about consumers was for the most part an expensive and time-consuming process. Large swaths of the media sector became dependent on advertising revenue, and on the whole, business was good.[80] Advertising expenditures settled in to account for between 2 and 3 percent of U.S. GDP.[81] Media empires were created as advertising became a "leading edge of global consumerism," serving the ideological and market-building needs of a profitable and astonishingly productive industrial economy.[82]

Things began to shift as the U.S. economy slumped into what Robert Brenner calls the "long downturn," a worldwide period of debilitating stagnation that began in the 1970s and dragged into the early 1990s.[83] To mitigate what became a crisis of profitability, businesses began to reorganize systems of production, finance, and consumption on a global basis.[84] This was a complex and uneven process that hinged on investment in heretofore publicly funded information and communication technologies, from computers to telecommunications networks. Dan Schiller has shown that while commodification of information has always been involved in capital accumulation, the last fifty years have seen information and communication technologies become a vital pole of growth for an emergent "digital capitalism."[85] The political mobilization of private sector interests played a significant role in these changes. In the United States and elsewhere, policies of privatization, deregulation, and "free trade" achieved mainstream orthodoxy under the moniker of neoliberalism.[86]

Compelled by a changing political economy, the marketing complex embarked on its own lurching reconfiguration around information and communication technologies and the systematic integration of consumer data into advertising practices.[87] In the 1980s, ad agencies began to use computer databases to target specific audience demographics through tactical ad placement across media channels.[88] "Customer relationship marketing" strategies such as loyalty programs used data to establish lasting connections with high-value consumers while excluding those deemed undesirable.[89] Though it had been around for many years, consumer surveillance was now seeping into advertising's mainstream.[90] During this period, audience fragmentation and the shifting demographics of the U.S. population put national mass advertising under increasing strain.[91] In 1965, an ad campaign could reach 80 percent of eighteen- to forty-nine-year-old women by purchasing three television commercials; a few decades later, it required nearly a hundred prime-time spots to achieve the same result.[92] For major marketers, these trends threatened a loss of control over a changing media system that had long been dictated by their interests.[93]

By the 1990s, the marketing complex was keenly attuned to the emergence of a new crop of interactive media that included the World Wide Web. The web was simultaneously a danger and opportunity, at once conceivable as advertising's next frontier and its mortal wound. Among the greatest threats was that interactivity would provide individuals with new kinds of media autonomy—perhaps even the power to excise advertising altogether. To turn threat into opportunity, the marketing complex needed the support of the federal government, as well as a push from the investor class of Silicon Valley. The politicians made the rules that governed the web's commercialization, while the venture capitalists, chasing monopoly profits, supplied the cash. Propelled by this structural inertia, the web became what Joseph Turow calls a "test bed" for data-driven advertising.[94] This is the jumping-off place of this book.

Chapter Outlines

In the midst of the economic recession of the early 1990s, policy makers at the highest levels of government were determined to spur growth through free trade agreements and deregulation of telecommunications and finance. In this context, the public sector and noncommercial origins of the internet were jettisoned so that private enterprise could take over to commercialize the digital revolution. Chapter 1 tells this story through examination of internet policy making under the first-term administration of President Bill Clinton. The chapter sketches a genealogy of Clinton's laissez-faire internet agenda, which stemmed as much from neoliberal ideology as from political expedience and the instrumental power of business interests to shape public policy. Many marketers were initially skeptical that the clunky web platform could work as a sales channel, but industry leaders quickly understood that a noncommercial or advertising-adverse medium would undermine their dominant position in the U.S. media system. Chapter 1 shows how the marketing complex ramped up to work with the U.S. government to ensure that the new media, whatever the particular format, would develop in alignment with marketers' overarching business needs.

Drawing on archival records from the Clinton Presidential Library and other sources, the second chapter looks closely at the key articulation of Clinton's second-term internet policy agenda, a document called the *Framework for Global Electronic Commerce*. This chapter develops a case study around the *Framework*'s creation to show how "private sector leadership" was reaffirmed domestically, extended internationally, and applied directly to the burgeoning surveillance advertising industry. Zooming in on the mechanics of policy making debunks the notion that neoliberalism represents a minimalist, nonregulatory approach to governance and reveals the antidemocratic nature of internet commercialization. Public and private sectors worked in close quarters to harmonize their objectives for internet development, and despite disagreements in a few areas, they found a great deal of common ground. At the same time, civil society groups and everyday citizens were largely excluded from closed-door policy discussions.

Chapter 3 addresses the formative business models and technologies of the internet advertising sector. Discussions of surveillance often dwell on a particular technology like the HTTP cookie as a way to point to something concrete that enables consumer data collection. This chapter offers a counterpoint by emphasizing the logistical problems of the advertising business that web technologies were marshaled to solve. Instead of focusing on a specific technical innovation, it is more useful to examine the development of the ad network, a new breed of company that offered centralized ad delivery services to disparate publishers across the web. The most important of these companies was DoubleClick, an early pioneer and enduring market leader that was among the first to integrate surveillance into web advertising in a systematic fashion. DoubleClick exploited the flexible design of the web's communication protocols in order to build a unique system in which every ad served was also an opportunity to gather data about internet users. This created a foundation for the increasingly invasive forms of consumer surveillance that came to occupy the center of the internet advertising industry.

Ad networks propelled the scale and precision of online advertising far beyond what was available at the time, enabling the new industry to make a rapid generational leap. But this growth was dependent on a huge influx of capital that stemmed from the dot-com investment bubble that overtook the U.S. economy in the second half of the 1990s. The fourth chapter revises the legacy of the dot-com bubble as generative of surveillance advertising, looking at the period through the lens of a marketing/finance feedback loop. Internet advertising companies deployed venture capital to roll out new services, acquire competitors, and invest in infrastructure, all while operating at stunning losses. The bubble also played an important role in generating early demand for web advertising. Tech start-ups were among the web's biggest ad spenders, legitimizing the commercial internet at a time when many traditional marketers were still ambivalent about its prospects as a sales channel. The stock market bubble ultimately functioned as a catalyst to surveillance advertising, providing ample material and ideological resources while helping to undermine alternative media revenue models.

Chapter 5 gets to the heart of surveillance advertising's construction. As the financial bubble intensified in the late 1990s, a cadre of ad networks began to reconfigure their business model, shifting focus away from web publishers toward a much greater prize: the massive ad budgets of national marketers. Leveraging outsized financial valuations, ad networks expanded their service offerings, effectively launching a surveillance arms race to improve targeted advertising. I use the lens of platformization to highlight several interconnected trajectories of this buildup, including the creation of new surveillance practices and the broadening of ad networks' ambitions to, as DoubleClick's CEO put it, become the "operating system for advertising on the net."[95] Platformization represented another milestone in internet advertising's evolution whereby web publishers, retailers, and marketers alike—effectively the whole commercial internet—were compelled by market competition to plug into the developing infrastructure of surveillance advertising. Although these systems often remained ungainly, the platform strategy set a template for the modern surveillance advertising monopolists.

Chapter 6 chronicles the country's first public debate over internet privacy. In the late 1990s, a popular backlash against the merging of offline and online data produced a potential crisis for the marketing complex. An emergent advocacy community pressured Congress to consider opt-in legislation mandating that companies obtain prior consent from users before collecting their data. Seeing affirmative consent as a threat to the developing surveillance advertising business model, a coalition of marketing trade associations and newly formed online ad industry groups successfully lobbied to maintain the regime of advertising self-regulation. As advertising became a driving force of the internet's commercialization, political leaders chose to let the industry continue to regulate itself, even as it became clear that the sector was solidifying around practices that were obliterating the privacy norms of the day.

By the end of the decade, a sociotechnical infrastructure for surveillance advertising had been established. Although the financial mania of the dot-com bubble did not last, the business practices, technical infrastructures, and political framework of surveillance advertising endured. The final chapter brings this history up to date, connecting the dots between the first and current generations of surveillance advertising. The chapter focuses on Google, which achieved early success in internet advertising without collecting user data but then changed course after it acquired a relic from the 1990s: the ad network DoubleClick. Google's embrace of consumer monitoring marked the ascendance of the surveillance advertising model, effectively ending the debate about whether market forces would provide solutions to internet privacy issues.

The formative moments of any new technology are particularly salient for structuring its future development.[96] Early policy interventions could have limited surveillance advertising in a number of significant ways, but once momentum and capital accrued, it became increasingly difficult to alter course. With an accommodating political economic framework, surveillance was cemented as the internet's primary business model. When Google and Facebook went on to build advertising empires in the intervening years, they relied on more than just clever technology and heaps of venture capital. They also banked on the political premise that ubiquitous data collection would be permitted by default and that they would be free to build the tools of mass surveillance and targeted persuasion without being held to public account.

In the Introduction of the tenth anniversary edition of *No Logo*, Naomi Klein reflects on the nature of her research for the original book. She notes that once you begin to look deeply into advertising, the conversation broadens to include everything "from how products are made in the deregulated global supply chain to industrial agriculture and commodity prices. Next thing you know you were also talking about the nexus of politics and money that locked in these wild-west rules through free-trade deals. . . . In short, you were talking about how the world works."[97]

Surveillance advertising has been driven by the overarching imperatives of global capitalism: the profit motive; the struggle to find new areas of investment in age of the "long downturn"; the commodification of information; and the hope that the internet's commercialization would engender a new economy free of the painful contractions that plagued previous decades. So although this book is principally about the construction of surveillance advertising on the internet, it is also about the dynamism of a capitalist economic system that must continually push the boundaries of marketing and finance as sites of expansion. To be clear, my argument is not that the internet—past or present—has been totally and irrefutably dominated by commercial interests. To a greater extent than mass media or proprietary computer networks, the public internet has facilitated a range of activity unbound by the discipline of markets. Unlike cable television or Microsoft's Xbox Live gaming network, the web is home to many noncommercial undertakings, including efforts to critique and counter surveillance advertising. But the marginalization of such activities compared to the commercial fortunes of Google, Facebook, and their ilk is undeniable.

The history of surveillance advertising is in many ways the story of the internet's assimilation into the capitalist political economy. This does not mean that internet advertising developed smoothly or without resistance. Numerous people and institutions pursuing myriad objectives have influenced the internet's evolution, which remains ongoing and uneven. There is thus a practical truth to media critic Bob Garfield's quip that attempting to write about the internet is like "sketching the Kentucky Derby."[98] But every race eventually produces winners and losers. Three decades after the introduction of the World Wide Web, it is clear who has won and who has lost.

The contemporary internet is not the only one that could have been constructed. The current iteration—heavily integrated into overbearing systems of commercial surveillance—was built with intention for reasons that can be explained. For those who are interested in changing course, it is important to know how we got here in the first place.

1 THE REVOLUTION WILL BE COMMERCIALIZED

WASHINGTON, D.C., 1993. There were challenging questions in the air, and it was the job of the Information Infrastructure Task Force (IITF) to provide some answers. This group of federal officials, assembled on the order of newly elected President Bill Clinton, was charged with developing a master plan for the rollout of the National Information Infrastructure (NII). One immediate trouble spot was that no one knew exactly what that meant. There was a sense that some form of communications revolution was under way, particularly in the area of networked computing.[1] But even among high-level policy circles, there was little certainty about which technologies and services were about to be revolutionized. Nor was there consensus about what to call the coming technological wonder. Was it the NII? The internet? Or, in the preferred phrase of Vice President Al Gore, the information superhighway?

In its initial report, the IITF opted for a safe approach of covering all bases. The NII was described as "a wide and ever-expanding range of equipment including cameras, scanners, keyboards, telephones, fax machines, computers, switches, compact disks, video and audio tape, cable, wire, satellites, optical fiber transmission lines, microwavenets, televisions, monitors, printers, and much more."[2] For all of the ambiguity, there was one idea that the group quickly came to discuss with confidence and uniformity. This was the understanding that whatever technological form it took, the communications revolution was on a path to undermine individual privacy on a massive scale.

The task force reached this conclusion after convening a privacy working group to examine the relationship between interactive technologies and the growth of private sector consumer databases.[3] In a series of reports between 1993 and 1995, the group warned of an "increased risk to privacy in the evolving NII" owing to the automatic generation and capture of personal data around an increasing array of communication activities.[4] They noted that networked computing was making it easier than ever to collect, store, transmit, and reuse consumer information. Although privacy policy in the United States had heretofore focused primarily on how government agencies handle personal data, the IITF observed that "the private sector now rivals the government in acquiring and using personal information."

Among the group's top concerns were forecasts of "on-line profiling," a method of marketing research that compiled consumer information in ways that were "previously impossible or economically impractical." They elaborated:

> Before the NII, in order to build a profile of an individual who had lived in various states, one would have to travel from state to state and search public records for information about the individual. This process would have required filling out forms, paying fees, and waiting in line for record searches at local, state, and federal agencies, such as the departments of motor vehicles, deed record offices, electoral commissions, and county record offices. Although one could manually compile a personal profile in this manner, it would be a time-consuming and costly exercise, one that would not be undertaken unless the offsetting rewards were considerable. In sharp contrast, today, as more and more personal information appears on-line, such a profile can be built in a matter of minutes, at minimal cost.[5]

A parallel study by the National Telecommunications and Information Administration (NTIA) affirmed the idea that the commercial internet would bring increased privacy risks and again pointed to consumer profiling as an area of particular concern.[6] In a notable passage, the NTIA argued that market forces would induce "providers of telecommunications and information services to become more sophisticated and aggressive" in their data collection efforts.[7] As these government analysts understood it, the commercialization of the internet was about to unleash a vast market for personal information that would propel new and existing companies alike to develop surveillance capacities in direct tension with consumers' privacy expectations.

Both the IITF and NTIA warned that current regulations around electronic data collection were inadequate for the technological and market changes ahead. The analysts framed the problem as about balancing the competing social goods of individual privacy on the one hand and the economic benefits of "free flow of information" on the other. Building on a decades-old conception of "fair information practices," they sketched out a privacy framework grounded in two basic principles: notice and choice.[8] The idea was that people should be given notice about data collection practices so that they may choose whether to participate or not, but also that certain standards of privacy protection must apply universally.

The NTIA explicitly rejected what it called a "pure contractual approach" where individuals and businesses would hash out the rules around data collection among themselves on a case-by-case basis.[9] Such an approach requires, at minimum, a competitive marketplace so that consumers can "walk away from transactions that do not provide adequate privacy protection, secure in the knowledge that other offers will be readily available."[10] Warning of the historical lack of competition in the telecommunications sector, the NTIA advocated instead for a uniform set of privacy safeguards. Without universal protections, the agency argued, consumers would be at a considerable disadvantage in the coming privacy marketplace. A free market for privacy would inevitably mean that the most powerful internet companies would be "free" to dictate data practices without fear of competitive reprisal. Consumers would be forced to submit to unwanted surveillance or abstain altogether from using the new communications services.

From today's vantage point, this early analysis is striking for two reasons. One is just how accurate the government's predictions were, especially considering they were written at a time when internet advertising was still considered a fringe experiment. While many marketers were focused on "interactive TV" and CD-ROMs, the wonks at the IITF and NTIA understood that the internet was an infrastructure for collecting and processing data, and that commercializing these functions would unleash an unprecedented wave of consumer surveillance. The analysts also thoughtfully discussed policy options for mitigating the privacy harms that were sure to flow from this scenario. Although one can disagree with their approach to addressing such harms, their basic diagnosis was correct: If we leave this to markets, a privacy disaster awaits.[11]

The second striking thing is how little these warnings actually mattered. Despite credible analysis of the dangers of commercializing personal information on the internet, decision makers at the highest levels made it a priority to give business free rein to do just that. As I explain in this chapter and the next, the bedrock organizing concept for federal internet policy in the 1990s was the maximization of private sector control. In matters of consumer data, this mandate was implemented via a sustained pattern of government inaction grounded in the faith that markets would solve any privacy problems that might arise. Time and time again, beginning with the state's own early warnings, calls for universal privacy safeguards were ignored in favor of a patchwork of industry "self-regulation"—the very conditions that the NTIA had identified as inimical to privacy protection.

With the support of the White House, Congress, and the Federal Trade Commission (FTC), an emergent internet advertising sector framed the policy vacuum as a victory for "consumer empowerment."[12] Privacy became a market transaction like any other. Individuals were "free" to bargain with companies over their data collection practices, "empowered" to take their privacy into their own hands. By the end of the 1990s, the first generation of the surveillance advertising industry was firing on all cylinders, enabled by a near total lack of regulatory constraint or public interest commitment. The current state of commercial internet surveillance is a direct continuation of this policy foundation, itself an element of the federal government's broader efforts to privatize and commercialize the internet as quickly as possible. On the whole, business interests have been well served by this half-baked implementation of market-based privacy controls—and everyone else, much less so. Why, then, were serious reservations about consumer surveillance swept under the rug at the time when they might have mattered most?

New Democrats on the Information Superhighway

"It's the economy, stupid." This was the unofficial slogan of Bill Clinton and Al Gore's 1992 presidential campaign, waged in the midst of a lingering recession. Although there is nothing remarkable about politicians campaigning on the economy, Clinton's platform foregrounded the unique role of information technology as an "engine of growth."[13] Prosperity, Clinton argued, hinged on the country's capacity to develop and commercialize advanced technology, especially in the domains of computing and telecommunications. Clinton's selection of Al Gore as running mate was strategic in this regard. As a member of the House and Senate, Gore had been a leading proponent of federal investment in information technology and an evangelist about the broad social gains that would flow from a new American communications revolution.

On the campaign trail, Clinton and Gore spoke about their vision for an "information superhighway," a high-speed communications network that would revitalize the flagging economy by spawning "dozens of new information industries" and providing cutting-edge services to businesses, schools, and hospitals.[14] Most people in the United States had little personal experience with computer networking, so the "information superhighway" was a useful metaphor to encapsulate the bundle of futuristic applications envisioned by the campaign. As the *New York Times'* John Markoff summarized, "Scientists, engineers, or product developers far from each other could collaborate because their computer screens would become a sort of electronic blackboard for everyone to work on," while a "couch potato could summon any movie ever made by pushing a button."[15]

Like the interstate highway system that Gore's father championed in the 1950s, the information superhighway promised to distribute a wide range of economic and cultural opportunities by mitigating intractable problems of distance and cost. But unlike the interstate, which President Eisenhower's secretary of commerce called "the greatest public works program in the history of the world," the information superhighway would not be implemented as public infrastructure.[16] Over the course of Clinton and Gore's first term in office, their internet policy coalesced around a very different idea: "The private sector must lead."[17] Over and over, internal correspondences, policy documents, and public statements reiterated this point. The revolution would be commercialized, and the private sector would be in control.

The notion of private sector leadership rests on the idea that markets are the best mechanism to distribute the social benefits of a powerful new information technology—a belief certainly espoused by the Clinton policy apparatus. If Ronald Reagan framed supply-side tax cuts as the primary means to "lift all boats," Clinton and Gore positioned the commercial internet as the best mechanism for generating broad-based prosperity gains. The government's main job was to help get things moving and then get out of the way. But there is more to it than this.

Clinton's devotion to market-based public policy did not spring forth spontaneously on the day of his inauguration. Below I sketch a genealogy of Clinton's laissez-faire internet agenda, which stemmed as much from political expedience and the power of business to shape public policy as it did from ideology. The internet's commercialization—and the specific policy decisions that enabled surveillance advertising to flourish—reflected a reorientation within the Democratic Party toward the interests of the technology industry and away from working-class politics. There were important structural dynamics at play as well, including the overriding need for U.S. capital to locate new areas of profitable investment in the face of rising global competition. These and other capitalist imperatives motivated the formative internet policy agenda, placing powerful economic "pressures and limits" on political decision making.[18]

Any given public policy choice must be understood within its historically specific political context.[19] For 1990s internet policy, this means paying close attention to the neoliberal consensus presided over by Clinton and Gore, as well as broader shifts within the Democratic Party that transpired over the preceding decades. As Jennifer Holt argues, neoliberalism "placed great faith in market solutions to economic and social problems, and by the end of 1980s, was the predominant philosophy guiding American political and economic policy."[20] Scholars including Wendy Brown and David Harvey have helped to chart the history of the neoliberal political formation, which reached new heights during the formative years of internet policy development.[21]

Long before he was mocked by late-night comedians for allegedly claiming to have invented the internet, Al Gore was more of an Atari person. As a U.S. House representative from Tennessee in the early 1980s, Gore became part of a group known as the "Atari Democrats."[22] This was an informal coalition of legislators from primarily affluent districts that cultivated a political niche by touting the economic importance of the technology sector and pledging to reform the government's relationship to tech companies. As Representative Tim Wirth, another prominent voice in the movement, told the *Washington Post* in 1982, the Atari Dems wanted to shift from a politics of redistribution to a "politics of growth."[23] A few months later, Wirth and a handful of other Democrats split from their party's mainstream to join conservatives in an effort to relax antitrust enforcement and provide tax incentives for tech companies that wanted to cooperate on research and development efforts.[24] The *Christian Science Monitor* called it a "modern Marshall Plan" for the U.S. tech sector, whereby Congress would "stimulate private funding" instead of providing direct government investment.[25]

Preaching a gospel of technology development through increased public–private partnerships and relaxed regulatory scrutiny, the Atari Democrats gained influence and institutional support throughout the 1980s. Jerrold Schneider points out that the movement picked up steam in the midst of rising campaign expenses, particularly related to the growing costs of television advertising.[26] Atari Dems were among the first in their party to recognize a new source of political patronage in the technology and finance sectors, which had until then been a relatively untapped source of campaign funding.[27]

The group carved out a political niche among the donor class and won the support of a number of Democratic strategists who wanted the party to break from its New Deal lineage.[28] Lily Geismer links the rise of the Atari Democrats to the party's movement away from its traditional working-class base.[29] Technology was positioned as the domain of scrappy entrepreneurs and meritocratic markets, a rhetoric designed to appeal to a fresh voter base of suburban white-collar workers. It is important to emphasize, as Geismer does, that New Deal policies were designed in large part to benefit white male workers and their families while excluding women, people of color, and other marginalized groups. At the same time, New Deal industrial policy generally gave labor a seat at the table to serve as a counterweight to the influence of the ownership class.[30] It favored equitable distribution of profits over uninhibited growth. Retreating from this balance, the Atari Democrats represented an insurgent movement that sought to use tech industry boosterism as a tonic to cleanse the Democratic Party of antagonism to business power. The "Atari" moniker fell out of fashion after the eponymous gaming company failed spectacularly in 1983 (the name was originally a gibe anyway). In search of another label for the group, some newspapers began using the term "neo-liberals."[31]

The neoliberal platform was institutionalized and amplified by the Democratic Leadership Council (DLC), an organization created in the wake of Reaganism to foment a so-called bloodless revolution within the Democratic Party, moving it toward the political center. The DLC's founder, Al From, was an experienced party operative who argued that in order to win elections, the Democrats had to jettison populism, excise the influence of labor unions, and fully embrace market-based policies and limited government.[32] Many from the Atari Democrat coalition, including Al Gore, joined the cause. With messaging that focused on individual opportunity and responsibility, the DLC and its associated think tank, the Progressive Policy Institute, churned out a raft of what were essentially conservative policy proposals on issues from free trade to welfare reform. As Jacob Hacker and Paul Pierson point out, a crucial element of the DLC's "reformation project" was to cultivate relationships with generous political donors, particularly those attracted to the organization's business-friendly outlook.[33] One of the DLC's first policy initiatives argued against the minimum wage.[34]

Representing the party's progressive wing, Jesse Jackson began to call the DLC "Democrats for the Leisure Class."[35] Despite this internal pushback, the DLC's calls for reform were bolstered as the Democrats lost three successive presidential elections in the 1970s and 1980s.[36] It was clear to party elites that something needed to change. As Joseph Stiglitz put it: "One couldn't win an election just standing up for the poor and in modern America, everyone saw themselves as middle class."[37]

In 1990, the DLC announced its charismatic new chairman: Arkansas governor Bill Clinton. Known for his affable nature and a willingness to confront what From called "liberal sacred cows," Clinton was a rising star among the Atari Democrats' successors, a group that became known as the "New Democrats."[38] As he geared up to run for president, Clinton plotted out a distinctive path to electoral victory, a centrist "third way" between what he framed as big-government liberalism and small-government conservatism. His platform was incongruous in some respects, juxtaposing outwardly progressive stances on health care reform, reproductive rights, and environmental protections with regressive positions on social programs and crime crackdowns. When he accepted the Democratic Party's presidential nomination in 1992, Clinton underscored his commitment to a market-oriented policy platform and pledged to create a government that would "expand opportunity, not bureaucracy."[39] Crosscutting this policy mishmash was the promise of a coming communications revolution.

Third Way Internet Policy

Clinton's defeat of incumbent George H. W. Bush solidified the neoliberal transformation of the Democratic Party's mainstream. It was clear from the beginning of Clinton's presidency that internet development would be a flagship test case for the New Democrats' third way policy program. One month into office, Clinton previewed his internet agenda in a document called *Technology for America's Economic Growth*. The commercialization of the information superhighway, now rebranded as the National Information Infrastructure (NII), was highlighted as a "major priority."[40]

Here it is useful to distinguish between privatization and commercialization. Privatization—transferring the ownership, management, and control of internet backbone systems from public to private hands—formally began in the late 1980s under the Bush administration and was not completed until 1995, several years into Clinton's first term.[41] As Shane Greenstein points out, privatization only occurred "after the internet had already incubated under government stewardship for a considerable time in the 1970s and 1980s."[42] Whereas privatization is about handing over control of the pipes, commercialization is about building businesses and markets on top of the newly privatized infrastructure. Clinton inherited and carried out the privatization effort, but his administration was the primary policy architect for the internet's commercialization.

Clinton convened the Information Infrastructure Task Force to set the federal policy agenda for these overlapping initiatives, which included establishing the formative regulatory framework for online advertising, privacy, and consumer surveillance. From 1993 to 1995, the IITF crafted a series of blueprints for internet privatization and commercialization, a complex task that required surveying a wide range of policy domains and mapping out the government's strategic objectives.[43] Although there were many substantive goals on the table, including universal internet service, telemedicine, network security, and educational applications, the IITF's most basic and important function was to demarcate the roles of the public and private sectors in internet system development.

As New Democrats, Clinton and Gore saw themselves as reformers not only of their own party but of an archaic industrial political economy beleaguered by a bloated and technologically backward federal government.[44] They came to view the government's role not as the builder or provider of public information services but as an accelerator and steward of private sector internet development, which, once overtaken by market forces, would generate broad social gains. The state, Clinton argued, had not kept pace with technology advancements, and as a result, "Government regulations have tended to inhibit competition and delay deployment of new technology."[45] Framing his administration as a new chapter in the federal government's relationship with the tech sector, Clinton pledged to "play a key role in helping private firms develop and profit from innovations."[46]

In September 1993, the IITF released its inaugural policy framework: *The National Information Infrastructure: Agenda for Action*. First among nine objectives was "to promote private sector investment."[47] Though the government would play a role through "carefully crafted" policy actions, the *Agenda for Action* made it clear that "the private sector will lead the deployment of the NII."[48] In order to promote "vibrant competition" and "spur economic growth," the administration pledged to work with

Congress to reform the nation's telecommunications sector to carve a path for the internet's commercialization.

This initiative became the Telecommunications Act of 1996, a major legislative overhaul that cleared away decades of public-interest regulation to aggressively implement a free market approach. According to David Horowitz, "The broad change was that the public interest [would] be secured not by regulation but by competition."[49] Letting the private sector lead meant not only deregulation but also an abdication by the government of nearly all operational responsibility to see to it that communications systems served a public good. "The point of government regulation, pure and simple, became to help firms maximize their profits," writes Robert McChesney. "That was the new public interest."[50] As such, critical media scholars have argued that so-called deregulation is better understood as reregulation.[51] The rules are not so much eliminated as revised to prioritize commercial interests.

This approach was applied fervently to internet development, as spelled out in the subsequent *Framework for Global Electronic Commerce*, the most comprehensive statement of the Clinton administration's internet policy program. Released in 1997, the *Framework*'s opening section reads: "Commerce on the internet could total tens of billions of dollars by the turn of the century. For this potential to be realized fully, governments must adopt a non-regulatory, market-oriented approach to electronic commerce, one that facilitates the emergence of a transparent and predictable legal environment to support global business and commerce." Elaborating on this theme, the *Framework* laid out guidelines for internet policy development across a range of domestic and international issues. I discuss the creation of this document in detail in chapter 2. For now, it is enough to note that the *Framework*'s first principle doubled down on the approach laid out in the 1993 *Agenda for Action:* "For electronic commerce to flourish, the private sector must continue to lead. Innovation, expanded services, broader participation, and lower prices will arise in a market-driven arena, not in an environment that operates as a regulated industry."[52]

Joseph Stiglitz, among the most distinguished of elite economists, chaired President Clinton's Council of Economic Advisors, and in that role, he participated in policy discussions around telecommunications reform and internet development. After leaving the White House for the World Bank, Stiglitz wrote a book reflecting on his "ringside seat in government decision making" during the "roaring nineties."[53] Part of the book tells the story of telecommunications deregulation, which Stiglitz attributes to an ascendant "free market ideology" within the Democratic Party.[54] "While the demand for deregulation had long been there," he writes, "the politics of the nineties provided the supply."[55]

It is an oversimplification to characterize the New Democrat movement as a sudden and sharp right turn. As Rick Perlstein points out, neoliberalism's rise within the Democratic Party's mainstream reaches back to Jimmy Carter.[56] A close reading of Clinton's early policy proposals shows that his administration tried to thread the "third way" needle to a greater extent than critics often admit. Clinton's standard 1992 stump speech included progressive proposals on issues such as universal health care and student loan forgiveness.[57] One of his administration's first successful legislative initiatives was a tax hike on the wealthy.[58]

Nevertheless, once in office, Clinton governed like a conservative in significant respects. Across a spectrum of issues, including social welfare, criminal justice, and the federal budget, the New Democrats yielded the terms of political debate to conservative framings, which led to policies that negatively affected workers and marginalized groups. The Violent Crime Control and Law Enforcement Act of 1994 stands out as a particularly egregious example. The bipartisan legislation, part of what Michelle Alexander calls "the new Jim Crow," put the United States on a fast track to mass incarceration, with disproportionate effects on people of color.[59] Two decades later, Clinton apologized. "I signed a bill that made the problem worse," he said. "And I want to admit it."[60] Today, 20 percent of the world's prisoners are locked up in the United States, a country that makes up less than 5 percent of the global population.[61]

These social policies reflect the same neoliberal consensus that was readily applied to technology issues. With few exceptions, America's political elites governed from what appeared to be a shared understanding that technological change was rapidly outmoding the structures of government regulation and that the only credible response was to tear up the old rules. This is what Jean-Christophe Plantin et al. call the "retreat from the modern infrastructural ideal," where governments turned away from public utility-style regulation to embrace privatization and so-called free market approaches to networked computing.[62]

Of course, this policy record reflects not only the trajectory of the New Democrats but also the impact of the 1994 Republican revolution. Clinton began his presidency in a strong political position, with Democratic majorities in both houses of Congress. Then in the 1994 midterm elections, the GOP won both the Senate and the House of Representatives, the latter of which had been reliably Democratic for four decades. The speaker of the House, Newt Gingrich, dug in immediately, leading the GOP in a series of budget battles that resulted in two government shutdowns during Clinton's first term. The Republicans maintained complete control of Congress for the remainder of Clinton's presidency.

Despite roiling partisanship, the two parties found common ground on a number of economic issues, particularly regarding telecommunications and media deregulation and the commercialization of the internet. These were areas in which the "New Democrats could join forces with the Old Republicans," writes Stiglitz.[63] The difference between the parties' approaches was that, as Paul Starr put it: "the Republicans wanted to jump off a cliff, while the Democrats wanted to scramble down . . . preserving a bit of protection for those population groups which might otherwise be mistreated."[64]

Hungry for campaign contributions, both political parties saw an opportunity to forge ties with the rising technology sector, particularly among the software and computing companies that had not been as historically dependent on regulation as, say, the telecommunications industry. "Whereas AT&T, for example, had given millions over the years in political contributions," writes Leslie David Simon, "IBM did not even have a political action committee."[65] Generally speaking, the Republicans held a home-court advantage in terms of business support, but Clinton and Gore, with their New Democrat bona fides, became reliable champions of commercial technology. There was a sense that the New Democrats wanted to "earn their pro-business stripes by pushing deregulation still farther than it had gone before."[66]

Internet policy grounded in free market orthodoxy proved politically expedient for the New Democrats. As organizations like the DLC understood well, the success of the party's class reorientation depended on its ability to secure a strong donor base among ascendant industries such as technology and finance. As Jill Lepore writes, the Democrats' abandonment of the "working class for the microchip" turned out to be a lucrative fundraising strategy.[67] In 1990, the communications and electronics sector donated more money to House Democrats than Republicans by a near 2:1 margin.[68]

A transcript of a 1996 conference call between Clinton, Gore, and a handful of Silicon Valley leaders is illustrative of the success of the Democrats' neoliberal turn. The call was led by notable venture capitalist John

Doerr, who explained: "This is a pretty unusual event. We're announcing today that seventy-five executives from the technology community are endorsing Bill Clinton and Al Gore to be president and vice president in 1997. . . . Seventy-five high-tech executives are saying whether it's the economy, reducing the deficit, shrinking the size of government, creating jobs, or in opening world markets, this administration gets it."[69] Near the end of the call, Clinton remarked: "I thank those of you who crossed party lines for making a leap not only for your companies and your employees, but for our country."

Shortly after Clinton's reelection, Doerr and crew were invited to the White House to discuss economic policy issues. According to the official program notes for the event, Doerr and the other tech leaders who "provided political support during the campaign" sought to "establish a working relationship with the administration in order to help shape the administration's technology agenda and provide input on economic and regulatory issues that impact high technology industries."[70] Over two terms in office, Clinton and Gore deepened their ties to Silicon Valley, meeting with many tech executives including Marc Andreessen, Jeff Bezos, and Steve Jobs.

The budding courtship between the New Dems and the technology sector was something of a coup for the Democratic Party in terms of political patronage, but it paid mighty dividends to the private sector as well. As I describe in chapter 2, Clinton and Gore extended the idea of public–private partnership to the policy-making process itself by inviting business interests to extensively participate in internet policy formation. In a remarkable book that blends policy analysis with historical tell-all, former AT&T and IBM lobbyist Leslie David Simon provides a glimpse into the extent of corporate access in this formative period of internet policy making. Simon, who is generally approving of Clinton's stance on private sector leadership, notes that the Clinton policy team "had not come to this understanding accidentally."[71] In fact, business interests had "mounted an aggressive campaign to shape the administration's policy from the beginning."

From the very start of Clinton's first term, the computing, telecommunications, and media industries were invited to give policy guidance in official capacities such as the advisory council for the NII, which served as a private sector counterpart to the IITF. Traditional lobbying was prevalent as well, often though trade groups like the Information Technology Industry Council, which put out over thirty-five policy documents in 1995–96 alone and by 1999 was publishing a "high tech voting guide" that rated members of Congress according to their friendliness to tech business issues.[72] Another industry group, the Computer Systems Policy Project (CSPP), reportedly arranged for a wish list of policy proposals to greet Clinton on his desk as he entered office in January 1993. According to Simon, CSPP materials were widely read within the administration, to considerable effect. Among the group's principle recommendations was that the "development and deployment of the [NII] must be led by the private sector, guided by the forces of a free and open market."[73]

As for the Republicans, Gingrich struggled somewhat to prove his technology chops (once suggesting an inane program of means-tested tax breaks to help poor families buy computers), but his free market credentials were strong indeed.[74] Gingrich maintained close ties with the Progress and Freedom Foundation think tank, an early proponent of telecommunications deregulation, and he was happy to make deals with the president on such matters.[75] In addition to defunding the government's Office of Technology Assessment, Gingrich stewarded the House's overwhelming bipartisan passage of the Telecommunications Act of 1996, unanimously approved by the Republican majority.

Despite its policy successes, the neoliberal consensus was not all pervasive, impermeable, or unchallenged. It involved what David Hesmondhalgh calls "struggle and negotiation."[76] Throughout the early 1990s, there was a fair amount of contestation among government and private sector interests on various fronts, including pitched battles over internet content deemed indecent (e.g., pornography) and encryption controls. However, such disputes were overshadowed by the broad agreement over privatization and commercialization. There was little room for alternative ideas regarding the fundamental order of things. For example, before Vice President Gore was a proponent of internet commercialization, he had been a strong advocate for public investment in computing infrastructure development. During the 1992 campaign, and even into the first few months of governing, Gore argued that state-funded internet provision would be necessary to ensure that the information superhighway would be available to all, rather than a "private toll road open only to a business and scientific elite."[77]

In mid-December 1992, the president-elect and the vice president–elect held a televised roundtable on the state of the U.S. economy. Panels of executives, academics, and civil servants dialogued with Clinton and

Gore on live television. One notable exchange subtly illustrated the powerful voice of business in setting the technology policy agenda. Robert Allen, the chairman of AT&T, remarked that outside of providing incentives to the private sector, the government should steer clear of the task of building the new information networks.

Gore responded: "It does seem to me that government ought to play a role in putting in place that backbone. Just as no private investor was willing to build the interstate highway system but once it was built, then a lot of other roads connected to it. . . . Most people think [the internet] ought to be built by the Federal Government and then transitioned into private industry. You didn't mean to disagree with that view when you said government shouldn't play a role, did you?"

"Yes, I may disagree," was Allen's soft-spoken reply, prompting more than a few chuckles from the room. Clinton quipped, "I was hoping we'd have one disagreement," then quickly changed the subject.[78] The deadpan delivery of Allen's opposition to public infrastructure was understated, but his message may have well been shouted into a bullhorn. He was speaking not only for AT&T but for the whole of the U.S. business sector. At a foundational level, the notion that the government would fund the new information infrastructure or steward the development of public interest applications was anathema to a broad swath of private sector interests. A 1994 investment forecast from Deloitte & Touche illustrates this impulse in remarkable fashion, warning, "Network owners counting on advertising and transactional revenues to offset heavy capital investments could be reluctant to go along with steps designed to encourage users to browse through the county council's agenda or exchange videos of the latest high school soccer games instead of ordering things from information and merchandise vendors."[79] In other words, if it don't make a buck, it ain't worth doing. Visions for the information superhighway that lay outside of profit making were a threat and needed to be reined in. The real task at hand was to stimulate economic growth and global competitiveness. Everything else was a distraction.

This sentiment was widespread among the industry groups working closely with the federal government to develop both the broad strokes of internet policy, and, as I show in chapter 2, the specific regulatory environment for advertising and commercial surveillance. Vice President Gore's rapid evolution on the issue of public infrastructure is indicative of the efficacy of business lobbying efforts. In an "extraordinary turnabout," Gore quietly abandoned his position on publicly funded infrastructure, instead taking up a star-crossed effort to stash universal service and common carrier provisions into the coming avalanche of deregulation.[80]

Interactive Media as Threat and Opportunity

Much of the meat and potatoes of Clinton's first-term internet policy agenda dealt with infrastructural topics such as the privatization and interoperability of internet backbone systems. Issues more directly related to commercialization, such as advertising and privacy, were part of early policy discussions but were not taken up fully until Clinton's second term. For the marketing complex, however, advertising and privacy were not back-burner issues at all. By 1994, marketers had embarked on a concerted lobbying effort to ensure that lawmakers stuck to the principle of "private sector leadership" as they moved from privatization to commercialization. This political project began in earnest as marketers began to understand the internet simultaneously as a promising new business opportunity and a threat to their long-standing position at the top of the commercial media food chain.

By the time Clinton and Gore introduced the concept of the information superhighway on the presidential campaign trail, the marketing complex was already buzzing about "interactive media." In the same way that the term "print" evoked an array of media channels from local newspapers to national magazines, the term "interactive" had become a catchall for marketing at the intersection of personal computing, telecommunications, and cable television. Reading the advertising trade press during this period reveals that the new interactive media generated a great deal of hype, but also skepticism within marketing circles.[81] Would the new media be a game-changing opportunity for growth or another passing fad?

Early on, there was incredulity about interactive media that, according to *Advertising Age,* had sprung up "almost overnight."[82] Of course, things like computer-based online services had not actually appeared out of nowhere. In fact, a portion of the ad industry's early skepticism stemmed from the fact that some practitioners felt like they had been down this road before with less than stellar results. They recalled failed attempts to commercially develop early networked information services such as videotex and teletext, which transmitted text-based data over telecommunications lines and broadcast signals.[83] These were followed by a more successful crop of computer-based online services such as CompuServe, Prodigy, and America Online (AOL). Although some of these systems had experimented with advertising, they remained largely funded by sub-scriptions.[84] Content publishers had also begun to test floppy disk and CD-ROM formats, though these too had relatively little advertiser buy-in.[85]

Things changed after the 1992 election. Clinton and Gore were now promoting the National Information Infrastructure from the White House rather than campaign stops. Led by AOL, commercial online services began to attract new subscribers at a significant rate. Cable and telecommunications companies touted plans to develop "interactive television," or "iTV," services to bring electronic shopping, content on demand, and household-level target marketing into the mainstream.[86] Most importantly, the trade press began covering a new technology called the World Wide Web. Though it was a fringe medium compared to AOL or CompuServe, the release of graphical web browsers signaled the web's potential to attract a larger user base.

It was around this point that some leaders within the marketing complex began to take the new interactive media more seriously as both an exciting business opportunity and credible threat to business as usual. The trade press began to argue more forcefully that the web was worth paying attention to, even if it had yet to take popular hold. *Advertising Age* ran more stories on the web in the first two months of 1995 than it did in all of 1994.[87] Whatever this was, it was no teletext.

A key element of the emerging narrative was that interactive media was finally going to put consumers in charge. "If the remote control was the great equalizer in the battle between advertiser and television viewer," wrote Chris Anderson, then interactive media "may shift power completely to the hands of the consumer."[88] This was a vision of the advertiser–audience relationship that was markedly different from the status quo. Advertising has always been a game of cat and mouse among advertisers and consumers. "Ever since the start of their industry in the nineteenth century," writes Joseph Turow, "advertising organizations have been deeply worried about finding efficient ways to persuade people to buy their products."[89] Although industry rhetoric tends to downplay this framing, the heart of the enterprise is adversarial: capture people's attention and try to persuade them to action, whether they ask for it or not. Commercial media environments are structured to facilitate this game through conventions like the commercial break, the full-page ad, the half-time show sponsorship, and so on.

At one level, advertisers understood that interactivity would add new dimensions to the game of capturing consumer attention. The industry has historically adapted to keep up with social trends, especially those produced by new communications technologies. Many marketers hoped that interactive platforms would present fresh opportunities to "go beyond the one-way flow of traditional media" in order to engage consumers in more meaningful ways.[90] But advertisers also worried about more fundamental changes. If interactive media was really going to prioritize individual agency, then this suggested the possibility of a media environment where advertisers no longer held structural advantages in the game of cat and mouse. Worse yet, perhaps they would no longer get to play at all.

Practitioners and analysts began to express concern that the ad industry could be "left behind by technology," as one headline put it.[91] Martin Nisenholtz of the Ogilvy & Mather Direct agency was among the earliest to call his colleagues to action, warning, "If you have no role in the development of the [internet] business, you probably won't have a role in its future. It's not a foregone conclusion that advertisers will be involved with this."[92] Although some observers in the trade press were skeptical that any media platform could develop in the United States without advertising support, others were not so sure.

By the end of 1993, Gerald Levin, CEO of Time Warner Cable, had pledged to invest $5 billion to build a next-generation interactive television service.[93] Dubbed the Full Service Network, the goal was to bundle video programming, home shopping, electronic games, and other applications into a new kind of subscription platform. Other cable and telecommunications companies announced similar initiatives, kicking off a frenzy of speculation about the future of interactive advertising. As John Malone, head of cable giant TCI and perhaps iTV's greatest evangelist, put it: "Rather than a structure designed to satisfy advertisers . . . everything will be organized to satisfy the needs of the individual consumer."[94] Time Warner executives drove the point home by suggesting that advertising might not be a necessary component of interactive TV. If consumers were willing to pay the full costs of program delivery, Time Warner signaled it might be able to provide "network TV shows without commercials."[95]

There is a long history of advertising industry pushback against innovations that give people more control over their media engagement. The television remote control, VCR home recorder, and pay-per-view distribution technologies were all seen as highly disruptive to compulsory advertising. But none of those threatened to upend the basic structural arrangement of the advertising funding model to the same degree. "The revolution is now," warned an *Advertising Age* editorial. "Who controls this media—advertisers or the John Malones of this world—is now being determined."[96]

The advertising industry's reaction was dictated most strongly not by advertising agencies or the trade press but by major national marketers, otherwise known as the people who write the checks. Already concerned with the fragmenting of mass audiences and consumer aversion to increasingly ad-cluttered media environments, big marketers grew anxious about their status on the information superhighway. Perhaps the most important call to arms came from Edwin Artzt, chairman of Procter & Gamble, then (and now) among the world's largest advertisers.[97] In 1994, Artzt gave a high-profile address to the American Association of Advertising Agencies that called on the industry to seize control of interactive media development in order to create the "greatest selling tool ever conceived."[98] Inaction, warned Artzt, meant that advertising might not have a future in the new media world. It was a moment of awakening for marketers and the advertising industry that depended on their patronage. As the *Washington Post* reported: "Now the head of Procter & Gamble, a man as important to U.S. advertising as turnips are to a pig, has said out loud what many only agonized over in private: Someday there may be no commercials on the tube."[99]

Even though he never mentioned the internet by name, the structural and political implications of Artzt's remarks are significant. The man was not simply musing that it might be a good idea to see what this whole interactive thing is all about. This was a rallying cry to maintain the fundamental political economic order of the U.S. media system. It was a call to reaffirm the notion that media exist to serve the interests of advertisers and that the new media, whatever form they may take, must be brought into this alignment. When commercial radio shook up the world of print advertising in the 1930s, Artzt recalled, advertisers took control of broadcast programming and "molded the environment to fit our needs. . . . Now, we're going to have to grab technology in our teeth again and make it work for us."[100]

Matthew McAllister frames this moment as expressing a love–hate relationship that centered around the issue of control.[101] Marketers loved the prospect of more control over consumer information in order to target messages to specific consumers, but they were deeply concerned about failing to extend the economic control they have historically wielded over media systems to the emerging internet. Writing in 1995, McAllister argued: "If advertisers sense that computers [and the internet] offer them more control than they had before, then they will exploit these digitized opportunities to the hilt. If advertisers sense that computers offer less control than they had before, then they will do everything they can to turn that around."[102]

Political mobilization became a central part of marketers' efforts. Artzt called on industry leaders to craft a "legislative and regulatory game plan" to ensure that advertising would continue to have pride of place in the media hierarchy. The first order of business was to build a cross-industry coalition to advocate on behalf of the advertising funding model itself. "We're limited only by our creativity," said Artzt, "and our ability to prove that it's in everyone's interest to involve advertising in these new media."[103] The information superhighway was still a nebulous concept in 1994. Without a clear understanding of how interactive media would pan out, and lacking any guarantee that whatever platforms emerged would be ad supported, the marketing complex adopted an anticipatory strategy to shape the entire regulatory environment in their favor. Lobbying the federal government to support the advertising funding model rather than any specific iteration, the strategy was like arranging the pieces on a chess board to their own advantage before committing to any individual moves.

There were differences of opinion about what exactly interactive advertising would look like, but consensus quickly formed around the notion that marketers, ad agencies, and publishers needed to work together to ensure that advertising would be the economic engine of the new media. A few months after Artzt's speech, the marketing complex launched a multifaceted lobbying effort to advocate for just that. Leading the charge was a brand new trade organization called the Coalition for Advertising-Supported Information and Entertainment (CASIE), which represented marketers and advertising agencies. Artzt took a leadership role, and throughout the second half of the 1990s, CASIE ran a number of campaigns to support its primary mission of creating "an environment where advertising revenue is the key funding source for the large majority of information and entertainment sources in the evolving world of media."[104]

To make this case, CASIE and others leaned heavily on an argument about the benevolence and necessity of advertising's subsidization of media. The core idea is that funding from advertising is the one and only means to support a media system that is both accessible to all people and free from government control. By offsetting the costs of content creation and distribution, the argument goes, advertising makes media affordable (even free!). And by attracting funding from a diverse range of businesses, advertising ensures media's independence from the heavy hand of state censorship. In what the trade press described as a "politically winning argument," the industry shrewdly linked the notion of the advertising subsidy to the concept of universal internet service, a policy objective particularly near and dear to Vice President Al Gore.[105]

In the summer of 1994, Procter & Gamble dispatched another executive, Robert Herbold, to testify at an NTIA hearing on universal service held as part of that agency's work with the IITF. Herbold argued that without advertising support, the Clinton administration would be unable to achieve its goal of universal internet access. On an ad-free information superhighway, warned Herbold, "the less moneyed will be stranded at the side of the road."[106] Connecting universal service to the ad subsidy became a staple of the marketing complex's lobbying playbook, and evidence suggests that the argument was well received among policy makers. After hearing from Herbold, the NTIA issued a formal request for further comment on "the efficacy of advertising as a vehicle for funding universal service in the 21st century."[107] In the words of John Kamp, vice president of the Four As advertising trade group and former FCC staffer, "Clearly we made progress because there seemed to be agreement that advertising will pay for a lot of this."[108]

In the next chapter, I take a closer look at how the advertising business model was normalized in the politics of internet commercialization and explore how business interests worked hand in hand with government officials to craft the foundational policies of surveillance advertising.

A FRAMEWORK FOR GLOBAL ELECTRONIC
   COMMERCE

THE FORMAL PRIVATIZATION of the internet backbone was completed
in 1995. Heading into his second term, President Clinton's internet policy efforts were increasingly focused on the net's commercialization. In
1996, the White House began to develop a renovated policy agenda for
internet commerce. Clinton tapped a close advisor, Ira Magaziner, to
lead this initiative and draft what became the White House's *Framework
for Global Electronic Commerce*. Released in mid-1997, the *Framework*
outlined a plan for internet commercialization that served as a guideline
for domestic and international policy and laid out the federal government's approach to internet advertising and privacy. This chapter develops a case study around the creation of this policy agenda to show how
"private sector leadership" was reaffirmed domestically, extended internationally, and applied directly to the nascent surveillance advertising
industry.

Magaziner's papers, archived at the Clinton Presidential Library, provide a firsthand look at how the *Framework* was drafted. Reading this
archive in conjunction with relevant press coverage, speeches, interviews,
and the *Framework* itself provides an opportunity to compare side by
side the substance of this historically significant policy statement and
the behind-the-scenes blueprints of its construction. The archive shows
who was consulted as the *Framework* was written, which issues were of
concern and contested, and which were taken as givens.

In addition to the substance of policy formation, the *Framework* case
study also illustrates what might be called the praxis of neoliberalism, or
how political ideology is made concrete through everyday practices of

policy making. Neoliberalism is surely among critical scholarship's most overburdened terms, but I use it here to suggest a set of ideas about the proper relationship between the state and the private sector that rose to prominence in the 1980s and 1990s. A core element of the neoliberal framework is that the primary goal of public policy is to facilitate "free markets," which are unquestionably the best mechanisms to serve human needs.[1] Beyond that, government action should be minimal.

The Magaziner archive presents an opportunity to zoom in on the routines and mechanics of neoliberal policy making in the Clinton administration. This perspective reveals contradictions in the neoliberal theory of governance that are expressed in a disconnect between the way officials describe their approach to public policy and the actual practices of policy making itself. In particular, the story of the *Framework*'s construction debunks the notion that free market policies represent a minimalist, nonregulatory form of governance. It shows instead that foundational U.S. internet policies were created via processes that were heavily skewed toward corporate interests and misrepresented to the public as a kind of cyber-enhanced exercise of participatory democracy. Industry and government worked in close quarters to harmonize their objectives for internet development, and despite disagreements in a few areas, they found a great deal of common ground. At the same time, advocacy groups and everyday citizens were largely marginalized from closed-door policy discussions. At one level, this case study suggests acute government capture by business interests. But the deeper story is not a one-off exposé of government co-optation. It is about the interplay of private sector instrumental power and political ideology, both of which reflect the imperatives of a capitalist political economy running full steam ahead to commodify the new sphere of interactive media.

Drafting the *Framework*

The *Framework* outlines the Clinton administration's vision for a transnational capitalism led by the United States and supported by a "global information infrastructure." Intended to serve as the basis for all federal internet policy, the *Framework* was accompanied by a presidential directive that instructed "all department and agency heads to review their policies that affect global electronic commerce and to make sure that they are consistent with the five core principles of this report."[2] The five principles were:

1. The private sector should lead.
2. Governments should avoid undue restrictions on electronic commerce.
3. Where governmental involvement is needed, its aim should be to support and enforce a predictable, minimalist, consistent, and simple legal environment for commerce.
4. Governments should recognize the unique qualities of the internet.
5. Electronic commerce over the internet should be facilitated on a global basis.

There are significant parallels here with the Clinton administration's first-term policy agenda from 1993. Most important is the consistent demarcation and hierarchy of roles for the public and private sectors. Business was in the driver's seat. The state's primary purpose would be to support the internet's commercial development. The *Framework* sent a strong signal that the Clinton administration would not only defer to the private sector on many areas of domestic policy but would also advocate on behalf of U.S. business interests as internet markets proceeded on a global basis.

Magaziner's papers provide a firsthand account of how the *Framework* was written. The archive shows that the policy positions advanced in the document were the outcome of sustained collaboration with an array of business interests and, to a much lesser extent, organizations from civil society. Those at the uppermost strata of private industry were afforded privileged access to Magaziner and his staff as the *Framework* was drafted. Records show that Magaziner repeatedly engaged with corporate executives and trade groups through correspondence, meetings, and speaking appearances. This priority access meant that the private sector's interactions with Magaziner were far more numerous and impactful than those of civil organizations, whose motivations more often extended beyond purely economic concerns.

The *Framework*'s iterative drafting process illustrates this lopsided dynamic particularly well. Starting in fall 1996, some eight months before the paper's official release, Magaziner's office made a series of working drafts available to select business leaders for comment and consultation. The final document went through more than a dozen such revisions. Although the comprehensiveness of the archive is unknown, the available evidence includes correspondence addressing the substance of the *Framework* from thirty-seven private organizations. Broken down by category, comments were submitted by eighteen corporations, thirteen industry trade associations, and six civil society organizations such as think tanks and advocacy groups. Ten of the eighteen companies represented were Fortune 500 firms in 1997 including IBM, AT&T, Citicorp, BellSouth, Bank of America, SBC Communications, Microsoft, Sun Microsystems, and Oracle. Trade associations that were involved in the drafting process included the Information Technology Industry Council, Interactive Services Association, Direct Marketing Association, and Software Publishers Association. Advocacy groups and think tanks were more sparsely represented and included groups such as the Center for Media Education, Center for Democracy and Technology, and Cato Institute.

In addition to soliciting written feedback on drafts of the *Framework*, Magaziner met personally with top corporate decision makers to discuss industry policy concerns and objectives. For example, Magaziner met several times with Eric Schmidt, first as CEO of Sun Microsystems and later as CEO of Novell.[3] They discussed trade policy, intellectual property, and the general task of "working to see that digital markets reach their full potential."[4] A memo from the president of the Software Publishers Association illustrates the typical back-and-forth of these interactions: "My senior staff appreciated meeting with you earlier this month to discuss the proposal, and it is my hope that you will call on SPA for further comment as the administration revises it."[5]

As would be expected, many of these discussions reflected the pet issues of particular companies and trade groups. Those with strong intellectual property interests such as McGraw Hill and the Magazine Publishers Association argued for the importance of robust digital copyright protections.[6] Multinationals such as IBM, Microsoft, and AT&T stressed the need for harmonization of international trade policies and strong federal action to fortify U.S. technology sector interests in global markets.[7] Joseph Stiglitz's summary of the lobbying he encountered while chairman of the White House Council of Economic Advisors maps nicely to the general discourse around the *Framework* drafts. "I observed three almost unfailing principles among those who came to us for help," Stiglitz recalled. "First, businesspeople generally oppose subsidies, for everyone but themselves. . . . Second, everyone was in favor of competition, in every sector but their own. . . . And third, everyone was in favor of openness and transparency, in every sector but their own."[8]

The companies and trade associations of the marketing complex did not stray from this pattern, lobbying Magaziner's office about their concerns related to advertising and data collection. While still harboring uncertainties about how internet advertising would play out, marketers remained broadly interested in interactive media's potential to use consumer data to improve the efficiency of advertising. Their political efforts broadened from the basic task of securing advertising's role on the internet to include specific pleas for a business-friendly data collection regime. These goals were realized in the *Framework,* which explicitly endorsed ad funding as a driver of internet development and confirmed the Clinton administration's intent to apply a self-regulatory approach to internet privacy. As in other policy areas, lobbyists played a central role in the *Framework*'s treatment of these issues.

The Magaziner archive contains extensive correspondence from advertising trade groups and companies, including the American Association of Advertising Agencies, Direct Marketing Association, and ad agency giant Leo Burnett. As the *Framework* drafts evolved in consultation with these groups, Magaziner added a dedicated section on advertising that echoed industry arguments about the importance of ad subsidization and self-regulatory principles. "Advertising will allow the new interactive media to offer more affordable products and services to a wider, global audience," the document stated.[9] Although some countries restrict advertising in various capacities, "in principle, the United States does not favor such regulations." It is worth emphasizing that this language was not present in any of the *Framework* drafts dated before January 1997, when a batch of comments arrived from advertising interests, including a detailed memo from Leo Burnett that argued that "the continued exponential growth of this medium can only be facilitated by the substantial investment of the private sector in supporting this media through advertising."[10] It was as if the lobbyists had channeled Dallas Smythe, who wrote in 1981 that "the fiction that advertising supports or makes possible the news, entertainment, or educational content has been a public relations mainstay of the commercial mass media."[11]

If the White House's endorsement of an advertising-subsidized internet was a culmination of the marketing complex's earlier lobbying efforts, the *Framework*'s treatment of privacy pointed to internet advertising's immediate future. In a dedicated section, the Clinton administration outlined its position on internet privacy and data collection. While noting the potential for privacy harms, the *Framework* officially endorsed a set of fair information practices to be implemented via private sector self-regulation. Such principles as "notice and choice" were important "if people [were] to feel comfortable doing business" online.[12] The administration anticipated that technological innovation and market competition would "offer solutions to many privacy concerns" and pledged to "engage its key trading partners in discussions to build support for industry-developed solutions to privacy problems."

Again, these points are in near total alignment with those made by industry groups as they commented on drafts. "We strongly believe that advertising industry self-regulation efforts should be promoted, endorsed and supported," wrote an executive from Leo Burnett.[13] The Direct Marketing Association argued that notice and choice principles were the cornerstone of "consumer empowerment" and must be "the basis of U.S. position and strategy."[14] Anyone raising concerns about commercial data collection was to be dismissed as a "privacy zealot." "Private databases do not pose the serious threat to civil liberties that government databases do," concurred the Cato Institute. The point of consumer data collection is "simply to sell people things."[15]

The *Framework* made it clear that President Clinton's promise to let the private sector lead would apply to internet data collection, though there was one caveat. Pointing to children's information as an area of concern, the *Framework* issued a warning: "We believe that private efforts of industry working in cooperation with consumer groups are preferable to government regulation, but if effective privacy protection cannot be provided in this way, we will reevaluate this policy."[16] The inclusion of this language likely reflects campaigning from media advocacy groups led by the Center for Media Education, who lobbied Magaziner on issues of children's data collection. Children's privacy represented a crack in the armor of industry self-regulation, a weak spot that activists would attempt to exploit in the coming years. Chapter 6 addresses this policy battle in detail.

In 1997, amid a rapidly changing internet advertising landscape, the *Framework* was significant in that it represented the White House's "first real stake in the ground" on privacy issues.[17] The policy statement built on the earlier analyses of the Information Infrastructure Task Force and National Telecommunications and Information Administration discussed in chapter 1, but it ignored key elements of their recommendations. Those reports warned that without universal safeguards, a market-based approach to internet data collection would inevitably erode privacy norms. The NTIA argued that it was unreasonable to expect that companies facing market pressure to collect data would bargain fairly with consumers around privacy protections. By endorsing self-regulation, the

Clinton administration signaled that it would ignore its own prior analyses and listen to industry instead. Everyone seemed to agree that companies should abide by "fair information practices," but no one that mattered thought the government should be in the business of creating or enforcing any rules. The market would sort things out.

Supporters of self-regulation framed the government's position as a "user-empowerment approach to protect consumer interests."[18] Although it was far from certain that this policy would benefit internet users, there was no doubt that it was a major victory for the marketing complex interests who helped write it. The federal government had done more than give advertising-funded internet development its official imprimatur, however. In its endorsement of self-regulation, the state had promised the advertising industry a kind of privacy that internet users would find increasingly difficult to come by: the right to be left alone.

Antidemocratic Policy Making

Beyond specific policy demands, nearly universal among industry comments on the *Framework* drafts was the request for continued influence over internet policy making. For example, the Information Technology Industry Council trade group praised the *Framework*'s market-led approach but cautioned Magaziner to "apply this principle faithfully" while keeping in close consultation with industry for "guidance and advice."[19] America Online requested that the Clinton administration explicitly "acknowledge the private sector's role in advising our government" because "those involved in building businesses on the internet" were "in the best position to understand the need for and implications of government action or inaction."[20] For AT&T, "the active involvement of the private sector" was "of highest priority," while Oracle went so far as to suggest the appointment of "an equal number of private sector representatives" to Magaziner's team of federal policy makers.[21]

While corporate lobbyists demanded a permanent and prominent seat at the policy-making table, advocacy groups were largely marginalized. Non-business-oriented advocacy organizations account for about one tenth of *Framework*-related correspondence contained in the Magaziner archive. A note likely written by a member of Magaziner's staff indicates that the civil liberties organization Center for Democracy and Technology received a "leaked copy" of the *Framework* draft and thus was not initially consulted in an official manner.[22] Comments on a letter from the Center for Media Education are even more evocative of the peripheral status of advocacy groups. The bluntly phrased remark "not crazies, doesn't seem to be an ambush," penned in the margins of a request for a meeting with Magaziner, suggests that before a meeting was considered, the lone progressive advocacy group in the mix had to be vetted regarding its sanity.[23] None of the available evidence suggests a similar level of scrutiny was applied to corporate executives and trade association lobbyists.

All told, the *Framework* was a near total victory for the private sector, including those elements interested in advertising and consumer surveillance. The policy-making process itself turned out to be perhaps the greatest implementation of the New Democrats' promise to reinvigorate public–private partnerships. The *Framework* was the result of close collaboration among the government and industry, whose agents did not agree on everything but universally agreed on the main thing. Above all else, the internet would be an engine of private profits.

A memo from Electronic Data Systems, the information technology services giant founded by Ross Perot, illustrates both the degree of public–private collaboration and the business sector's general sense of satisfaction. The correspondence, forwarded to Magaziner by an EDS executive, was prefaced with a note indicating that the document was "not meant for further distribution, but for Ira [Magaziner] to understand how pleased we are with the direction of the *[Framework]* white paper."[24] The opening paragraph is worth quoting in full:

This paper is excellent! . . . The theme of this policy announcement, to encourage industry leadership in developing electronic commerce with a market-driven industry self-regulatory approach should be applauded and strongly supported. In almost every area of the paper, the policy approach is supportive to EDS business objectives and the needs of U.S. industry in global markets. Although 'the devil is always in the details,' the policy initiative will greatly assist us in shaping similar policies in other foreign markets. The Administration has done an excellent job in this new electronic commerce area and EDS should find ways to tell them so publicly. We will meet with Ira Magaziner and other senior Administration officials to express our satisfaction with the paper and to determine how EDS can play a role in shaping follow-on implementation.[25]

Shortly after the *Framework*'s public release in July 1997, thirteen technology sector CEOs, including Microsoft's Bill Gates and Intel's Andy

Grove, issued a joint statement of approval.[26] Companies and trade associations distributed press releases praising the administration's technological savvy and bold vision. Many of these organizations were directly involved in the drafting process, including the Software Publishers Association, which issued this statement: "The Clinton administration holds the keys to driving electronic commerce on the information superhighway. With this report, they handed us the keys for a Corvette—not an Edsel. They clearly understand the potential of electronic commerce to pump billions of dollars into the American economy over the next few years."[27]

One of the takeaways from this case study is that formative internet policy in the United States was created through what can only be described as an antidemocratic process. Critical scholars including Patricia Aufderheide, Jennifer Holt, and Robert McChesney have written extensively about America's history of antidemocratic policy making in the domains of communications and media.[28] In the absence of robust popular activism, communications policy has generally been dictated by "elites and self-interested commercial interests."[29] As Aufderheide notes, "The public is endlessly invoked in communications policy, but rarely is it consulted."[30]

Hewing closely to this historical pattern, policy makers cultivated the appearance of democratic participation in writing the *Framework* but did not follow through in any substantive way. In late 1996, the White House website posted a draft of the whitepaper and invited email comments from the general public. "What we wanted to do was reach out and consult with as many people as possible to try to get a wide series of views," reported Magaziner, and "for that reason, we . . . treated it as a virtual document."[31] This was held up as an example of the democratization of public policy making in the internet age. Whether motivated by a genuine commitment to democratic principles or not, the move also functioned as a cynical public relations tactic. It was a way to demonstrate the White House's technological savvy while also claiming democratic legitimacy for the elite political project of commercializing the internet.

A few months after the *Framework*'s release, Magaziner did not disagree with an interviewer's suggestion that making a draft publicly available online had contributed to a "more direct form of government emerging from the internet."[32] Instead of mentioning the disproportionate levels of private sector access, Magaziner responded by saying, "We heard from hundreds of people we never would have heard from in Washington. . . . I think it will have a profound effect on future government procedures."[33]

By this account, the *Framework* was more than just enlightened internet policy; it was enlightened policy making.

Indeed, the Magaziner archive contains dozens of printed email messages from citizens interested in internet policy. This batch of correspondence, the comprehensiveness of which is not specified by the archive, includes its share of antigovernment missives, but it also features some authentic feedback pertaining to privacy and security issues. More than a few commenters wrote to the White House to seek assurances that their personal and financial information would not be abused when conducting transactions online and requested that the government address these concerns. Limited citizen participation notwithstanding, all available evidence undermines the notion that the *Framework* was written through some experiment of participatory cyberdemocracy. Among the most jarring examples is that the first draft of the report posted publicly online was actually at least the ninth version, which had already been written in consultation with private sector elites well before becoming available on the White House website.[34]

As political leaders assembled to plan a national strategy for internet development, they could have easily convened public hearings and debates.[35] A broad range of stakeholders might have been brought together to have public dialogues about the country's collective goals for the communications revolution that politicians and business leaders had been promising for several years. What Americans got instead was a glorified digital suggestion box and the assurance that private enterprise would unerringly steer the country into a prosperous digital future.

Like all neoliberal policy initiatives, the *Framework for Global Electronic Commerce* was part of a political project to narrow the field of legitimate government action. Even if the New Democrats could not explicitly endorse the conservative project of shrinking the state to a size where it could be "drowned in the bathtub," they agreed that the proper role of government should generally be confined to facilitating private sector growth.[36] As stated in the *Framework*, in order for the internet to fully realize its potential, "governments must adopt a non-regulatory, market-oriented approach to electronic commerce, one that facilitates the emergence of a transparent and predictable legal environment to support global business and commerce."[37]

Neoliberal governance proceeds from the basic tenet that markets stand alone as the natural and benevolent mechanism of social ordering and that state action invariably gums up the works. Of course, the truth is that the government always plays a structuring role, even if the result is creating a business environment in which companies can "operate in a relatively unhindered way."[38] There was never any real question about whether or not the state had a part to play in internet system development. The 1993 *Agenda for Action* identified the government's role as "essential" to that project. The real questions were always about whose interests would be prioritized and whose would not. To paraphrase Herbert Schiller, internet development was a matter of "power for whom and for what?"[39]

From this ideological baseline, government action that supports capital expansion and profit making is normalized and framed as nonregulatory or noninterventionist. Ira Magaziner described his policy approach as fundamentally "cautious about government action," while explaining that his team "did not start with any ideological position."[40] At the same time, public initiatives that do not overtly serve business interests are delegitimized as government interference or the overreach of a "nanny state."[41] Under these conditions, free trade agreements and deregulation are worthy government projects. Social welfare programs, labor protections, and, yes, internet privacy safeguards are all sent to the chopping block.

This is the contradictory logic of a neoliberal political economy that enabled the marketing complex to demand self-regulation on privacy issues with its right hand while clamoring for a new regime of copyright protections with its left.[42] It is the rationale behind marketers' insistence that government support of advertising-funded media is the only way to keep media free of government control. It is how AOL was able to remain coherent when calling for a "market-driven approach" to internet policy while simultaneously petitioning the government to take "aggressive" action to shape global markets to serve the interests of U.S. companies.[43]

The case of the *Framework* reveals protracted government/private sector partnerships rather than minimalist state intervention. Early in the drafting process, internet policy positions were hashed out with corporate stakeholders down to the last detail. Instituting a moratorium on international and domestic taxation of electronic commerce, pursuing global harmonization of intellectual property protections, and outwardly supporting an advertising-based digital media economy do not indicate a government unwilling to get involved the operation of so-called free markets. Rather, the policy positions laid out in the *Framework* and the processes by which they were constructed clearly demonstrate the unwavering support of the U.S. government for private sector business imperatives.

Instrumental Power and Structural Imperatives

The principle of "private sector leadership" articulated in the *Framework for Global Electronic Commerce* exemplifies the neoliberal political consensus that solidified in the 1990s. Throughout this period, free market orthodoxy was applied not only to the internet, telecommunications, and media sectors but also to banking, finance, and international trade agreements such as NAFTA. Each of these areas doubtless saw a fair share of dedicated lobbying, but there were also overarching political economic forces at play. Clinton's internet policy fits into a larger neoliberal agenda that was shaped by both instrumental and structural factors. Vincent Mosco defines instrumental power as "the ways a dominant class uses the state to achieve its ends."[44] Here the emphasis is on "how the capitalist power structure shapes the state's major policy decisions."[45] The case study of the *Framework* demonstrates this kind of instrumental power.

Attention to instrumental power is complimented by a structuralist approach, which "focuses less on processes of class rule and more on the why of class rule." It "considers the vital functions the capitalist state must satisfy in order to maintain the system on which the state depends for its survival."[46] From a structural perspective, neoliberal internet policy grew out of political and economic elites' response to the "long downturn" that began in the 1970s.[47] As I outline in the Introduction of this book, a debilitating profitability crisis prompted elements of the private sector to reorganize in earnest around computing, communications networks, and global "commodity chains."[48] This included political efforts to shape domestic and international policy around expanded investment opportunities in technology, telecommunications, and media. Although both mainstream political parties in the United States were receptive to these initiatives, the Democrats were quickest to embrace technology as a means to drive "growth, not redistribution."[49] The story of the *Framework* is not simply about New Democrats bowing to the demands of a handful of powerful corporations (that is, instrumental power). It is also about how the Clinton administration commercialized the internet as a matter of national strategic interest in the face of increasing global competition and domestic economic stagnation. Staring down these structural factors,

Clinton made jump-starting the growth of the U.S. private sector a priority from day one.

The neoliberal ideology that provided justification for the internet's commercialization was produced as a political project of the capitalist class, a concentrated effort to overcome crises of profitability.[50] In other words, instead of replacing a politics of redistribution with a "politics of growth," as the New Democrats claimed, neoliberals pursued growth by reversing the flow of redistribution from top down to bottom up. The evidence of their success is overwhelming. The wealth gap between the owning class and everyone else has steadily increased over the last forty years. According to Gabriel Zucman, the richest 1 percent of the U.S. population now possesses around 40 percent of total household wealth.[51] In 2019, the ratio of CEO to typical worker compensation was 320 to 1.[52]

While the rich have gotten richer, real wages for working people have remained stagnant for decades.[53] As Elise Gould shows, the story is "not only rising inequality in general, but also the persistence, and in some cases worsening, of wage gaps by gender and race."[54] Economic inequality is a multifaceted phenomenon, but it clearly reflects the power of elites to shape public policy around issues like taxation, antitrust, trade, and the evisceration of organized labor, which once functioned as a political counterweight to the instrumental power of the capitalist class.[55] The internet's privatization, commercialization, and laissez-faire approach to surveillance advertising fit squarely within this trajectory and deepen its entrenchment.

David Hesmondhalgh points out that neoliberalism's ascent involved "struggle and negotiation" and that "policy is not utterly at the mercy of the wealthy and powerful." In an argument that adds nuance and complexity to a process that might seem overdetermined by economics, Hesmondhalgh notes that policy is always the product of a "balance of social forces" that are deeply impacted by structural inequalities of various kinds, including the uneven distribution of resources among those seeking political influence.[56]

This was certainly the case in the construction of the *Framework*, where access to the policy-making process was highly unequal across intersectional categories of difference. In addition to the lopsided access between business elites on the one hand and everyone else on the other, there were almost certainly severe inequalities along lines of gender and race. Although it would be challenging to find archival sources specific to the inequalities of the *Framework*'s policy formation, reasonable conclusions can be drawn from broader studies of diversity among corporate and government elites during this time period. For example, researchers analyzed the makeup of the boards of directors of Fortune 1000 companies in 1997, concluding that the average board size was eleven people, among which 1.1 were women and 0.7 were racial minorities.[57] Similarly, women made up just 3 percent of top managers in Fortune 1000 firms.[58] Although public policy may not always be dictated by the wealthy, the *Framework* represents a moment when ruling class interests prevailed, as articulated by a narrow group of white male elites.

To conclude this chapter, I want to emphasize the *Framework*'s role in spelling out a self-regulatory policy foundation for internet advertising that carries on to this day. The neoliberal consensus around internet commercialization narrowed the terms of debate around advertising, privacy, and commercial surveillance. Victor Pickard calls this process of contraction "discursive capture," whereby dominant political economic narratives take hold and "systematically write off alternative policy options."[59] For most of the 1990s, questioning the desirability of internet advertising or consumer data collection was beyond the bounds of legitimate discussion. Self-regulation was the only "serious" idea on the table. Recall the internal government studies from the Information Infrastructure Task Force and the National Telecommunications and Information Administration outlined in chapter 1. As early as 1995, these groups cautioned that, absent a universal regulatory framework of privacy protection, market forces were sure to unleash a torrent of consumer surveillance. That these warnings went unheeded reflects the potent mix of neoliberal ideology, instrumental power, and structural imperatives that characterized this crucial period of policy formation. As I show in chapter 6, a real policy debate occurred only at the end of the decade after activists pressured Congress to respond to increasingly invasive consumer monitoring practices. By then, surveillance advertising was well on its way to becoming the preeminent internet business model.

Magaziner's papers reveal how discursive capture played out regarding matters of internet privacy and data collection. As the *Framework* was being drafted, policy makers examined a proposal to create a new federal privacy agency. One of the earliest mentions of this idea came from a 1996 letter to Magaziner from Marc Rotenberg of the Electronic Privacy Information Center. Rotenberg suggested that a dedicated privacy regulator was necessary because "market solutions do not work."[60] Observing that there was "no part of the government that has privacy as its primary mission," staff from Magaziner's office and the National Economic Council discussed how a privacy regulator might be empowered to "create and administer legally enforceable regimes of fair information practices."[61] Their correspondence noted, however, that such a proposal "would be inconsistent with Administration policy to date."[62]

The final version of the *Framework* did not include any trace of the discussions about a federal privacy regulator. A later memo from Magaziner's archive hints at why the proposal never saw the light of day. Summarizing the views of a privacy working group staffed by the Department of Commerce and the White House Office of Management and Budget, the memo states: "There was a general agreement in the group that . . . a comprehensive regulatory role across all sectors would be inappropriate."[63] The reason? The majority of staffers "thought it would be viewed unfavorably by the business community and therefore counterproductive."[64] In this formulation, the only valid public policy goals are those that align with business interests. Anything else is "counterproductive."

Des Freedman's concept of negative policy helps to clarify the dynamics of the neoliberal praxis outlined in this chapter and is especially apt to explain Clinton's self-regulatory approach to surveillance advertising. Freedman points to policy makers' unwillingness to develop regulation out of "fear of undermining innovation or of imposing bureaucratic restrictions on market activity."[65] Negative policy is found "not in policy visibility, but policy opacity, not decision-making, but non–decision making."[66] For Freedman, negative policy refers not simply to inaction but to "the options not considered, the questions that are kept off the policy agenda, the players who are not invited to policy table, and the values that are seen as unrealistic or undesirable by those best able to mobilize their policy-making power."[67]

The story of the *Framework* document, told through archival records, is a vital part of the larger history of the coevolution of the internet and global neoliberal capitalism. It illuminates the concrete practices of internet policy development that supported the buildup of surveillance advertising on the internet. The outcome of Clinton-era negative policy was a political void that provided open terrain for companies to experiment with advertising business models that depended on harvesting consumer data. The next chapter looks at these how these companies became the first generation of surveillance advertisers.

3 THE WEB GETS A MEMORY

WHILE THE POLITICAL FOUNDATIONS of surveillance advertising were being secured, the companies of the marketing complex still needed to hash out how to make advertising work online. This involved not only building technical capacities to deliver ads but also establishing a set of practices and norms for conducting business. The data collection elements of targeted advertising often receive the most attention, but it was the intersection of data collection and networked ad distribution that enabled internet advertising to make its first generational leap. This operational structure was prototyped in the mid-1990s by companies that created so-called ad networks to distribute banner ads to disparate sites across the web, which provided unique opportunities to gather and combine user data. Many of the large-scale surveillance advertising operations conducted today by companies like Google and Facebook descend from this basic ad network model. Indeed, the most important ad network of the 1990s, DoubleClick, was acquired by Google in 2007 and now makes up a major division of its advertising business.

In this chapter, I trace the development of ad networks in the context of web advertising's first three years, from 1994 to 1997. The story of ad networks, and DoubleClick in particular, demonstrates how scattered commercial practices and flexible technologies were brought together to form a particular business model that rendered data collection and ad distribution one in the same. By systematically coupling banner ad delivery with data gathering, and by working to ensure that such practices were enabled as default web browser settings, ad networks set the stage for surveillance advertising's subsequent growth. The early success of the ad network business model, premised on the integration of tracking technologies like the HTTP cookie, catalyzed an important shift in the web's configuration of user privacy. As companies adapted the web's open protocols to make them more suitable for advertising, the interactive media landscape, originally designed to keep users anonymous, became increasingly organized around tracking and identification.

By the mid-1990s, it was increasingly clear that the personal computer, not the television, would be the gateway to the interactive media future.[1] The cable industry's vision for interactive television had failed to materialize, but the growth of commercial online services like AOL catapulted the internet to the forefront of new media. The World Wide Web emerged as the predominant internet application due in no small part to Netscape's "killer app," the graphical web browser.[2] Although AOL and the like were originally walled-garden services, a burgeoning market of dial-up internet service providers offered direct access to the web. Facing this competition, commercial online services were compelled to incorporate web browser functionality, thereby opening up their walled gardens and giving millions of their subscribers access to the public web.[3]

Even though the web was interactive media's breakout star, it remained a troublesome advertising platform at this early stage. Online services already had several years of experimentation with advertising and the results were underwhelming. Prodigy, a partnership between IBM and Sears, had been among the first online services to implement ads, but it was forced to scale back its program after "slow-drawing, screen-hogging ads gave subscribers fits."[4] Responding to the backlash, Ted Leonsis, president of AOL, pledged never to put ads on his company's network. "Here we have this beautiful new interactive medium and we're trying to put a 200-year-old idea on top of it," he said. "It doesn't work."[5]

Though Leonsis would not keep his promise for long, the sentiment was animated by a mythos of anticommercialism ascribed to the denizens of cyberspace. "Academic, international, and apparently free, the internet developed into an almost militantly egalitarian and cooperative community," recalled Netscape's cofounder, Marc Andreessen. "Virtually nobody made any money from it directly."[6] According to the chairman of Delphi Internet Services, another commercial online service, the internet was nothing less than "the last bastion of socialism."[7] It is difficult to gauge the impact of these perceived cultural barriers to business development. What is more certain is that advertisers were flummoxed by the web's hodgepodge of often clunky technologies and general lack of polish. Even with the enhancements of the graphical web browser, computing power and bandwidth were limited, which introduced all manner of technical and creative constraints for would-be advertisers. Although the entire enterprise was characterized by trial and error, early adopters looked for points of familiarity where they could.

The first web advertisements appeared in the fall of 1994. The most prevalent format was the banner ad, known in the industry as display advertising because it mixed text and graphical elements in a manner similar to print and outdoor media. These electronic billboards were largely static images placed on high-traffic websites, with the objective of attracting users' attention as they navigated through content. But unlike other forms of display advertising, web banners offered a layer of interactivity. They could be configured as hyperlinks, enabling users to click through to visit a new website, dictated by the ad's sponsor. One of the first banner campaigns foregrounded this element of interactivity. AT&T sponsored a series of ads on the website HotWired.com that read: "Have you ever clicked your mouse right here? You will."[8] People who clicked were transported to AT&T's website, which featured information about long-distance telephone services and links to a handful of experimental sites created by fine art museums. The campaign didn't make much sense, but it was clear that web advertising's early adopters were leaning into the novel concept of interactivity.

Print publishers were among the first media outlets to test out interactive spaces, and they struggled with decisions about whether to pursue advertising, subscription funding, or both. Some partnered with commercial online services like AOL, but many began creating their own websites, as did increasing numbers of marketers themselves.[9] Still, the bulk of the Madison Avenue ad industry establishment moved online fairly slowly in this early period. Many traditional marketers were willing to bide their time, letting others make the first forays into a challenging and unproven new medium. In 1995, web ad spending barely registered on the scale compared to more established media, but rapid growth was just around the corner. "The promise of [interactive media] is here," said Jeffrey Katzenberg, chairman of Walt Disney Studios. "The delivery and demand are a bit further over the horizon."[10]

The marketing complex's aggressive political mobilization around the advertising funding model discussed in previous chapters should not be confused with the initial hesitation of individual advertisers to spend serious money the web. There is an element of contradiction in the fact that the industry worked to ensure that the internet would become an advertising medium, but remained reluctant to commit significant resources once the ad funding model was more or less secured. But the political campaigns led by the likes of the Coalition for Advertising-Supported Information and Entertainment were defensive in many ways. Their primary goal was to eliminate the chance for new media to develop with autonomy from advertising funding. As I argue below and in the next several chapters, it did not take long for the marketing complex to come online, nor to again band together to wield influence over the particulars of internet development. Ironically, the political efforts of the marketing complex's old guard helped to generate the conditions for a crop of technology-focused upstarts to take a leadership role in the web's growing advertising economy. But there were challenges along the way.

Ad Networks in Dodge City

The most important impediments to early web advertising were logistical. For marketers and ad agencies accustomed to relatively streamlined processes for buying ad inventory, the day-to-day business of web advertising was a labor-intensive guessing game played on unfamiliar technical terrain. Although the conventions of television and print advertising were well established, the web lacked the standard practices, formats, and metrics that greased the wheels of off-line ad channels. There was "no standard reference for what an on-line ad should cost or look like," noted the *Financial Post*.[11] Also missing were the "viewer statistics advertisers in other media take for granted." Invoking the image of the lawless American colonial frontier, one practitioner compared the situation to "Dodge City," admitting, "The structure's a mess right now."[12]

As Joseph Turow argues, early web advertisers achieved a watershed moment with the implementation of the mouse click-through as a standard measure of value for banner advertisements.[13] For advertisers, the click was compelling because it offered a measure of verification that was unique to interactive media and provided a quantifiable representation of consumer intention. Although clicks could not be attributed to individual web users, they could be tallied to get a general sense of a banner's level of engagement. In short order, the click-through rate—the percentage of ad impressions that generate clicks—became a universal metric for evaluating the efficacy of banner ad campaigns.

Nevertheless, the practice of buying and selling ad space online remained cumbersome for most advertisers and publishers. Every aspect of a campaign, including the specifics of the creative elements, the placement and duration of ads, and expected audience exposure had to be negotiated.[14] David Shen, an early employee at Yahoo, recalls inputting banner rotation schedules by hand into a spreadsheet that served as the master template for the portal's advertising operations.[15] Web publishers were flying by the seats of their pants, in many cases trying to drum up business without dedicated ad sales personnel.

Advertising distribution—the placement of ads on publisher sites and the coordination of campaigns—was one of the industry's most important operational hurdles. Although internet usage was growing quickly, audiences were unevenly scattered across thousands of websites and online services. There were limited means to replicate the scale of mass advertising favored by many national marketers, and it was unclear how campaigns of any meaningful size could be managed across such a decentralized medium. "If the web is a 100,000-plus channel universe in which each site is its own program," noted *MediaWeek*, web advertising "is an exasperating reflection of that chaos."[16]

Finding opportunity in this disorder, a new breed of advertising company emerged: the ad network. Blending long-established practices of ad sales outsourcing with the interactive properties of the new digital medium, ad networks positioned themselves as intermediaries between web publishers looking to sell ad inventory and marketers looking to reach sizable audiences. Their point of intervention was logistical, utilizing the technical affordances of web communication to facilitate the distribution of advertising on a large scale. As the first organizations to create simple and efficient systems for banner ad distribution, ad networks built an organizational and technical infrastructure to support subsequent innovations in collecting and deploying user data for targeted advertising.

Beginning in 1996, a core group of ad networks developed a business model that enabled online advertising to expand in a more systemic fashion and primed its embrace of consumer surveillance. No company was more important in these efforts than DoubleClick, described by the *Wall Street Journal* as a "trendy cyber-agency leading Madison Avenue's uncertain charge" into the realm of interactive media.[17] DoubleClick found a foothold in the new web advertising market not through some breakthrough technology but by providing contracted sales labor and streamlining the process of buying and selling banner ads. DoubleClick and peers like WebRep compiled groups of publisher clients and deployed sales teams to entice marketers to buy banner inventory bundled across networks of different sites. The aim was to relieve publishers of the sales burden while giving marketers a single point of access to make buys at relatively large scale.

These companies called themselves ad networks to mimic the conventions of broadcasting, hoping to provide a sense of familiarity to marketers. DoubleClick even gave itself call letters, dubbing its first bundle of sites WCLK.[18] This explicit comparison to television reflects the fact that for all of the hype surrounding interactive media, the nuts and bolts of early web advertising focused in large part on building basic economies of scale, simplifying a chaotic business landscape, and coordinating sales labor. To these ends, ad networks worked to standardize banner formats and units of sale, such as cost per thousand ad impressions (CPM), helping to ease transaction costs and enable comparisons across publishers.

Ad networks' services were immediately attractive to web publishers for whom the cost of hiring sales personnel was prohibitive.[19] Even for those with deep pockets, expertise in the evolving online platform proved to be a scarce resource. By early 1996, major media companies, including CBS and NBC, arguably among the best positioned to sell their own ad inventory, hired outside firms to handle sales.[20] So did important web publishers like Netscape, who contracted DoubleClick to monetize the influx of traffic to its corporate site, which was set as the default home page on its popular Navigator browser. The web publishing sector experienced a rush for sales personnel with any modicum of interactive experience; they would take "anyone who [could] translate web gobbledygook into language that marketers [could] understand."[21]

Although ad networks were novel on the internet, outsourcing ad sales and bundling disparate audiences were not new ideas. On the contrary, ad sales representation was in many ways the original business model of the adverting agency.[22] As early as 1889, J. Walter Thompson sold ad space across some thirty magazines such as *Harper's* and *Cosmopolitan*.[23] By facilitating bundled ad distribution, writes Richard Ohmann, early agencies like Thompson "opened up an economic space not previously demarcated and put themselves solidly in it."[24] As turn-of-the-century print advertising grew, ad agencies expanded their purview to include copywriting, media planning, and market research. J. Walter Thompson in particular pioneered a full-service agency approach that enlarged the industry's scope by centralizing a range of marketing functions and iterating to create new ones. Daniel Pope argues that the emergence and broadening of ad sales representation played an integral role in the "making of modern advertising" and the commercialization of print media.[25]

A century later, ad networks like DoubleClick followed in Thompson's footsteps, expanding on ad sales representation toward a more full-service approach. DoubleClick developed proprietary technologies to not only improve and enlarge banner advertising distribution but also to centralize control over these processes. DoubleClick's management came to view its core business as facilitating "the logistics of internet advertising on a large scale."[26] DoubleClick facilitated this mission by merging with Interactive Advertising Network (IAN), another start-up that had developed a system to deliver ads to many disparate websites from a central web server. Describing the deal's rationale, IAN's cofounder Kevin O'Connor told *Advertising Age*, "We realized we had the same goals: [DoubleClick] had the sales and we had the technology. It was a merger made in heaven."[27] Foreshadowing the company's future emphasis on building centralized ad technologies, it was IAN's O'Connor, rather than DoubleClick's management, who led the new company as CEO.

DoubleClick's new ad-serving technology leveraged the disaggregated nature of the web's communication protocols to consolidate the delivery and coordination of banner ads. Here's how it worked. Behind the scenes, a website that appears to load as a unified entity is really an amalgamation of various media elements assembled by the browser. In a basic setup, a web browser might receive all the files that make up a web page from a single server, but this two-party configuration is not a technical requirement. Different website elements can easily be stored across multiple servers and then compiled into a unified web page with no apparent change in the final display or functionality. For example, in the earliest days of web advertising, a publisher like Fast Company would generally host all of the files that constituted its website on its own servers, including any ads, even if ad sales were contracted out to a network. This scenario changed as ad networks began offering centralized ad serving. So when Fast Company joined DoubleClick in 1996, it outsourced not only its ad sales operation but also its ad delivery and campaign management functions. Setup simply required adding a few lines of code to Fast Company's site to instruct web browsers to retrieve banner ads from DoubleClick rather than its own server. DoubleClick would handle the rest. Advertising online, once a confusing and laborious process, suddenly became the "easiest [business] model for a web startup to implement."[28] Rather than fiddling with ad tech or chasing down user subscriptions, all web publishers needed to do was "contract their revenue growth to an ad network and focus on building an audience."[29]

Because it was largely invisible to web users, the ad network system became known as third-party advertising. When an individual web user (the first party) visits a web publisher (the second party), there is an expectation of communication among the two parties. Working behind the scenes to deliver ads from unaffiliated servers, ad networks were third-party intermediaries into what was previously a two-party exchange. By building their own distribution infrastructure via centralized ad servers, DoubleClick and other ad networks were able to offer publishers fully outsourced advertising services, ameliorating the need for sales labor but also handling key operational functions like ad delivery, campaign management, and billing. As the financial services website Edgar Online told the *New York Times*, working with DoubleClick allowed the company to "focus on what we're good at, the selling and marketing of S.E.C.-based products, but not on what we're not good at—dealing with ad agencies, trafficking ads, and sending advertisers reports."[30] Third-party ad servers swiftly became an industry mainstay, giving marketers and their ad agencies more convenient means to reach economies of scale in their media buys—and, as we shall see, opening new possibilities for targeted messaging. As one ad network executive put it, "What we think will drive growth is an automated system that can do all of the ad buys in real time and automate the results."[31]

As the web proliferated and more ad networks cropped up, "the challenge facing media planners" shifted from "finding sites on which to advertise to knowing which tools to use for help."[32] Competing with ad networks, other companies emerged to offer iterations of self-service ad tech management. Among the most important of this group were NetGravity and Accipiter, start-ups that provided turnkey ad servers to web publishers that did not wish to outsource ad sales or bundle their inventory in a network.[33] Like ad networks, these software-based tools were far more efficient than manual ad placement. Yahoo reported using NetGravity's system to go from a three-person staff managing five ad campaigns across twenty web pages to a team of two managing seventy campaigns across sixteen thousand pages.[34] As the technology improved, the time delay for executing and modifying ad campaigns was effectively reduced to zero. Banners washed over the web at an increasing pace. By late 1997, DoubleClick alone was serving approximately 750 million ads per month, and capacity was growing.[35]

Beyond the Banner

The logistical improvements brought by ad networks were significant, but the young industry encountered other equally vexing problems. As banners spread, their novelty began to wear thin. It was something of an open secret among web publishers that the majority of users simply did not click on ads. Banners were like poison ivy: Most people steered clear, and those who did click once or twice usually kept their distance after that. This was especially troublesome because so much of the hype surrounding the web's commercialization hinged on its interactivity, which was supposed to enable marketers to engage consumers directly rather than simply shout in their general direction, only to be ignored. Without robust interactivity, the low-bandwidth web seemed a poor substitute for existing branding platforms like television. As marketers began to grumble about low click-through rates, the online ad industry responded with a flurry of activity centered on ways to move "beyond the banner."[36]

Some web advertising companies attempted to enhance banners with "rich media" experiences and pop-up formats that were harder to ignore, but the idea that gained the most traction among advertisers was that ads simply needed to be more "relevant" to consumers. Greater personalization of messaging was positioned as a solution for reining in the chaos of an interactive medium that seemed to give consumers greater control over their media experiences.[37] Of course, personalization required increased knowledge about web users, which dovetailed with evolving needs for data collection and user identification in other sectors such as internet retailing and banking. What the web needed was a memory. The problem was that it was designed to forget.

The web's communication protocols were originally created to facilitate series of discrete data transfers, not persistent connections. Rather than preserve a continuous "state" of communication among parties, web protocols saved precious computing resources by operating in a "stateless" condition.[38] Data was sent back and forth as a string of stand-alone communication events. It was possible to catalog information about certain user interactions—servers could count clicks and capture glimpses of immediate browsing history—but it was difficult to attach such actions to individuals. This made web browsing functionally anonymous but limited the scope of commercial applications. For example, in order for online shopping to function, websites had to be able to recognize that a given series of actions (like putting items into a shopping cart) were connected to a single user. As the *Wall Street Journal* put it, without the means to tell one person from another, websites were destined to remain "poor shopkeepers."[39]

Seeking to improve the relevance of ad targeting, internet advertisers found it especially pressing to develop the web's capacity to recognize and remember individual users. Ad companies and publishers began to work on solutions that required users to register and log in, but it was Netscape, maker of the leading web browser software, that developed a scalable fix to the problem of statelessness. This was the HTTP cookie, an innovation that enabled web servers to uniquely identify web browsers. Cookies effectively allowed websites to say, "Here, hang onto this file and show it to me the next time you ask me something. It will remind me who you are and what we've already talked about."[40] Passing a cookie identifier back and forth created a continuous communication state between browsers and servers, which facilitated a range of new data collection practices on the web. Released as an open technical standard, cookie functionality was quickly integrated into all major browsers and put to a variety of uses spanning e-commerce, credentialization, and personalization.[41] It was not long before *Network World* described cookies as "a de facto standard" web protocol.[42] This widespread implementation altered the web's trajectory by introducing a new capacity for surveillance into what had effectively been an anonymous communications environment.

The internet advertising industry seized on cookie technology as a means to improve ad targeting and relevance. Before cookies, ad metrics companies such as I/PRO had attempted to glean information about web traffic patterns from the routine records stored in server logs. Some degree of analysis was possible using metadata such as IP addresses, but as I/PRO's founder explained, without a system of unique identification, server logs were "ungainly veins."[43] No company was able to reliably divine the activities of individual users without forcing people to register and log into websites. Cookies were a game changer in this regard, offering any business on the web an unobtrusive means to link online actions with individual web browsers. Because they were built into the web's standard communication protocols, cookies were automatically passed back and forth behind the scenes during the browsing experience. Voluntary site registrations and user questionnaires became outmoded by new methods of data collection that did not need to bother with "the trouble of getting the user's permission."[44] By 1997, the Internet Advertising Bureau trade group endorsed cookies as "an essential part of member companies' business strategies."[45]

Cookie Monsters

Although the broader advertising sector recognized cookies as an opportunity to improve ad targeting, only ad networks had the capacity to integrate data collection into ad delivery operations on a large scale. This gave ad networks a unique vantage point to track individuals as they moved about the web across seemingly unaffiliated sites. Cookies were flexible and could be hitched to any number of routine data transactions between web browsers and servers. Third parties could deposit cookies through websites for which they were not the primary hosts, provided that they served at least some element of the page. Any component would do, be it an image, a chunk of text, or a far-flung banner advertisement.

Ad networks capitalized on this opportunity, shrewdly embedding cookies into the banners served to sites across their networks. Each time a banner was served, a cookie was sent with it. This created and maintained a data channel between an ad network like DoubleClick and every user who visited any of its client websites.[46] Leveraging this reciprocity, DoubleClick transformed its ad delivery system into an apparatus for systematically gathering information about web users and their behaviors. Dispersed across the web via ad networks' central servers, banner ads became conduits for circulating cookies on a scale and scope that far exceeded anything in practice at the time. Although any web publisher could deploy cookies on its own site to recognize return visitors, ad networks had the ability to connect the dots as users moved from site to site. Significantly, the appropriation of cookies gave ad networks a way to develop improved user tracking and profiling capabilities and to make a renewed business case to publishers, marketers, and investors regarding the viability of targeted banner advertising.

In the hands of ad network developers, cookies added an unprecedented level of granularity to existing advertising techniques, spawning early forays into what later became called behavioral advertising.[47] The regularly updated information stored in cookie files provided the crucial mortar used when building databases of user profiles, enabling surveillance of individual web browsers as a proxy for individual consumers. These capacities were enhanced because they were deployed over sprawling ad networks. More than simply adding a larger volume of consumer information, data collection via ad networks qualitatively changed the possibilities for profiling and ad targeting. One of the most popular innovations was termed clickstream analysis, which involved tracking the movements of individual web browsers over time. This enabled ad networks to compile browsing histories that included information about the time, duration, and order of the sites users visited. As *Forbes* explained, after receiving an initial DoubleClick cookie, "whenever you visit any of the sites [in the network], the DoubleClick server picks up the [cookie] ID number and tucks away information about your visit. Gradually it builds a pretty complete dossier on you—and your spending and computing habits."[48]

DoubleClick moved aggressively into profiling, depositing 40 million cookies and compiling a database of 10 million unique user profiles in its first year.[49] To get a sense of scale, DoubleClick's profile database was 60 percent larger than the entire subscriber base of America Online, at the time the nation's largest internet service provider.[50] In 1997, DoubleClick branded its technology under the label DART, which stood for Dynamic Advertising, Reporting, and Targeting. The DART system could serve targeted ads in near real time by cross-referencing its user profile database with information collected on the fly. The company's tag line during this period highlighted its dynamic targeting capabilities with the promise to deliver the "right message to the right person at the right time."

The DART software, deployed across DoubleClick's network of publishers, represented the first major incarnation of the data-driven surveillance advertising that industry boosters had been promising for years. When asked whether DoubleClick could "enable an advertiser to reach women aerospace engineers who like sports in Southern California," CEO Kevin O'Connor responded, "If you work for Lockheed [Martin] in Orange County and you're accessing the sports scores for women's soccer, we've got you."[51] As *Crain's New York Business* observed, "No one else [was] doing it in nearly as sophisticated a fashion."[52]

Although some major publishers such as Microsoft and the *New York Times* kept ad services largely in house, Forrester Research declared that "the future of web advertising belonged to ad networks rather than single websites."[53] DoubleClick, among the best positioned to capitalize on network effects and economies of scale, emerged as a market leader. The industry was by no means a well-oiled machine, but the services provided by ad networks made it more practical and enticing for marketers to allocate portions of their ad budgets online. Boosted by the start of what would become the dot-com financial boom, online advertising spending in the United States reached nearly $1 billion in 1997, closing in on spending totals for outdoor media ($1.4 billion).[54] As *HotWired* described it, "The days when the net seemed to exist outside the laws of capitalism [were] just about over."[55]

Revolt of the Developers

The original technical specification for HTTP cookies was created at Netscape by a team led by Lou Montulli, one of the company's first software developers. As Montulli told the *New York Times*, the goal was to create a tool with the flexibility to be put to many different uses, including "things we hadn't thought about."[56] One such thing was the online ad industry's increasingly widespread use of cookies to power surreptitious data collection. Montulli was no privacy hawk, but he was troubled by the way cookies had been appropriated by ad networks to engage in third-party tracking. Working with colleagues, Montulli drafted a revised technical specification that disabled third-party cookies by default, requiring users to opt into advertising from the likes of ad networks.[57] Although Montulli had no problems with data-driven advertising on a first-party basis, he "didn't want cookies to be used as a general tracking mechanism" without explicit user consent.[58]

This is how David Kristol, an engineer at Bell Laboratories and respected member of the internet standards community, came to be accused of corporate subversion. "I got an outraged call from Kevin Ryan [CFO of DoubleClick] expressing his unhappiness and accusing me of trying to sabotage his business," he recalled.[59] Kristol had coauthored the new cookie specification with Montulli and submitted it for review with the Internet Engineering Task Force (IETF), a volunteer standards setting community that developed internet protocols.

The ad network executive's anger was indicative of a groundswell of industry aggravation related not only to Montulli and Kristol's proposal but also to a spate of unwanted public attention. The news media had recently discovered the existence of cookies and was beginning to raise questions about online privacy.[60] More worrying still, the Federal Trade Commission was gearing up to hold a workshop to discuss web privacy issues. Though there was little evidence to suggest that President Clinton's administration would derail web advertising's trajectory, the White

House had not yet officially endorsed a self-regulatory approach to internet data collection.

Upon catching wind of Montulli and Kristol's revised cookie proposal, internet advertising companies went on the defensive, inserting themselves into what might have otherwise been seen as an obscure technocratic issue. As one industry representative put it: "What concerns us is the tone of the proposal, which is that advertising is not good for us, so we want to avoid it. That begs the question, how is the web going to be funded?"[61] Tellingly, the new cookie specification was not actually against web advertising. Nor was it against the use of cookies for tracking and personalization. Nor was it even against third-party advertising when conducted on a voluntary, opt-in basis. What the specification opposed was hidden third-party surveillance as a default setting on the web. The proposal took specific aim at the lack of transparency involved in third-party cookies and the absence of user control over their use. As Kristol explained, "Short of turning off automatic image loading, a user could not avoid receiving third party cookies."[62]

A debate began within the IETF not only about whether third-party surveillance was a threat to user privacy and autonomy but also about whether the organization should be involved in privacy issues in the first place. Public email archives reveal heated discussions about the overlapping technical and social dimensions of this issue.[63] Proponents of the revised standard conceded that it could produce some fallout by limiting otherwise acceptable cookie practices, but they opted for a "conservative method," preferring to err on the side privacy.[64] Others contended that tracking was a necessary component of web advertising and that disrupting third-party cookies would destroy ad networks and the growing number of publishers that depended on them for revenue.[65] Drawing a distinction between legitimate advertising and unaccountable surveillance, Kristol argued that restrictions on third-party cookies would undermine "business models that relied on tracking users, not the advertising business itself."[66]

Among the most strident opposition to the proposal came from an employee at Microsoft who argued that the "free market will do a better job of protecting user's rights" than a restrictive standard.[67] The commenter warned that if the IETF tried to implement such "social engineering," the organization would become irrelevant by showing companies that it was a "dangerous place to create standards."[68] "After all," the commenter wrote, "vendors want to work with an organization where they are partners in the standards process, not its target." It is worth noting that Kristol and others had explicitly reached out to industry representatives from the start of the discussion, but only a few organizations elected to participate early on. It was only after the revised specification proved a threat to the developing surveillance advertising business model that industry took notice.

Instead of engaging in a real debate about the privacy costs of its emerging business model, the ad sector ran interference while organizing to support a competing standard that left third-party tracking alone.[69] Leading this countereffort was the chief technology officer at Engage Technologies, a company on its way to becoming one of DoubleClick's biggest ad tech rivals.[70] Like the broader political mobilization of the marketing complex, this was another example of competitors joining forces to advance a common interest in shaping the web's features toward surveillance.

With all the back and forth, the deliberation process at the IETF slowed to a crawl, dragging on for months. Reaching an impasse, Kristol withdrew the provision to limit third-party tracking.[71] There would be no official pushback from the internet standards community on advertising and privacy issues. Ultimately, the power to implement any standard rested with the browser software makers, of which there were only two of significance. Netscape and Microsoft controlled nearly the entire market, and as such, their decisions became "de facto standards," regardless of the IETF's technical specifications.[72] Both companies participated in the IETF discussions to some degree (Montulli was still a Netscape employee), but in the end, they were unwilling to support third-party cookie restrictions.

It could have been that Netscape and Microsoft were simply focused on other business objectives and therefore reluctant to dedicate resources toward privacy concerns. As the product manager for Navigator put it, "We expect this to blow over. We just don't consider it a significant issue."[73] Kristol's own reflection is that while Netscape and Microsoft were giving web browsers to consumers for free, they were selling servers and related software to businesses. It simply was not worth the trouble to potentially "anger their paying customers by disabling third party cookies."[74] As Rajiv Shah and Jay Kesan argue in their study of the cookie standards-setting process, "the implication is that society cannot expect firms to meet or adequately protect unprofitable societal concerns."[75]

In some ways, the software design decisions made by Netscape and Microsoft years earlier had set the stage for the resolution to this standoff. The first iterations of Netscape's Navigator browser implemented cookies entirely behind the scenes. There were no options for users to manage cookies; nor was there any indication that they were being placed on users' machines as they surfed the web.[76] From the start, cookies were infrastructural, a background technical feature meant to support a range of second-order practices. Only several years later, in the midst of the IETF debates and mounting public scrutiny, did browser makers add user controls over cookies.[77] But even then, browsers were configured to accept all cookies by default, including those from third-party ad networks. Had they wanted to support Montulli and Kristol's revised specification, Netscape and Microsoft could have easily reversed this design choice. Instead, they allowed third-party tracking to recede into the web's normal state of operation.

It so happened that adding user controls while leaving third-party tracking intact was the exact solution offered by Dwight Merriman, the lead engineer at DoubleClick. Blocking third-party cookies "should be available to the user as an option," he wrote to the IETF, but all cookies should be enabled "by default."[78] The reason? Disabling third-party cookies automatically was "basically equivalent to not allowing them at all, because 99% of the population will see no reason to change the default" setting. Some within the IETF working group disagreed. "That Double-Click has formed a business model around a loophole in the original cookie draft is not, as I see it, any reason to compromise the privacy of future web users," wrote one participant. "I think it is deplorable that you would ask to modify an agreed-to standard for your commercial gain."[79]

Deplorable or otherwise, leaving third-party cookies as the default configuration was a significant victory for ad networks and the surveillance advertising business model at large. "Because the vast majority of Web users never bother to change their cookie preferences," summarized *Advertising Age*, "the effect on companies that use cookies as targeting tools will be minimal."[80] Research on the power of default settings corroborates this conclusion. As Rajiv Shah and Christian Sandvig have shown, defaults place significant power to regulate human behavior in the hands of technology designers, particularly when adjusting settings is left to the underinformed, as was the case for the majority of web users in this period.[81] In his work on digital rights management systems, Tarleton Gillespie argues that objectionable practices like surveillance "seem to be more palatable to users when they arrive as an organic part of a new technology, rather than being imposed on a technology already in existence."[82] The IETF's unsuccessful challenge to third-party cookies was a moment of what Gillespie calls "technological regulation," which helped to ingrain surveillance not as a political question of design but simply how the internet works. This is precisely what would be expected in the regulatory void of the government's neoliberal approach to internet privacy.

Cookies are still used today, but they are by no means the only mechanism of internet surveillance. Overemphasizing their functional role, or that of any particular technology, obscures one of the key lessons of this history. It is not only what cookies did (identify browsers and collect data) but also how they were deployed that helped set the web on the trajectory of surveillance advertising. Cookies were the first widespread implementation of consumer surveillance deployed natively within a media platform. Integrated into the web's communication protocols, cookies built a capacity for surveillance into the technical guts of the web in the early stages of its development and popularization. Implemented behind the scenes, cookies normalized surveillance as part of the default experience of internet use. In their appropriation of cookies, ad networks set up the technical foundations for the increasingly invasive forms of consumer surveillance that followed. As ad networks grew, so did surveillance advertising, and the fundamental character of the web was transformed from anonymous to identifying.

The following years saw an expansion and refinement of the business models and technologies of surveillance advertising. By the late 1990s, DoubleClick and handful of other ad networks were clear industry leaders. Although still not profitable, they were earning revenue and relentlessly promoting themselves through public relations and their own advertising campaigns. And while falling short of fully satisfying the demands of marketers, the sophistication of their ad-serving systems and the scope of their reach surpassed contemporary alternatives and continued to point to the intensified use of the web as a medium for consumer surveillance. As the chief executive of the Engage ad network told *BusinessWeek*, coming to appreciate the value of consumer data was his industry's "single most important revelation."[83] The next chapter examines how surveillance advertisers were given a major boost, materially and ideologically, by the dot-com investment bubble, which propelled the U.S. economy into the twenty-first century.

4 THE DOT-COM BUBBLE

BETWEEN ROUGHLY 1995 AND 2000, the U.S. economy was overtaken by a financial market boom and bust that centered on the commercialization of the internet: the dot-com bubble. The speculative investment of this period contributed significantly to the buildup of surveillance advertising. Soaring investment markets and the growing internet advertising sector entered into a pattern of mutual reinforcement that began in 1995 and intensified until the bubble collapsed in 2000. This chapter outlines the consequences of this marketing/finance feedback loop. The influx of investment capital provided a big boost for many online ad companies, allowing them to rapidly expand their advertising capacities and market share under the prevailing business strategy of "get big fast." Most concretely, leading ad networks like DoubleClick raised large amounts of capital, which enabled them to pursue aggressive growth strategies while operating at losses.

The bubble also played an important role in generating early demand for internet advertising. Brimming with investment capital, dot-com startups were among web advertising's biggest spenders. This helped legitimize the medium for traditional marketers who began to move online in earnest during the bubble's later stages. Large internet advertising outlays were rationalized through a new economy discourse in which traditional measures of economic valuation like profitability were superseded by metrics of publicity such as brand recognition and "mind share." Advertising thus became an important dot-com business strategy: necessary not only to acquire customers but also to attract the next round of vital investment capital. The bubble ultimately functioned as an accelerant to surveillance advertising on the web, providing ample material and ideological resources while helping to undermine alternative media revenue models like subscription content.

The financial bubble grew out of a complex array of factors, but it was driven by risk capital investment, a term used here to indicate the short-term speculative investment typical of entities such as hedge funds, private equity firms, and venture capitalists. In contrast to something like a mutual fund that pursues incremental growth over a number of years, risk capital investment seeks above-average returns through rapid deployment and strategic exit under careful consideration of market conditions. During the dot-com period, risk capital was deployed most significantly by venture capital firms (VCs) largely based in California's Silicon Valley. VCs establish high-value investment funds constituted by agreements among the firm's principals (general partners) and outside investors (limited partners). Under the management of the principals, funds are invested across a portfolio of start-up companies in cascading series of financing rounds that are usually conditional on growth benchmarks. A basic VC game plan might look something like this: Invest in a start-up with significant growth potential, spend capital to swiftly increase market share, and then realize profits by cashing out via an initial public offering (IPO) or acquisition deal.

In the mid 1990s, VCs began to home in on the internet as the next great investment opportunity. Many believed that the recently privatized interactive medium would foster a range of new "winner take all" markets with vast commercial potential. In order to exploit this potential to its fullest, risk investors promoted what David Kirsch and Brent Goldfarb call the "get big fast" strategy of business development.[1] Modeled after the monopolistic successes of companies like Microsoft and Intel, get big fast was a "bet on a future state of the world in which a select group of 'winners' would dominate the e-commerce landscape."[2] Rather than pursue incremental growth, the aim was to saturate a given market as quickly as possible in order to secure "first mover" advantages, minimize competition, and reap the resulting superprofits.

The first internet company to successfully use this strategy was Netscape Communications. Now best remembered for developing and popularizing Netscape Navigator, the graphical web browser, Netscape's implementation of get big fast was just as consequential, serving as a proof of concept for a flood of follow-on VC-backed start-ups. In 1994, Netscape secured a $5 million investment from the prominent venture capital firm Kleiner Perkins Caufield & Byers and used the funds to swiftly push its Navigator browser to market.[3] Pursuing market share, Netscape gave its software away for free and partnered with computer manufacturers and internet service providers to increase distribution. By the middle of 1995, Netscape had won nearly three quarters of the web browser market.[4] Citing future competitor Microsoft as an inspiration, Netscape's young cofounder, Marc Andreessen, summarized the rationale: "Market share now equals revenue later and if you don't have market share now, you are not going to have revenue later."[5] Microsoft's fundamental lesson here was to go for product ubiquity—a plan that required substantial resources.

Looking to raise more investment capital, Netscape went public in August 1995. Trading began so frantically on the day of the IPO that the company's share price nearly tripled before the market opened, then closed at more than twice the original offer price. Worth $21 million one year before, Netscape's valuation instantly jumped to over $2.2 billion, netting the company and its investors huge sums.[6] As PBS's *Frontline* would later report, the IPO was an "historic and prophetic moment on Wall Street."[7] It was historic because the explosive demand for Netscape's stock took the financial world by surprise and kick-started widespread speculative investment in the internet sector. It was prophetic because it legitimized the get big fast strategy that "came to define an entire generation of internet technology companies," otherwise known as dot-coms.[8]

Annual VC investment surged over the next five years, growing from about $7 billion in 1995 to nearly $100 billion in 2000, then receding to less than $40 billion a year for the next decade.[9] Most of this capital went to businesses seeking to commercialize the internet. In 1999 and 2000, the peak years of the bubble, internet companies scooped up nearly 80 percent of VC investment.[10] The dot-com start-up population ballooned, as did the value of individual funding commitments. Companies that only a few years earlier "would have been happy to receive a few million in venture funding routinely [received] up to ten times that amount."[11]

Following the path broken by Netscape, hundreds of dot-com companies held IPOs between 1995 and 2000. These included household names like Yahoo, Amazon, and E*Trade, as well as more specialized companies like the DoubleClick ad network. Many dot-coms continued to raise money beyond the IPO by issuing follow-on stock offerings, and a large number of internet-related businesses attracted financing outside of public markets. All told, an estimated 24,000 internet-related firms raised $256 billion from public and private investors during the bubble.[12] To better understand the relationship of the financial bubble and surveillance advertising, it is necessary to take a closer look at how these companies spent their risk capital windfalls.

The Marketing/Finance Feedback Loop

The dot-com bubble generated a kind of marketing/finance feedback loop in which the most important business competency was attracting investment capital. This was achieved to a significant degree through advertising and public relations, whereby companies sought to demonstrate their potential to become dominant in a given online market: to get big fast. Dot-coms with a strong market position and favorable media profile found it much easier to attract investors, while securing risk capital through IPOs and other means was deployed as a public relations event in its own right. At the same time, companies that had secured investment funding spent heavily on advertising to further build market share and enhance brand image, which in turn aided more fundraising. This feedback loop between marketing, finance, and the new internet medium directed significant investment toward transforming the web into an advertising channel, supporting and accelerating the broader efforts of the marketing complex.

What is often overlooked about Netscape's success in the financial markets and the dot-com phenomenon more generally is the fundamental role that marketing communications played in all stages of the bubble's investment processes. Standard investment analysis holds that a company's valuation should be based on objective indicators of business performance and underlying market fundamentals. The field of behavioral finance adds a layer of complexity, showing that factors like brand awareness and public image—elements that are heavily influenced by marketing communications but that are difficult to account for on financial statements—can also be important determinants of a company's valuations and fundraising outcomes. As Robert Shiller argues, "The role of the news media in the stock market is not, as commonly believed, simply as a convenient tool for investors who are reacting directly to economically significant news itself. The media actively shape public attention and categories of thought, and they create the environment within which the stock market events are played out."[13]

During the dot-com bubble, advertising and public relations became important drivers of financial valuation, in many cases superseding more conventional metrics. A crucial detail of Netscape's financial story is that on the day of its wildly successful IPO, the company had not recorded a single dollar of profit. This set in motion an investment rationality for the dot-com era in which profitability, a long-standing rule of thumb for companies filing IPOs, was suddenly seen as outmoded. In 1995, Netscape was an outlier. Almost two thirds of new stock issuers had profitable operations when they held initial public offerings. By the first quarter of 2000, fewer than one in five companies were profitable at the time of their IPO.[14] The outlier had become the norm.

Netscape's IPO triggered a retreat from the profitability standard. A new valuation model was articulated by professional investment analysts whose pronouncements were reproduced by uncritical and at times obsequious media coverage. Perhaps the highest-profile example is a series of reports from investment bank Morgan Stanley that downplayed established economic markers (such as cash flow) in favor of indicators related to growth potential. A proliferation of metrics such as "mind share" signaled the upswing of marketing-based asset valuation models that depended heavily on advertising and public relations.[15]

Howard Kurtz demonstrates the extent to which investment analysts were given media platforms to espouse marketing-based asset valuation models and the degree to which such practices were encouraged by media owners and professionals who often had vested interests in keeping the bubble going strong.[16] The "rhetoric of the new economy was hot and glamorous."[17] It spawned a subgenre of internet investment market news (especially on cable television) and was featured more generally across mainstream media outlets. This developing media discourse had material consequences. As Nigel Thrift argues, "Telling the new economy story worked, and worked to the extent that it began to re-describe market fundamentals."[18] In practice, marketing-based valuation models created incentives for dot-com companies to pursue market share, measured perhaps most directly by web traffic, in order to attract investment and bump up their stock prices.[19]

Digging deeper into the VC/IPO risk investment process illustrates precisely how dot-coms utilized marketing communications to meet these objectives. Following Netscape's pattern, the timeline for most dot-coms was to first secure funding from venture capital firms and/or wealthy angel investors, then hold an IPO as soon as possible. Demonstrating forward momentum was essential to fundraising. More important still was to show the potential to become a household name and win a given internet market. To this end, it became increasingly necessary to generate positive media publicity, or investment buzz, across all stages of the investment process, but especially when approaching an IPO.

Netscape's media acumen was critical to its fundraising success. As cofounder Jim Clark put it, "Anyone starting a company that doesn't try to influence the press's impression surrenders the future to fate, a tremendous mistake."[20] Shrewd deployment of advertising and public relations was critical for securing venture capital and holding a successful IPO. In other words, the emerging characteristics of the speculative financial bubble encouraged dot-coms to allocate inordinate resources to marketing communications. On this point, the Morgan Stanley analysts were clear: "For now it's important for companies to nab customers and keep improving product offerings: mind share and market share will be crucial."[21]

Netscape's IPO was consequential because it demonstrated that financial success could be achieved through advertising and public relations in the absence of profitability. Subsequent dot-coms and investors took the lesson to heart as branding became "essential for web companies" seeking capital.[22] After starting a dot-com, journalist and would-be internet entrepreneur Michael Wolff quipped that his "primary job was now to get the company's name in the paper."[23] "Publicity," Wolff noted, "is the currency of our time."[24]

In this context, dot-com start-ups routinely hired advertising agencies and public relations firms to launch strategic communication campaigns in order to attract attention from potential investors. As one internet executive declared, "You've got to get an [ad] agency to show VCs that you are making progress with your business plan; having an agency is a comfort factor for VCs." Some observers noted that dot-com ad campaigns seemed to be "disproportionately skewed" to investor publics in order to "generate confidence."[25] During one eight-month period in 1999, TBWA/Chiat/Day, an agency known for its edgy creative work, reported meeting with no fewer than 174 dot-coms as potential clients.[26]

Dot-coms raised billions of dollars from IPOs during the bubble, a significant portion of which went directly to fund marketing communications. Retailer E-Stamp committed nearly two thirds of its $110 million IPO earnings to "ads, marketing and brand-building" efforts.[27] Likewise, online insurance peddler HealthExtra used its IPO to finance a $25 million ad campaign.[28] Goldberg Moser O'Neill, an ad agency with Interpublic, claimed that its dot-com clients planned to spend in excess of $1 billion in the fourth quarter of 1999, roughly equivalent to the annual U.S. ad spending of McDonald's and Burger King combined.[29]

Advertising spending data are more meaningful when compared across business sectors. One method for gauging a given company or industry's relative emphasis on marketing activities is to compare sales and marketing expenses as a percentage of revenue, known as the SME ratio. A study commissioned by *Advertising Age* found that the dot-com sector had an average SME ratio of 94 percent in the fourth quarter of 1999, meaning that the typical dot-com spent 94 cents on sales and marketing for every incoming dollar of revenue.[30] Although high SME ratios are not uncommon among new businesses, dot-coms allocated disproportionate resources to sales and marketing efforts compared to off-line retailers, which averaged SME ratios of 25 to 40 percent.[31] These data show that the dot-com sector funded marketing communications, and advertising in particular, at rates that far outpaced comparable off-line businesses. This trend can be attributed in part to certain large-scale branding efforts via traditional media channels. This was most pronounced in television, where dot-coms bought ad inventory at premium rates, including collectively purchasing seventeen ad spots during the 2000 Super Bowl.[32] Yet the majority of traditional media spending came from an unrepresentative cluster of the most highly capitalized internet companies.[33]

Although Super Bowl commercials were noteworthy expenditures, most dot-coms spent the bulk of their ad dollars on a medium much closer to home. In 1996, six of the top ten online advertising spending leaders were dot-coms.[34] The list included Excite, Netscape, Infoseek, Yahoo, Lycos, and CNET, all of which had recently held IPOs. Infoseek spent 60 percent of its advertising budget online, while Yahoo spent nearly all of its ad dollars on the same.[35] In 1997, all but CNET again ranked among the top ten online spenders. More generally, dot-coms and companies in the computing and technology sectors, like Microsoft and IBM, accounted for more than half of all online ad spending in 1996 and 1997 and about 40 percent in 1998.[36] In 1999 and early 2000, a group of about eighty well-capitalized dot-coms paid for over three quarters of all web advertising.[37]

Online advertising represented a small fraction of total U.S. ad spending at the start of the bubble. By 2001, it had surpassed outdoor media and trade publications.[38] Annual outlays more than tripled from 1996 to 1997, more than doubled from 1997 to 1998, doubled again from 1998 to 1999, and grew by 75 percent from 1999 to 2000.[39] Dot-coms drove this growth, offsetting the more tentative outlays of traditional marketers. Some traditional advertisers experimented with banner advertising and corporate websites as early as 1994, but others were hesitant to move ad dollars online in any systematic manner until the end of the decade. Although only intermittently available, ad impressions data confirm this. In the second and third quarters of 1999, the ten largest dot-com marketers collectively purchased over 7.5 billion banner ad impressions, more than double the amount purchased by the top ten traditional marketers over the same period.[40]

In addition to providing material support for ad spending, the bubble helped to foreclose alternative media funding models. Publishers considering user subscriptions ran into the powerful headwind of "get big fast." "Our investment bankers were urging us not to charge [for content]," said the cofounder of financial news site TheStreet.com.[41] Although start-ups did not need to be profitable to get funded, they were required to sketch out plans for future revenue, particularly in the bubble's later stages. As Ethan Zuckerman notes, dot-coms were not universally excited about adopting the advertising business model. It just so happened that advertising was the "easiest to market to investors."[42] Advertising became a kind of default business plan for dot-coms who could not risk losing market share by attempting to charge consumers for content or services.

Propped up by risk capital, dot-coms maintained robust marketing budgets even as burn rates—industry jargon for negative cash flow—climbed steadily. These expenditures were legitimized through a new economy discourse, or what Patrice Flichy calls a "frame of representation," that helped to coordinate the activities of the period.[43] The new economy discourse was steeped in "mythologies of entrepreneurial risk taking" and promises of monopoly profits for those who could dominate yet untapped internet markets.[44] Vincent Mosco characterizes the period as being overtaken by a "myth of the digital sublime" whereby the dot-com designation "conferred a mythical power that allowed firm[s] to transcend accepted marketplace conventions."[45]

The new economy was a compelling narrative that not only justified spending large sums on advertising but also made it effectively mandatory. As technology writer and free market evangelist Kevin Kelly wrote, the new economy meant a new set of rules for conducting business: "Those who play by the new rules will prosper, while those who ignore them will not."[46] The new rules maintained that while dot-coms would eventually need to attract actual customers, their immediate priority was to generate excitement among investors and stockholders. A portfolio manager with the investment firm Neptune Capital Management spelled out what this meant: "In the internet world, you have to look for the dominant player. We're not looking for profitability. Now, we're only looking for growth."[47] For dot-coms pursuing get big fast, advertising was the gateway to the next round of essential investment capital. "If budget-busting advertising campaigns or product giveaways are what it takes to propel your company into the ranks of web giants, well, that's okay," wrote *Fortune* magazine. "Profligacy pays."[48] For the venture capital firms and investment banks that exploited the financial mania to collect substantial investment pay-outs and service fees, profligacy paid quite well, at least during the bubble's upswing. As John Cassidy notes, "Instead of using the stock market to build companies, venture capitalists and entrepreneurs use[d] companies to create stocks"—a strategy that was remarkably lucrative.[49] In 1999, U.S. venture capital firms collectively realized a return of nearly two and half dollars for every dollar they invested.[50]

Venture capitalists used advertising and public relations to build valuation before exiting investments via IPO markets. Execution of this strategy was dependent on VCs' exerting managerial influence within the boardrooms of their portfolio companies.[51] As the *Wall Street Journal* reported, "When it comes to the marketing craze among web-based start-ups, the most powerful advertising executives aren't in the advertising business at all. They are the people of Sand Hill Road, Silicon Valley's venture-capitalist enclave."[52] In late 1999, an estimated 80 percent of venture funding provided to internet companies was spent on advertising.[53] This is indicative of the instrumental power of an investor class that deployed marketing communications as a means to deliver returns on speculative investment. Inflating demand for internet advertising was in many ways an externality of this moment of financial capitalism.

Ad Networks Get Big Fast

Beyond creating the primary source of demand for internet ads, speculative investment also played a more direct role in launching the internet advertising industry. Advertising start-ups raised billions of dollars in risk capital in the dot-com period. The ad network DoubleClick and its main competitor, CMGI, epitomized this trend. Bolstered by public and private investment, these two companies grew to become the new industry's top dogs. The balance of this chapter offers a case study of DoubleClick and

CMGI, showing how these companies used risk capital to support the development of surveillance advertising on an increasing scale.

As Michael Indergaard observes in his study of New York City's "Silicon Alley" district, DoubleClick's "prowess for developing technology was matched by a knack at raising capital."[54] Founded during the bubble's early stages, DoubleClick was led by an executive team that counted fundraising and internet advertising evangelism among its primary competencies. CEO Kevin O'Connor was an outspoken figure who saw public relations as a pillar of the company's growth strategy.[55] Kevin Ryan, hired in 1996 as chief financial officer and later succeeding O'Connor as CEO, was a former investment banker and senior vice president at United Media, a syndication service owned by the newspaper conglomerate E. W. Scripps.[56] Under their leadership, DoubleClick repeatedly used risk capital to fund aggressive business expansion. In June 1997, DoubleClick secured its first private financing in the form of a $40 million venture capital investment.[57] This was the largest private financing for a dot-com start-up outside of Silicon Valley to date, valuing DoubleClick at over $100 million and making it "far and away" the most exciting internet company in the New York area in the eyes of the business press.[58] It was a seal of approval from the investor class, bolstering DoubleClick's brand and the still unproven internet advertising industry more generally.

DoubleClick emerged as a figurehead of New York's dot-com start-up scene, "setting benchmarks for risk-taking" and catalyzing a wave of internet investment from traditionally more conservative East Coast venture capital firms.[59] Capitalizing on the stock market's simmering infatuation with dot-coms, DoubleClick held an IPO just eight months after its first private venture round.[60] The IPO provided another $62.5 million and generated further publicity. In what was described as "one of the hottest IPOs of the year," DoubleClick's stock rose 57 percent on the first day of trading, resulting in a company valuation of more than $400 million.[61]

As CEO Kevin O'Connor put it in his signature bombast: "Our goal is to deliver every ad in the world to every consumer."[62] The timing seemed right for such audacity. Capital and publicity were available in spades. Over the next several years, DoubleClick raised money whenever it could, netting over $1 billion by the end of the decade.[63] As more and more capital poured into the dot-com sector, the value of individual stocks rose sharply. This was especially true for top-tier companies like Double-Click, whose market capitalization—the total value of its outstanding shares—increased from $424 million at the end of 1997, to $1.9 billion at the end of 1998, to $10.7 billion at the end of 1999.[64]

"Flush with cash and possessing a highly touted stock," DoubleClick set out to "dominate the internet advertising business."[65] In its annual shareholder reports between 1997 and 2000, DoubleClick outlined its plan "to significantly increase its operating expenses in order to expand its sales and marketing operations, to continue to expand internationally, to upgrade and enhance its [ad-serving] technology, and to market and support its solutions."[66] DoubleClick was going all in on the notion of internet advertising as a winner-take-all proposition. "It's clear what the market's telling us," said O'Connor. "They want to give us a lot of money, so we take it and we invest. Why? Because this is the biggest thing that's ever hit. Market share is everything."[67]

One of DoubleClick's primary competitors during this period was the internet holding company CMGI. If DoubleClick was the "godfather of the ad services game," then CMGI was the "web giant nobody knows."[68] With roots in direct marketing and software development, CMGI was reconfigured in the early 1990s as a kind of hybrid venture capital/holding company for internet businesses.[69] One element of CMGI's strategy was to build a portfolio of interlocking subsidiaries whose operations were meant to enhance each other. Seeing DoubleClick's success in the targeted advertising sphere, CMGI's chief executive David Wetherell was drawn to the idea that consumer data could function as grist for his "virtuous circle" business plan.[70]

CMGI maintained investments in audience aggregators such as Lycos, a leading search portal, and GeoCities, a large network of user-created web pages, as well a number of internet advertising start-ups.[71] In an attempt to create synergies among these holdings, CMGI created Engage Technologies to develop technology for consumer profiling and targeted advertising. Wetherell believed his company could win the internet ad market by deploying Engage's targeting technologies across CMGI's portfolio of high-traffic websites. With his sights set on DoubleClick, Wetherell also bought a controlling stake in the web portal AltaVista, one of Double-Click's most important clients. The goal was not only to reach AltaVista's large user base with CMGI's ad systems but also to deprive DoubleClick of the opportunity to do the same.[72] In 1998, the *Wall Street Journal* highlighted the success of CMGI's investment portfolio, which had grown to include full or partial ownership of twenty-two dot-com businesses. CMGI also attracted investment from established tech companies, including Microsoft and Intel.[73] As the financial market reached a fever pitch in 1999, the value of CMGI's shares shot up 700 percent on the year, shattering the relative gains of the likes of Amazon (342 percent) and Yahoo (166 percent).[74]

Like the rest of their dot-com counterparts, DoubleClick and CMGI used public relations and advertising to keep the marketing/finance feedback loop churning. As DoubleClick's O'Connor told *Advertising Age,* "It's important to make sure [investors] know what your company is about and what you do."[75] O'Connor became a fixture in the business press and cable news networks, while CMGI was featured on the covers of *Business-Week* and *Fortune.*[76] CMGI's Wetherell was said to promote his companies "with the passion of a true zealot," even purchasing the naming rights to the newly constructed New England Patriots football stadium.[77] By late 1999, the two companies were the "toast of both the Street and the Valley," and each boasted market capitalizations that hovered around $10 billion—about the same as Omnicom, one of the world's largest advertising conglomerates.[78]

The advertising dot-coms were remarkably successful in raising capital, but what did they do with it? The answer mirrors the plot device of *Brewster's Millions,* the 1985 comedy where Richard Pryor's character has to spend a ridiculous sum of money as fast as possible on the condition that if he succeeds, a vastly bigger fortune awaits. For DoubleClick, CMGI, and a few other contenders, the promised fortune was the elimination of meaningful competition in the internet advertising market. The goal was to compete *for* the market, not *in* the market. So like Brewster, DoubleClick and CMGI went on a shopping spree of epic proportions to pursue acquisitions and other kinds of strategic partnerships designed to limit competition. The strategy was certainly in vogue, as concurrent waves of mergers in the media and telecommunications sectors were ongoing in the wake of the Telecommunications Act of 1996.[79] The free market orthodoxy discussed in earlier chapters permeated the internet space and provided political cover for all kinds of dot-com deal making. One key distinction of the internet sector mergers is that very little money actually changed hands in the execution of these transactions. Instead, stock was the primary currency. In the context of the bubble, market capitalization readily translated into purchasing power as inflated share prices made it viable to conduct stock-based acquisitions. As the influential venture capitalist John Doerr noted, the upshot of going public is that it provides an immediate boost to liquidity in order to buy out competitors and branch into new markets.[80]

In October 1999, DoubleClick acquired NetGravity, a major competitor, fully financing the transaction with $530 million in stock.[81] The takeover increased DoubleClick's customer base of web publishers by 50 percent, adding 350 new clients including high-profile sites such as CNN.[82] It also made DoubleClick the ad-services provider for more than half of the web's top fifty publishers, solidifying its status as the market leader. The deal was about "operating system dominance," said one observer. "They don't want to give [publishers] . . . another alternative."[83]

One month later, after overcoming opposition from privacy advocacy groups, DoubleClick finalized a merger with data broker Abacus Direct in another stock deal worth $1.7 billion.[84] DoubleClick intended to combine Abacus' consumer purchasing information with its own profile database in order to improve its ad-targeting capabilities.[85] Stock-based transactions of this nature were almost self-perpetuating in the sense that they sent share prices upward, providing even greater purchasing power to the combined entity. As one dot-com CEO told *Fortune:* "Valuation is a sign that investors are actually rewarding us for being aggressive."[86]

In early 2000, DoubleClick again exchanged stock for a 30 percent stake in the discount ad network ValueClick. The move was significant because it established "a beachhead for DoubleClick in the emerging cost-per-click advertising model," a market segment in which it had previously not maintained a significant presence.[87] Other DoubleClick acquisitions in this period included Opt-In Email and FloNetwork, providers of email marketing services; Flashbase, an online sweepstakes servicer; and @plan, which offered research services for media buyers. Through this series of stock-based transactions, the biggest fish in the online advertising sea grew significantly bigger.

Like DoubleClick, CMGI threw the weight of its financial valuation behind a push to become a "powerhouse in the rapidly emerging market for targeted advertising."[88] The company's primary tactic: using its highly valued stock to make strategic acquisitions. In 1999 alone, CMGI completed seven acquisitions of online advertising companies, all of which were financed through stock trades valued in total at nearly $2 billion.[89] As the CEO of one ad tech company told *BusinessWeek* upon its acquisition: "CMGI wants to become one of the cornerstone players of internet advertising, and they are investing in the backbone pieces to do that."[90]

Between 1999 and 2001, CMGI spent "a staggering $13 billion on acquisitions, nearly all paid for with its own stock," on an array of internet business in the ad sector and beyond.[91]

In addition to mergers and acquisitions, DoubleClick and other leading companies used risk capital to invest in technology development, real estate, data centers, and a significant expansion of sales labor. DoubleClick invested heavily in its core technology systems for ad serving and consumer profiling, including developing redundant capacity for emergency systems failure scenarios and investing in server architecture upgrades.[92] By late 1999, the company maintained about 650 ad servers across twenty data centers housed in the United States and abroad. In 1996, DoubleClick employed thirteen people at a single location.[93] Shortly after receiving venture financing, the staff was expanded to over a hundred people, and the company relocated to a high-rise at Madison Avenue and 26th Street, the heart of what became known as Silicon Alley.[94] After its IPO, DoubleClick began opening sales offices domestically and internationally, establishing some thirty locations throughout Europe, Asia, and Latin America.[95] By the end of 2000, DoubleClick's workforce had grown to nearly 2,000 with a sales staff of 1,040 people, including 380 working internationally.[96] CMGI had a similar trajectory, employing 6,000 people in fiscal year 2000.[97]

The outcome of this investment was a dramatic scaling up of ad-serving capacity among internet advertising's biggest companies. In its first thirteen months, DoubleClick delivered a billion and a half ads to more than 26 million unique users.[98] This was during the bubble's early stages and before the company received any risk financing. By 1998, the year of DoubleClick's IPO, the company served 34 billion ads reaching 46 million web users in a single month.[99] Although this initial upward trajectory was strong, it pales in comparison to the growth that occurred during the final two years of the bubble period, when DoubleClick's risk capital–fueled expansion enabled it to deliver a remarkable 621 billion advertisements in 2000.[100] In other words, the company served about 200,000 more ads on the average day in 2000 than it delivered in its entire first year of existence, just four years before. Although not operating at the same massive scale, CMGI expanded its ad-serving capacity as well. A significant portion of its growth came from within as CMGI invested heavily in various online publishers and retailers throughout 1998 and 1999, bringing new companies into the fold. By mid-1999, CMGI's AdSmart network comprised 300 websites and delivered over 2 billion monthly impressions.[101] A year later, CMGI's ad properties combined served some 8.6 billion ads a month.[102]

Although DoubleClick and CMGI were market leaders, they were not the only ones in the field. DoubleClick functioned as a kind of proof of concept for dot-com ad companies. By securing its initial investment from top-tier investment firms Greylock Partners and Bain Capital, Double-Click earned a seal of approval from the finance capital community, helping to establish New York's Silicon Alley as a hub of dot-com activity.[103] More importantly, DoubleClick's early successes helped pave the way for broader investment in the internet advertising sector. Between 1998 and 2000, at least nineteen internet advertising companies held IPOs, raising a combined total of over $1.3 billion. Notable among these were Value-Click, AdForce, FlyCast, 24/7 Media, MatchLogic, and Real Media, several of which were later incorporated, to varying degrees, into DoubleClick and CMGI.[104] Others such as 24/7 Media and Real Media became significant industry players by completing big mergers of their own.[105]

By 1999, several second-tier companies including AdForce, ValueClick, and FlyCast had reached the milestone of serving over 1 billion ads per month, while 24/7 Media was delivering 3 billion and Real Media, 10 billion.[106] No data on aggregate impressions are available, but some observers put the figure well into the hundreds of billions per month by late 1999.[107] Such estimates appear to be credible considering that Double-Click alone was delivering approximately 50 billion monthly impressions. In any case, the sheer volume of advertising on the web grew by an order of magnitude from 1998 to 1999 and again from 1999 to 2000, at which point it was estimated that three different companies—DoubleClick, CMGI's Engage, and 24/7 Media—had the capacity to reach over half of global internet users.[108]

As described in chapter 3, DoubleClick's foremost technological breakthrough was to unify targeted ad serving and consumer profiling into a reciprocal process of data transmission and collection. In this regard, increasing the scale of ad serving was about more than simply delivering as many ads as possible across as many sites as possible. It was also about expanding data collection, consumer profiling, and other data-driven advertising practices to reach increasingly segmented groups of consumers wherever they happened to be on the internet. As DoubleClick's Kevin O'Connor put it: "The great paradox with targeting ads is that the more you are micro-targeting, the more reach you have to have."[109] "Critical mass is important," added DoubleClick's

Kevin Ryan. "The bigger your [profile] database, the more targeted you can be."[110]

Consumer data became a central factor in "dictating merger and acquisition strategy for the industry's leading players," noted *Adweek*.[111] DoubleClick's acquisitions of competitors such as NetGravity not only reduced competition but also provided significant additional surveillance capacity.[112] Likewise, CMGI's controlling investment in AltaVista "vaulted [it] into the number three spot among advertising networks" in terms of reach, but it also provided an abundant new source of consumer data.[113] The portal's 10 million monthly visitors fed a steady stream of consumer information into the databases of CMGI's Engage advertising subsidiary.

At CMGI, extensive consumer profiling became the lynchpin of its virtuous circle investment strategy of vertical integration. Our "vision is to have the largest reach on the web and monetize that reach better than anyone else," noted a CMGI executive.[114] The goal was to "build interactive marketing services and infrastructure to generate revenue across that reach."[115] Portals like AltaVista and Lycos were positioned as hubs to funnel consumers through CMGI's roster of internet properties such as the financial information site Raging Bull, retailer Furniture.com, and genealogy site Ancestry.com.[116] Undergirding these connections were CMGI's advertising operations, Engage and AdSmart, which delivered ads for and collected consumer information from all CMGI-affiliated sites. As one journalist observed, "If CMGI has a core technology that weaves through its patchwork portfolio, it's the ability to track computer users through their every browser click."[117]

By the end of the 1990s, CMGI's Engage had stockpiled a profile database containing over 70 million entries, which it used to refine and develop new ad-targeting methods.[118] In the third quarter of 2000, nearly 50 percent of CMGI revenues came from online advertising.[119] Yet even this dramatic growth could not match DoubleClick, which through its much larger network and own spate of acquisitions had amassed a collection of 120 million user profiles—twelve times what it had at the start of 1997.[120]

An Industry without Income

The big asterisk to this story is that DoubleClick and CMGI were consistently unprofitable throughout this period. Like many dot-coms, they maintained balance sheets that contrasted sharply with their stock valuations. Although DoubleClick posted steady revenue growth through-out the bubble, its losses grew at a much faster rate. Revenue increases stemmed from the absorption of acquired companies and greatly expanded sales efforts, but these income sources were not nearly enough to make the company profitable. Warnings regarding its "history of losses and anticipated continued losses" appeared consistently among the mandatory disclosures of risk factors contained in annual SEC filings. Digging deeper, financial documents reveal that losses in 1999 more than doubled those from the previous year, while revenue grew at a significantly slower pace.[121] CMGI too was consistently unprofitable and by 2000 maintained a "burn rate" of around $50 million a month.[122] It was, in Michael Wolff's memorable, if inexact, phrase, an "industry without income."[123]

Risk capital was the critical enabling factor that allowed DoubleClick, CMGI, and their contemporaries to aggressively expand despite sustained losses. Whereas DoubleClick raised funds by repeatedly offering pieces of itself via the public stock market, CMGI primarily took the approach of engaging directly in speculative investment. Regardless of these tactical differences, the goal was the same: get big fast. As Candice Carpenter, CEO of the web publisher iVillage, explained, because investors "will accept losses at this juncture, we are able to rapidly acquire other companies and really build market share. This is a land grab."[124]

DoubleClick's SEC filings plainly state the connection between risk capital funding and growth. DoubleClick applied the capital raised via its initial public offering "toward the expansion of international operations and sales and marketing capabilities" in addition to financing general operating costs.[125] It is reasonable to conclude that subsequent capital infusions beyond the IPO were applied to similar purposes. How else could the company "significantly increase its operating expenses" year after year while continually losing money?[126] Likewise, CMGI's business model was "built on the stock market's enormous expectations for the internet."[127] As BusinessWeek put it: "As long as investors keep paying high prices for shares in his companies, [CEO] Wetherell will have the currency he needs to keep doing deals."[128] Reciting a refrain of the new economy discourse, Wetherell shrugged off concerns regarding profitability, maintaining, "It would be sinful to be making money on the internet right now, when it's growing this fast."[129]

CMGI directly applied funds from the sales of its appreciated investments in Lycos and GeoCities to finance its money-losing advertising operations such as Engage.[130] Likewise, DoubleClick used proceeds from its VC investments and public offerings to supply working capital to maintain business operations.[131] Amazon founder Jeff Bezos clarified what was really going on here: If "ecommerce had been subject to the regular discipline of the market, early setbacks would have been fatal. But consumers were not driving online commerce, Wall Street was."[132] Although Bezos was talking about online retailing, his observations hold true for the internet advertising market and the dot-com sector at large, which, not incidentally, produced the greatest portion of early demand for online advertising.

Temporary as it turned out to be, the dot-com bubble shielded surveillance advertising companies from the pressures of profitability, enabled their rapid expansion, and funded a significant buildup of consumer monitoring capacity. Eyeing a future beyond the bubble and seeking to conquer the online advertising market, DoubleClick kicked off a commercial surveillance arms race, bankrolled in large part by speculative capital. At the same time, ad network executives understood that they would need to attract major off-line marketers in order to prosper in the long term. In their efforts to woo the more recalcitrant elements of the marketing complex's mainstream, ad networks sought to reposition themselves as intermediaries for a broader range of targeted marketing communications, a process that involved bringing marketers themselves into the business of online data collection and exchange. This trajectory, which I call protoplatformization, is the subject of the next chapter.

5   SURVEILLANCE ADVERTISING TAKES SHAPE

IN THE SUMMER OF 1998, scores of marketing practitioners and executives convened in Cincinnati, Ohio, under unusual circumstances. They arrived at the behest of Procter & Gamble, one of the world's largest advertisers, to attend a conference dubbed the Future of Advertising Stakeholders (FAST) Summit. Many in attendance were direct competitors. Even representatives from Unilever, P&G's archrival in consumer goods, had made the trip. The summit's purpose was to coordinate a unified strategy among the marketing complex's heavy hitters to wring greater efficiency from the internet advertising industry. For the more than four hundred business leaders in attendance, working together to shape the trajectory of internet advertising superseded everyday competitive antagonisms.[1]

The convention was a spiritual follow-up to Edwin Artzt's 1994 address to the American Association of Advertising Agencies, in which P&G's top executive urged marketers to "grab technology change in [their] teeth" in order to create the "greatest selling tool ever conceived."[2] Back then, Artzt spoke in general terms about the nebulous "information superhighway." Four years later, it was evident that the dominant interactive medium was the World Wide Web. Over two days of keynotes and panels, the FAST coalition emerged with a stark message for the internet advertising sector. To borrow a phrase from both the Old Testament and Johnny Cash, interactive media had been weighed in a balance and found wanting.

As I show in previous chapters, the marketing complex had been successful in its political bid to ensure that advertising would have a prominent place in the new media future, but many traditional marketers remained ambivalent about the efficacy of online campaigns in practice. In particular, the prevailing banner ad format was not producing adequate proof of return on investment (ROI). Although data collection techniques developed by ad networks such as DoubleClick provided new opportunities for ad targeting, marketers were keen to point out that average click-through rates had plummeted to below 1 percent for most campaigns.[3] A novelty in 1994, by 1998, banners had grown increasingly pervasive and gimmicky—trends owed in no small part to the early successes of ad networks themselves. The *New York Times* compared banners to magazine scent strips and television infomercials, previously attention-grabbing ad formats that were now more likely to draw consumer ire than genuine interest.[4]

The ROI problem was compounded by the fact that ads were bought and sold according to numbers of impressions, not clicks. Today, many internet ads are effectively free if no one clicks on them because marketers only pay for click-throughs. This kind of performance-based pricing was far less common in the 1990s, when almost all ads were sold on the basis of cost per thousand ad impressions (CPM), a standard pricing system for print and broadcast media. Marketers began to question why they should pay for impressions on an interactive medium that did not seem to produce much interaction at all.

These criticisms featured prominently at the FAST Summit, underscoring one of marketing's primordial problems: how to quantify advertising's ROI. As early twentieth-century century department store magnate John Wanamaker reportedly put it: "Half the money I spend on advertising is wasted; the trouble is, I don't know which half."[5] For several years, marketing pundits and elements of the trade press had billed the web as the long-awaited solution to advertising's ROI problem. Targeted ads and click-through measurements were supposed to provide hard evidence about advertising's efficacy, helping everyone move toward a more efficient future of "one-to-one" marketing communications.[6] This strategy represented what Joseph Turow calls "a new twist on a late twentieth-century understanding of customer relationship management," whereby companies aim to develop sustained engagement with their most valuable customers and prospects.[7] A central idea of customer relationship management is that a majority of profits stem from the repeat business of a select group of high-value customers. As such, marketers must learn as much as they can about this group in order to cultivate lasting relationships and attract more customers with similar characteristics. This requires not only enhanced means to speak directly to specific audiences but also a greater capacity to collect and analyze information about consumer attributes and behaviors. The budding targeted advertising systems developed by ad networks seemed perfectly positioned to achieve these goals.

Yet internet advertising was not living up to marketers' expectations. One study found that just 16 percent of marketers were "satisfied with online ad measurement capabilities," while two thirds of companies surveyed by the Association of National Advertisers reported that insufficient information was a "key barrier to online advertising."[8] Marketers complained that interactive media was overhyped and stressed the need for better data to justify spending real money online.[9] Dangling billions of advertising dollars as a "carrot over the hungry heads of the online media world," marketers at the FAST Summit made it clear that in order to meet its potential, the internet needed to prove it could deliver strong ROI.[10]

As Martin Nisenholtz, president of the *New York Times'* newly established online division, put it: "We are struggling every day to sell advertising in an environment where advertisers, quite frankly, still don't know quite what this does for them. . . . The internet is only going to work as an advertising forum if the advertisers see it as a more efficient vehicle than mass marketing."[11] Nisenholtz's comparison to mass marketing was telling. Broad reach and powerful branding had long been the bread and butter of national marketers who spent billions on ad campaigns in order maintain a constant presence in the minds of consumers. The web's user base was growing fast, but it was still a long way from achieving the kind of scale and saturation readily available via broadcasting. Furthermore, this was the prebroadband era, which precluded the kinds of production values that big marketers were accustomed to. Limited bandwidth and network latency issues made it nearly impossible to deliver quality video and audio content. To prove its worth, the internet advertising industry needed to improve its capacity to target specific groups of consumers and demonstrate that online ads could move the needle of consumer behavior.

Protoplatformization

The internet advertising industry awakened to this challenge amid a convulsing dot-com stock market. Soaring company valuations driven by record levels of speculative investment were punctuated by sudden downturns and spates of postponed IPOs. This volatility contributed to a growing recognition among business leaders that the dot-com phenomenon was indeed a financial bubble. It was, as Netscape's Jim Clark put it, "too hot not to cool down."[12] Although ad networks such as DoubleClick continued to grow at a rapid clip, a large portion of the demand for their services still came from dot-com start-ups eager to drive traffic to their online storefronts and portals. Despite the safety net provided by speculative capital, even the biggest ad networks understood that they needed to court national marketers in order to prosper in the long run. Failure to do so could spell disaster, but the potential upside was enormous. The combined ad-buying power of the FAST alliance alone was an estimated $50 billion a year, more than twenty-five times the total spent on internet advertising in 1998.[13] As one ad industry representative reportedly told a group of marketers at the FAST Summit: "Just tell us what you want us to do and we'll do it."[14]

During this period, leading ad networks like DoubleClick and CMGI began to reconfigure their businesses around two overlapping objectives. The first, outlined in chapter 4, was to get big fast in order to squeeze out competition and secure a dominant market position in the web advertising sector. This involved using finance capital to buy competitors and invest in technology and labor. The second objective was to transition from a business model that primarily served web publishers (the supply side of the advertising market) to one that also provided services to marketers directly (the demand side). Up to this point, much of the industry had focused on helping publishers sell ads, leaving traditional ad agencies to help marketers buy them. Now, in their expansionary fervor, major ad networks attempted to facilitate both supply and demand, rolling out new products and services geared toward marketers and their ad agency proxies.

These efforts dovetailed to form a business strategy that prefigured what Nick Srnicek calls "platform monopoly."[15] In a platform monopoly, the goal is not just to successfully compete within a market but to facilitate the market itself as an essential intermediary. Successful platforms sit at the center of "multi-sided markets," connecting "distinct groups of customers who value each other's participation."[16] Using dot-com financial capital, ad networks began to create services not only for web publishers who got paid to host ads on their sites, but also for the ad agencies, marketers, and retailers who bought the ads and increasingly demanded proof of their results. Crucially, ad networks ramped up their promises to provide marketers with enhanced ROI. In a move that anticipated the platform monopolies of Google and Facebook, ad networks began a process of what might be called protoplatformization, constructing a sociotechnical infrastructure of business relationships and technical capacities to facilitate the capture and exchange of consumer information at an accelerating scale and pace.

DoubleClick was among the first to reorganize its business in this way. Although ad network executives did not use the term "platform monopoly," they described their objectives clearly enough. DoubleClick's CEO Kevin O'Connor framed the strategy in terms of "reintermediation."[17] O'Connor, who was something of an iconoclast, coined the term to invert the new economy rhetoric of "disintermediation," which promised to connect buyers and sellers directly on the internet, eliminating inefficient go-betweens. By contrast, reintermediation signaled DoubleClick's intention to leverage its market position and superior ad-targeting capacity to become web advertising's indispensable middleman. The objective was not only to "deliver every ad to every consumer" but also to broker the broadest possible range of advertising transactions, taking a revenue slice of each one.[18] DoubleClick was attempting to expand from providing a narrow band of outsourced ad services to web publishers to "building the infrastructure that makes marketing work in the digital world."[19]

The gold standard for the platform monopoly approach was Microsoft's unrivaled dominance in computer operating systems, which gave it inordinate power in the adjacent computing hardware and software sectors—and made it among the world's most valuable companies. Many dot-coms including Netscape, Yahoo, and DoubleClick sought to mimic Microsoft's playbook, even as the company underwent investigation by the U.S. Department of Justice for its anticompetitive practices. Making the patterning explicit, O'Conner described DoubleClick's intention to become the "internal operating system for advertising on the net."[20]

Protoplatformization meant that DoubleClick had to move beyond simply scaling up its existing ad network. Portals such as Yahoo and America Online had grown to the point where they too could put banner ads in front of large audiences. To differentiate itself, DoubleClick needed to create new markets to inhabit, generate sector-leading knowledge about consumer behavior, and develop better means to quantify ROI for marketers. This required not only attracting new marketer and publisher clients but also bringing those clients more squarely into the routine practice of consumer data collection and exchange. In other words, DoubleClick and its rivals sought to develop a shared capacity for internet surveillance among all entities of the marketing complex and to place themselves at the center of the burgeoning consumer data economy.

This platform monopoly approach was controversial to some in the broader advertising sector, where double dipping from both the supply and demand sides of the market was seen as a conflict of interest. But the growing market power of dot-coms like DoubleClick, coupled with the sense that old rules no longer applied in the new economy, enabled ad networks to chart this new terrain relatively unfettered by the norms of Madison Avenue. Engaging in a bit of revisionist history, the CEO of CMGI's Engage now exclaimed: "We've always thought the marketer is the one with the power, so we are innovating for them."[21]

The remainder of this chapter chronicles ad networks' efforts to become platform monopolies and outlines the broader implications of the late dot-com period (1998–2000) for surveillance advertising's development. The trend of protoplatformization expanded surveillance capacities and created strong market pressures for all commercial entities to participate in consumer data collection. It also opened the doors to increasingly invasive, manipulative, and discriminatory practices of behavioral profiling and ad targeting. In all of these ways, these early attempts to build platform monopolies prefigure important elements of today's surveillance advertising economy.

Open the Network, Close the Loop

One of the first prerequisites for platformization was breaking open the business model that helped launch ad networks to prominence in the preceding years. DoubleClick had made its bones by building the web's premier ad network, but now the exclusivity of the network model threatened to constrain the company's growth. Ad networks had relied on making ad targeting a premium service, available only to web publishers who signed on to exclusive partnerships. If you wanted to use DoubleClick's state-of-the art technology, you had to join its network and refrain from using others. This afforded DoubleClick leverage to charge steep prices (publishers often relinquished half of all ad revenue), but it restricted DoubleClick's ability to serve ads and collect data from nonaffiliated sites. Though DoubleClick garnered significant audience traffic across its stable of publishers, the company's activities were nonetheless confined by the network format. Wedded to exclusive partnerships, ad networks were ceding significant chunks of the market without so much as a fight.

DoubleClick was among the first to crack open the ad network model by relaxing exclusive partnership requirements and offering its DART ad-serving technology to web publishers as a stand-alone service. Selling its technology à la carte risked undermining its network business. O'Connor said the decision "almost ripped the company apart."[22] But to win the business of national marketers, the company needed to develop new products and move into new markets. The move proved successful, attracting hundreds of web publishers who wanted better ad-targeting capabilities but had balked at joining an ad network. DoubleClick launched in 1996 with approximately thirty participating web publishers.[23] By the end of 1998, DoubleClick's client roster had grown to 570 publishers representing thousands of websites, including premium sites like the *Wall Street Journal,* NBC, and CBS.[24]

Competing ad networks began to relax their terms as well, experimenting with nonexclusive contracts and systems for bartering unsold ad inventory. CMGI broadened the purview of its Engage advertising division to include clients outside of the holding company's portfolio.[25] Engage's Real-Time Visitor Intelligence service gave any web publisher the ability to tap into its proprietary profile database in order to deliver targeted ads and personalized offers.[26] No exclusive network contract was required. As promoted on its product page: "As soon as a visitor clicks on your website, you can use information about their previous internet activities to provide them with customized web pages, targeted ads, promotions, products and services—even if it's their first visit to your site."[27] So-called discount networks pitched low costs and ease of use to bring in as many publishers as possible. One such company, LinkExchange, compiled a massive network of more than 400,000 small-traffic websites.[28]

DoubleClick also created a system for swapping unsold, or remnant, ad inventory among publishers on a one-to-one exchange basis.[29] In the event that DoubleClick could not deliver a targeted ad—for example, if no appropriate consumer profile could be located—it would simply serve a default banner representing itself or one of its affiliates. In O'Connor's words, the goal of reintermediation was to ensure that there was "never an unused ad space."[30] Likewise, the CMGI property FlyCast developed a system to auction off remnant inventory at reduced prices across a network of a thousand sites that included premier publishers such as Yahoo.[31] Other companies in the remnant auction market included Adauction and Adbot.[32] As explained by Adauction's CEO:

> The online auction works for publishers because it complements existing sales programs without creating channel conflict. Unlike other outlets that

essentially replace the publisher's direct sales of advertising, the auction is similar to the inventory yield and management system that airlines use to sell off empty seats to brokers, travel agents and other companies. Ad availability and media are as perishable as an airplane reservation. The auction format helps efficiently sell advertising late in the sales cycle or, to complete the metaphor, just before the plane takes off.[33]

Expanding their range of publisher partners was only the beginning of ad networks' turn toward platformization. To attract marketer clients, ad networks needed to demonstrate that internet advertising could provide strong ROI. Targeting a potential customer with an ad was all well and good, but demonstrating a resulting action—say, a product purchase or newsletter signup—was far better. To this end, DoubleClick created a marketer-focused version of its DART ad-targeting technology, running a variety of programs under the heading "Closed Loop Marketing Solutions," which purported to show the "true relationship between advertising and sales."[34] The idea was to augment targeted advertising with so-called post-click analysis to better understand what users did (and did not do) after they clicked through banners to reach marketers' home pages and digital storefronts.

One of the most successful applications of post-click analysis was what is now known as remarketing or retargeting, a practice that should be familiar to anyone who has experienced an ad seemingly following them around the web. Remarketing enables advertisers to reconnect with users who previously clicked their ads or visited their sites by sending a follow up message, either through a customized ad or email. In 1999 DoubleClick introduced Boomerang, one of the web's first remarketing applications. The service was pitched as a way for marketers to reach "precisely the individuals who have displayed an explicit interest" in their products by delivering follow-up ads across any of DoubleClick's thousands of partner sites.[35] Ads could be targeted using a range of variables, giving marketers the capability to reach prospects who had previously visited specific pages on their sites, including those who visited but had not completed a desirable transaction like a purchase or email registration.

With remarketing, advertisers could deploy tailored ads with the capacity to follow specific users as they traversed the web. It was the online equivalent of a mattress salesperson slipping into the backseat of your car as you left the showroom, quietly riding along with you to your next destination, and then tapping your shoulder to remind you of the upcoming

President's Day sale extravaganza. Failing that, the salesperson might also approach others who happen to share your behavioral or demographic traits, under the assumption that they too might be in the market for a queen-size pillow-top mattress.

In order to work, remarketing and similar services required that new channels of communication be established among web publishers (where ads appeared), marketers (where consumer actions occurred), and ad networks (who coordinated and conducted the transactions). For example, DoubleClick placed invisible tracking codes on its marketer clients' sites in order to enable post-click functionality. More advanced services required marketers to give DoubleClick access to the guts of their online shopping applications and customer databases, effectively building a patchwork infrastructure for consumer data transmission among advertising partners with DoubleClick as the hub.

Closing the loop between ads and consumer actions was hardly a revolutionary advertising strategy in itself. This had long been the premise of direct response marketing like mail-in coupons and catalogs. Similarly, ad networks had been developing centralized surveillance systems since 1996. As described in chapter 3, the first generation of ad networks combined ad delivery and data collection into a unified process, enabling a kind of localized surveillance within the boundaries of a given ad network. But subsequent efforts to close the loop marked a new stage of internet advertising's development because they extended surveillance capacities beyond the websites where ads appeared to marketers' own home pages and storefronts, and eventually beyond the web itself.

Racing to achieve platform monopoly status, ad networks also sought to build bridges with the well-established world of off-line data brokering in order to enhance their consumer databases. This relied on extensive partnerships among all manner of data brokers, both new and old. By 1998, CMGI's AdKnowledge media buying service integrated an array of commercial data, including "audience demographics from [online ratings services] MediaMetrix and NetRatings; psychographic data from SRI Consulting; web site ratings and descriptions from NetGuide; and web traffic audit data from BPA Interactive."[36] Ad networks had used external data in limited ways for several years. DoubleClick was among the first companies to augment ad targeting with information obtained from the U.S. census and other public sources. Nevertheless, advertising in cyberspace remained largely separate from the marketing and consumption practices of the physical world. Consumer profiles were generally limited to information that was collected passively as people surfed the web. Profiles were linked to unique IDs but only contained personally identifying information when it was supplied actively—say, as part of a website registration or purchase.

These boundaries began to break down when CMGI's AdForce secured an exclusive partnership with the global information services conglomerate Experian to provide data for ad-targeting purposes.[37] The off-line data broker industry itself was undergoing an expansionary trend as companies like Experian began to transition from primarily providing financial information services to a much broader range of activity, including credit reporting and consumer profiling.[38] Ad networks were particularly keen to obtain consumers' off-line purchasing records, thought by many marketers to be a valuable predictor of future buying behavior. This is certainly what DoubleClick was after in its 1999 acquisition of Abacus Direct, a data broker that tracked the buying habits of some 88 million U.S. households.[39] "Advertisers rely on demographic information to target ads when they don't have anything else," said DoubleClick's Kevin Ryan, talking up the significance of the acquisition. "Transaction information is much better."[40] DoubleClick's move to integrate its profile databases with Abacus' records, which included personally identifying information such as names, addresses, and telephone numbers, caused a public relations debacle and enflamed a larger public policy confrontation. I explore this incident in more detail in chapter 6. For now, it is sufficient to note that although DoubleClick's intention to integrate Abacus' data with its own was the most prominent example of the increasing intrusiveness of surveillance advertising, it was by no means an outlier.

The Social Relations of Surveillance Advertising

One of the most troubling consequences of surveillance advertising's expansion in the late 1990s was the increased use of behavioral profiling to categorize people according to determinations of their social worth. In 1993, Oscar Gandy wrote a prescient book called *The Panoptic Sort*, which articulated a theory of information technology–based surveillance through which individuals and groups are "sorted according to their presumed economic or political value."[41] Looking at a range of examples, including credit reports and data from the U.S. Census Bureau, Gandy warned of an emerging system of classification that enabled "organized interests," whether selling shoes, insurance, or political ideology, "to identify, isolate, and communicate differentially with individuals in order to increase their influence over how consumers make selections among these options."[42]

One of Gandy's overarching concerns was that information technology–based sorting accelerates forms of discrimination in accordance with institutionalized biases of "race, gender, age, class, culture, and consciousness."[43] Surveillance advertising's proliferation in the dot-com period only moved such practices of "social sorting" further toward the front of the marketing complex's business agenda.[44] Joseph Turow has documented the progression of this trend whereby marketers increasingly use profile databases "to determine whether to consider particular Americans to be 'targets' or 'waste.'"[45]

Although the practice of tailoring ad messages to specific audiences is not new, online behavioral profiling is of a qualitatively different character than the probability-based methods used to analyze and target mass media audiences. For instance, consumer classification is greatly enhanced by surveillance practices that combine past purchasing records with online behavioral data and demographic information. The shift is significant. As Turow explains: "For decades, marketing and media firms learned as much as they could about social groups and then tried to target people they thought were members of these groups. The emerging process is almost the opposite: They learn enormous amounts about individuals, consign them to various groups, and then determine whether and how they want to deal with them."[46]

Aggregating data across the publisher/marketer divide put companies like DoubleClick in a unique position to experiment with intensified forms of behavioral profiling. In some instances, behavioral profiling meant collecting novel types of data, such as attempts to monitor the ads that users hovered over with their computer mouse but did not click. How long did they linger over the ad? What was clicked immediately after hovering? But more significant was the buildup of capacities to aggregate data from an expanding array of sources in order to develop more detailed browsing histories, analyze post-click behaviors, classify consumers in various ways, and otherwise pursue what Phillip Napoli calls "the rationalization of audience understanding."[47]

Consumer classification became an increasingly important component of the targeting algorithms that ad networks touted as the key to improve marketer ROI. CMGI's Engage reportedly created consumer interest profiles using a matrix of some 800 potential attributes.[48] With the help of the Internet Archive's Wayback Machine, it is possible to see a snapshot of Engage's 1998 product description for a service called Next-Generation Profiling:

> As a visitor browses through an Engage-enabled website, the Engage Suite software builds individual profiles based on the type of content viewed, the time spent viewing, and other factors including their frequency and recency of visits to a particular interest category. This information is processed by a patent-pending algorithm into profiles that include a user identification number, an interest category code, and an interest score to indicate a level of interest in a particular category. A single visitor can have several entries in the database—one for each observed interest category. As the number of recorded visits of a single visitor grows, the accuracy and depth of the profile is improved. Unlike static registration information, Engage profiles are constantly changing to more accurately reflect the current interests of an individual.[49]

It is one thing when extensive profiles, compiled from disparate off-line and online sources over which individuals have little knowledge or control, become the basis for the commercial messages they encounter on the internet. It is perhaps another when these processes dictate the availability of broader social opportunities and material necessities. As Lori Andrews asks: "When young people in poor neighborhoods are bombarded with advertisements for trade schools, will they be more likely than others their age to forgo college? And when women are shown articles about celebrities rather than stock market trends, will they be less likely to develop financial savvy?"[50] Assessing these outcomes, Joseph Turow laments the dissolution of a media landscape that, while flawed, offered a pluralistic balance of society-making mass media and segment-making niche media.[51] But even these critiques do not capture the full social costs of unrestrained consumer surveillance.

As early as 1999, the data broker Acxiom offered a service called Info-Base Ethnicity System that provided a "precise breakdown of ethnic, religious, and minority classifications" that could be matched with name, income, housing information, and other demographic data.[52] According to promotional materials, the service enabled marketers to target, or perhaps exclude, categories of consumers as specific as "full-figured African American women." By 2000, critics had coined the term "weblining" to describe the practice of denying people opportunities on the internet based on their marketing profile.[53] The concept derives from "redlining," a descriptor of earlier discriminatory practices whereby the boundaries of poor, often minoritized, neighborhoods were mapped in red to indicate that services such as banking or telecommunications need not be offered. Redlining gets to the root of the issue, which is a hardening of social inequalities, whereby surveillance advertising practices reproduce social discrimination and economic exploitation on the internet and beyond. In this scenario, the marketing complex is doing more than just sorting profiles according to different consumer typologies. It is also creating a system that, when functioning optimally, catalogs individuals as either valuable or worthless via a range of processes ultimately beholden to profit maximization.

Far from creating objective representations of the world as it is, consumer surveillance reproduces and often reinforces existing structural inequalities.[54] In 1993, Gandy illustrated the prejudicial capacity of the panoptic sort by recounting the systematic denial of credit to qualified applicants of color based on a discriminatory index of race embedded in preweb automated loan processing systems. As Tamara Shepherd argues, data-driven surveillance marketing "does not just reflect user desires, it produces them in ways that are differential according to already existing structures of privilege."[55] In other words, discrimination is most likely to be exercised against the interests of working-class people, people of color, women, and other groups who might be variously ascertained as "waste" by an inhumane surveillance advertising apparatus.[56]

Mass marketing was in many cases about selling as much as possible to as many as possible. Although this approach certainly continues, surveillance advertising was developed in no small part to mitigate the dissolution of the mass audience and the inefficiencies of mass appeals. Surveillance advertising is about boosting profits by selling more to the right people, the flip side of which is eliminating efforts to market to consumers deemed undesirable, and even pruning existing customers who fail to meet profitability standards. In a purely economic sense, these practices are justifiable if they produce efficiency gains that compensate for the loss of low-value customers. Wherever exclusion can be implemented more profitably than inclusion, we should expect increasingly stratified and discriminatory business practices within an increasingly stratified and discriminatory capitalism. In the United States today, there are few areas of social life that remain insulated from this logic. Health care, employment, housing, education—all are seemingly fair game.

Mark Andrejevic's concept of "digital enclosure," described as the ongoing construction of interactive spaces "where every action generates information about itself," provides another useful lens to make sense of the social relationships produced by surveillance advertising and the industry's move toward platformization.[57] In digital enclosure, the persistent monitoring of interactive spaces enables the production of information commodities (e.g., behavioral profiles), which become the property of those conducting the surveillance and over which the subjects of monitoring have little control. As digital enclosure has proliferated, the ironic outcome for those being watched is an "asymmetrical loss of privacy." Individuals are more scrutinized than ever, while the institutions conducting surveillance remain "stubbornly opaque."[58]

The trajectory of protoplatformization in the late 1990s was a key moment of digital enclosure on the internet. It began to normalize a default mode of media engagement whereby participation in interactive spaces required submission to surveillance, a reversal of interactivity's much-lauded emancipatory potential. The theory of enclosure is powerful because it highlights the deep connections between capital accumulation and social division. Its reference point is a Marxist understanding of the land enclosure movements associated with the historical transition from feudalism to capitalism. In addition to creating new propertied areas for the production of commodities, land enclosures created social divisions among those who owned and controlled land and those who did not. Whereas land enclosures formalized social cleavages around property ownership and control over the means of production, digital enclosures create class-like divisions around the ownership and control of interactive spaces and the information commodities produced therein.

Whether the object of enclosure is common land or behavioral information, the purpose is to wring profits from yet untapped social domains, to expand the sphere of commodification.[59] Beyond the business model of any given internet advertising platform, digital enclosure is an extension of the marketing complex's long-standing prime objective to generate high levels of consumption to match the output of an incredibly productive consumer capitalism. Ultimately, surveillance advertising as digital enclosure makes media engagement more productive for capital by creating new opportunities for information commodification, centralizing control over interactive spaces, and making it increasingly difficult for people to abstain from consumer surveillance.

Here Come the Marketers

Marketers began to adopt the web as an advertising channel in earnest during the later years of the dot-com bubble. Data compiled by *Advertising Age* showed that in 1998, just nineteen of the largest hundred national marketers advertised on the web. By 1999, that number had jumped to eighty-seven.[60] Between 1999 and 2000, the total number of marketers purchasing online advertising quadrupled.[61] Not only did more marketers come online, they also began to allocate proportionally more of their ad budgets to internet ads. A member survey by the Association of National Advertisers found that respondents had tripled their web ad spending from 1998 to 1999.[62] The total number of ad impressions purchased by the top ten traditional marketers increased by a factor of five from 1999 to 2000, while aggregate online ad spending more than doubled from 1998 to 1999 and nearly did so again from 1999 to 2000.[63]

As ad networks focused their services around providing marketer ROI, they outflanked and then won business from some of their biggest detractors: traditional advertising agencies. Although some agencies had been skeptical of upstarts like DoubleClick, they increasingly turned to "outsiders possessing technological muscle" to conduct web campaigns.[64] Of course, agencies partnered with ad networks largely in response to marketers' requests for "proof that their online campaigns [were] paying off."[65] Those that did not have the ability to meet these expectations were forced to contract outside help. A significant chunk of this business went to the protoplatforms, further contributing to the sector's consolidation. DoubleClick attracted business from big-name marketers including AT&T, Charles Schwab, IBM, Intel, and Microsoft.[66] By 2000, DoubleClick alone served some 4,400 marketer clients representing over half of Fortune 100 companies.[67]

Though DoubleClick served hundreds of billions of targeted banners, it bears repeating that banner ad impressions are just one measure of surveillance advertising's development. The platform monopoly strategy was an attempt to dominate online advertising by reintermediating every possible advertising transaction, regardless of any specific ad format or technology. Responding to an interviewer's suggestion that DoubleClick was simply "peddling banners," DoubleClick's Kevin O'Connor articulated the agnosticism of the platform strategy as such: "You're fixating on a single piece of real estate that happens to be shaped like a banner.

Our business is, we take bytes. . . . whether they're shaped like a banner or a pop-up or a sponsorship. . . . It could be a video, it doesn't matter. We take those bytes and we target them at consumers, and we watch how consumers react."[68]

O'Connor was right. DoubleClick and the other platform hopefuls were not just peddling banners. They were selling surveillance advertising as a plug-and-play service, facilitating their clients' participation in a widening dragnet of consumer data collection. As ad networks embraced platformization, options for linking up with centralized commercial monitoring systems proliferated. Publishers could join any number of ad networks, license ad-server technology, or use cloud-based applications to collect and combine data on web users. Marketers could use dedicated ad campaign management platforms and customer relations management systems to conduct new kinds of targeting such as remarketing. As O'Connor put it: "You can think of us as the Burger King of internet advertising. We give it any way you want."[69] Although perhaps not as easy as pulling up to the drive-through, the barriers for marketers and publishers to participate in surveillance advertising were being lowered dramatically.

As it became easier to participate in consumer surveillance, it also became more difficult to abstain. This was particularly true for web publishers, who became increasingly desperate to attract advertising support as alternative funding models like paid-subscriptions faltered and dotcom investment dried up. "If the money is right, many online publishers are willing to strike whatever sort of partnerships an advertiser might want," reported the *Wall Street Journal*.[70] "I don't see how any site cannot [collect user data]. Advertisers will demand it," said one marketing executive.[71] By 2000, the *Wall Street Journal* surmised that it was "too late to tinker" with tracking technologies such as cookies: "They power practically every online shopping cart and every paid advertisement. In less than six years, they've become part of the fabric of the web."[72] Corroborating the *Journal*'s claims, a series of studies by the Federal Trade Commission found the consumer surveillance was "nearly ubiquitous" online.[73] The FTC predicted "a 99% chance that, during a one-month period, a consumer surfing the busiest sites on the web will visit a site that collects personal identifying information."[74]

Throughout the late dot-com period, web advertising remained a work in progress. Marketers continued to press for strategic advantage and made hay of instances of targeting gone wrong—flogging home mortgages on sites aimed at teenagers, for example—that undermined the rhetoric of precision put forth by the surveillance advertising industry.[75] Well aware of the importance of positive publicity and the appearance of forward momentum for attracting clients and investors, online ad executives routinely oversold their capabilities. So there was a heavy dose of irony in statements like those by Paul Schaut, CEO of Engage, who told *Adweek* in 1999: "Now, we don't have to wave our arms to talk about the promise of profiling. We have arrived."[76] Ad networks had indeed greatly expanded their surveillance capacities, but the industry had not "arrived" in the sense of fulfilling any "promise of profiling." Claiming that the waving of arms was no longer necessary was in fact a vigorous display of arm waving.

It might be expected that the gap between the rhetoric and reality of surveillance advertising's execution would have curtailed marketers' adoption. National marketers in particular had been complaining about the web's shortcomings from the very beginning, but ignoring the internet was never actually an option. As Dan Schiller argues, confronted by the internet's exploding popularity and the threat of its noncommercial development, marketers "had little choice but to spring into action."[77] The example of Procter & Gamble is again illustrative. In the early 1990s, P&G was among the first to articulate the marketing complex's collective need to ensure that the new interactive media would serve the interests of advertisers. The company threw its early support behind the cable industry's "interactive television" projects, all of which withered as the web rose to prominence. Thereafter P&G became one of web advertising's most reliable complainers, convening the FAST Summit and trumpeting the medium's shortcomings regarding ROI. In 1998, P&G spent about one tenth of 1 percent of its U.S. ad budget on the internet.[78] "The current state of web advertising just isn't effective enough to warrant any truly meaningful investment from us," said Denis Beausejour, P&G's vice president of advertising.[79]

But even the world's biggest advertiser could not afford to sit out the internet. The coercive power of capitalist competition is inescapable. Between 1998 and 2000, P&G ramped up investment in its own corporate sites and quadrupled its online advertising budget. Lauding the company's "tremendous influence in leading the industry, along with its own real commitment to the medium in ad spending and creation of innovative, successful campaigns," *Advertising Age* named P&G its 1999 "interactive marketer of the year."[80] Beausejour, the same executive who had lamented the web's inefficiency a year before, explained the reversal in these terms:

"The interactive world is where consumers are going, where it's happening, and we need to be there."[81]

Beausejour was speaking for more than just P&G. Ultimately, all elements of the marketing complex—including the upstart ad networks—shared an overriding interest in maximizing the internet's utility for selling. As *Advertising Age* observed: "While industry leaders may disagree about the mechanics of developing internet ads . . . the most important aspect to come out of FAST is that parties who used to sit at opposite sides of the table are now working together to figure out how to make the internet work as an ad medium."[82] The push for increasingly rationalized forms of surveillance advertising was part of a broader effort by national marketers to mold the internet's development to suit their interests, beginning with the trade association lobbying that I outlined in the first chapters of this book.

The flashy dot-coms with billion-dollar valuations and the marketing titans with billion-dollar ad budgets often butted heads, but they quickly converged on the notion that consumer data was to be the lifeblood of the commercial internet. Although the particulars were implemented on a competitive and ad hoc basis, a surveillance advertising consensus had taken hold. Closed-loop advertising services like remarketing laid bare the structural composition of this arrangement, demonstrating that ROI required consumer monitoring conducted collaboratively by web publishers, marketers, and platform intermediaries. Simply collecting data on one's own customers and keeping that data in house would not be sufficient. Surveillance advertising would be, in key respects, a team effort.

DoubleClick executives came to argue that advertising's future hinged on new forms of cooperative business practices around the collection, analysis, and deployment of marketing data:

> It has become clear that the old business silos of direct marketing versus brand advertising, or offline versus online media development, or the marketing area versus the IT department, no longer make sense. The common trait possessed by the most effective marketers and advertisers is that they have broken down these walls and allowed the groups to learn from each other's experiences. Successful companies must aggregate customer data from various channels in order to have a holistic view of their customers. They need the ability to measure the effectiveness of their campaigns across these various media. They also need technology to integrate their sales, customer service, IT, marketing, and advertising efforts.[83]

Consumer surveillance became a focal point in the perpetual business struggle to maximize returns, which demanded breaking down the walls that separated marketers and their intermediaries, from ad agencies to publishers to online advertising companies. The protoplatformization of ad networks epitomized these developments. DoubleClick's NetGravity subsidiary worked not only with publishers but also with marketers and retailers, and its services became increasingly integrated with its clients' own growing customer databases. "Is the business consulting or hardware?" asked *Advertising Age.* "Once the server is installed, there's a lot of time, resources and intellectual property that gets shared among clients, agencies and third-party ad servers."[84] Institutional and operational distinctions were blurred to facilitate surveillance advertising and assert the marketing function online. "All this means vendors such as NetGravity will be working even more closely with advertisers, agencies and publishers in the future," said a company executive. "It's not a piecemeal approach."[85]

As more marketers began to participate in surveillance advertising, ad networks benefited from an enlarged capacity to aggregate data and the incremental entrenchment of their position as the most important strategic intermediaries—protoplatform monopolies—in the online advertising sector. This made the fortunes of market leaders like DoubleClick even as it structured the entire industry in important ways, tilting internet development toward ubiquitous commercial surveillance and increasingly discriminatory practices of behavioral profiling. Protoplatformization pointed to a future where a few big winners would dominate an internet advertising industry organized around the widespread collection and exchange of consumer data.

What is significant about this period is not DoubleClick's particular business history per se, but its leadership in enlarging the social domain of consumer surveillance and creating a prototype for surveillance advertising's subsequent propulsion by market forces. As I discuss in the Conclusion of this book, DoubleClick was purchased by Google in the mid-2000s and became an integral part of the search giant's embrace of surveillance advertising. But already in the dot-com era, competitive pressure pushed all marketers and publishers toward indiscriminate data collection. It was a classic race to the bottom in which participating in surveillance advertising became more or less mandatory. In order to get the most value from web advertising, publishers and marketers alike had to become more than buyers and sellers of banner ads; they had to become terminals of surveillance, continuously collecting consumer data and exchanging it with the platform hubs.

As *Adweek* reported, "No one really knows just what data matters. . . . Companies are tracking everything they can now, with the idea of figuring out what's important later."[86] "People are erring on the side of collecting too much data rather than too little," admitted one dot-com executive.[87] Ad networks were particularly voracious. DoubleClick boasted a database of 120 million user profiles in 2000, twelve times what it had at the time of its IPO two years before, and roughly on par with the total number of internet users in the United States at the time.[88] Competitors amassed immense profile caches as well, with CMGI's Engage at 70 million, Match-Logic at 65 million, and 24/7 Media at 60 million.[89] The trend was so pervasive that data systems provider Oracle reported a 30 percent increase in orders for enterprise-class data warehouses and explicitly linked the surge in demand to dot-coms looking to store hundreds of terabytes of data collected from the web.[90] At that time, only the largest brick-and-mortar businesses had databases requiring storage in the terabyte range, and even then only after years of data collection.

The web of the late 1990s became a surveillance free-for-all as monitoring exploded without regard for consumer awareness, let alone consent. The prevailing business logic accepted such practices as beneficial to consumers and necessary "for mainstream advertisers to do more than kick the tires of online advertising."[91] Significant political challenges arose only after DoubleClick and others announced plans to integrate web profiles with consumers' off-line personal information. The resulting political battles are the subject of the next chapter.

6 THE PRIVACY CHALLENGE

THE SURVEILLANCE ADVERTISING INDUSTRY grew quickly under the favorable political economic conditions of the dot-com period. Free of regulatory constraints and urged on by corporate appetites for consumer data, companies in the digital advertising sector led a surge of internet surveillance. By the late 1990s, nearly all of the web's most popular sites not only collected consumer data as a matter of course but also neglected to disclose such practices to their visitors.[1] Surveillance had been quietly integrated into the web's default user experience. Although commercial data collection initially flew under the radar of many web users, it did not go completely unnoticed, or unchallenged, for long.

This chapter chronicles the conflict between alliances of marketing lobbyists and an upstart group of privacy activists to shape public policy over issues of internet data collection, disclosure, and consent. In what was framed as a matter of individual privacy, these groups sought to influence online advertising's regulatory parameters amid growing public concern over online surveillance. The flash point was a controversy surrounding ad network DoubleClick's acquisition of data broker Abacus Direct. DoubleClick sought to merge its web-based consumer profiles with Abacus' off-line purchasing records, which contained names, addresses, and other personally identifying information. Although a common practice today, mixing online and off-line records was a boundary-pushing move at the time. But this was merely the highest-profile event in a more protracted confrontation over whether federal regulation would establish universal guidelines for internet privacy or whether industry self-regulation would remain the norm. As detailed in chapters 1 and 2, the Clinton administration took an early position that the private sector would lead internet system development in the United States, leaving the online ad industry to regulate itself. Judging by the lack of congressional pushback, the majority of federal lawmakers supported Clinton's stance. Between 1998 and 2000, the political class's commitment to industry self-regulation was tested as activists began to agitate against the resulting wave of unchecked consumer surveillance.

The political struggles of this period stand among what privacy activist Marc Rotenberg calls "the most historic events on the [United States'] privacy timeline."[2] The stakes were high for the marketing complex. Privacy issues resonated with the American public and cut across political party lines. At the height of the debate, Congress was persuaded to consider adopting opt-in legislation that would require companies to obtain prior affirmative consent from web users before collecting their personal data. This threatened to undermine the developing surveillance advertising business model, which required pervasive monitoring of internet users. Facing negative publicity and potential legislation, a coalition of marketing complex trade associations and newly formed internet advertising groups lobbied to solidify an opt-out status quo in which surveillance, not privacy, was the default setting.

Returning to the theme of "negative policy" analysis from previous chapters, this chapter draws attention not only to the successful implementation of industry self-regulation but also to the policy alternatives that were rejected.[3] For the marketing complex, the internet's commercialization and the development of surveillance advertising in particular required that public interest efforts to regulate online data practices be thwarted. Marketing trade groups had worked closely with the Clinton administration in the preceding years to establish a policy of advertising self-regulation, and they intended to maintain that arrangement. This chapter shows how privacy reforms were defeated by private sector coalitions and explains how federal support for advertising industry self-regulation endured to become the regulatory foundation for internet data collection heading into the twenty-first century.

Politicizing Internet Privacy

Elements of the marketing complex had been working for decades to legitimize and legalize commercial surveillance in many areas of social practice.[4] When the web came along, the marketing complex shaped public policy to bring the development of the new interactive media into alignment with their business interests. There was precious little democratic debate over these issues. Privacy became one of the few entry points for organized civic participation in the broader commercialization of the internet. When DoubleClick and other ad networks began collecting web browsing data in 1996, they had the benefit of working under cover. Few people who used the web were aware of tracking technologies like HTTP cookies, and fewer still knew of their appropriation by digital advertising networks. There were no privacy policies or data disclosures of any significance; nor was there any legal expectation that companies would provide them. Web browsing software simply loaded cookies by default in a background process effectively hidden from users.

Public awareness of online data collection was stewarded in no small part by the efforts of a coalition of civil society groups that began to challenge surveillance advertising. Organizations including the Center for Media Education (CME), Electronic Privacy Information Center (EPIC), and Center for Democracy and Technology (CDT) formed what Colin Bennett calls a "privacy advocacy network" to generate publicity and policy proposals around internet privacy issues.[5] CME was a tiny media reform organization whose mission was to "improve the quality of electronic media, especially on the behalf of children and families."[6] EPIC and CDT were privacy and civil liberties watchdogs, established to "focus public attention on emerging civil liberties issues" related to the internet. These groups took a leadership role in a broader advocacy network that worked against industry opposition to spur the federal government to act.[7]

The range of policy discussion during this period was largely confined to a neoliberal field that rarely questioned the validity of the market as the internet's core organizing principle.[8] Although public concern over internet data collection grew quickly, there were no mass protests or organized episodes of civil disobedience around these issues. Within these constraints, privacy activists practiced a form of Beltway activism that used the tools of mainstream politics and public opinion making. These included conducting research, writing reports, filing lawsuits, and bringing complaints to federal agencies like the Federal Trade Commission. Arguably, their most effective strategy was public relations. Privacy activists were quite successful in generating press coverage of their concerns and agenda, which helped force the first public conversation about internet privacy and data collection and prompted Congress to consider legislative action.

Founded by Kathryn Montgomery and Jeff Chester, CME was one of the first civil society organizations in the country to draw attention to internet privacy. Concerned about how data collection might affect children, CME began an investigation of the website Kids.com in 1995. The site was a popular destination for children, offering interactive games, sweepstakes, and contests. It was also a hidden surveillance operation. To access the site, users had to complete a lengthy registration questionnaire designed to capture personal information for marketing purposes. Children were asked to disclose their names, genders, media preferences, and even describe their "hopes and dreams" in order to populate profile databases that could be sold to marketers of cereal and soft drinks.[9] These initial findings prompted CME to expand its study to include sites created by marketers such as Disney, Kellogg's, and Pepsi. According to Chester, "children's issues were a good starting point" for privacy activists because they were "harder to argue against" and presented better opportunities to attract much needed funding.[10]

As the CME worked on its investigation, journalists began to report on the use of cookies for online tracking. The *San Jose Mercury News* was among the first U.S. newspapers to break the story, running an article under the headline "Leading Web Browsers May Violate Privacy of Users' Computers, Activities."[11] Continuing coverage by news organizations provided a publicity boost to privacy activists who were beginning to build more coherent advocacy networks around these issues.

The activists' primary objective became persuading Congress to create "legally enforceable rights to information privacy."[12] Janlori Goldman of the CDT argued that information privacy should be treated as a basic right and that internet participation should not hinge on "trading your privacy for some kind of benefit."[13] EPIC made the case that consumers should have the option to retain total anonymity online while preserving the freedom to do what they wish, including engaging in business transactions.[14] More generally, privacy activists criticized the lack of transparency in data collection practices, arguing that "average consumers did not know their activity was being tracked let alone how the information was being used."[15] They argued that consumers should be afforded access to and control over the information collected about them, including the right to opt out of data collection entirely.[16]

In the spring of 1996, CME released its findings in a report titled *Web of Deception*, which argued that marketers were invading children's privacy through "solicitation of personal information, tracking of online computer use, and exploitation of vulnerable, young computer users through new unfair and deceptive forms of advertising."[17] CME called for an immediate end to the collection of children's personal information and for clear separation between commercial messages and content directed to young audiences on the internet. The report generated stories in major newspapers at a time when there was little public knowledge about online marketing, let alone marketing geared to kids. Much of the prior attention given to children's internet use was focused on "indecent" content.[18] CME's efforts helped place internet data collection on the civic advocacy agenda and initiated a public shaming of the companies involved. The negative publicity was enough that General Foods postponed the launch of its new website for children in order to steer clear of the news cycle.[19]

Looking to attract the attention of regulators in Washington, D.C., CME also filed a formal complaint against Kids.com with the Federal Trade Commission. The allegations in the complaint were not about data collection or privacy per se but rather that the site's undisclosed surveillance constituted a deceptive business practice. Why not file a complaint about privacy directly? The simple answer is that the CME had no legal basis for doing so. Deceptive business practices fell under the jurisdiction of the FTC, but internet privacy did not. Nor did it fall under the purview of any federal agency, because the United States had no regulatory authority or legislative framework devoted to internet privacy issues. Kids.com and other companies were spying on children, but they were not breaking any internet privacy laws.

Apart from the Fourth Amendment's restrictions on illegal search and seizure, the most significant U.S. privacy legislation is the Privacy Act of 1974, which created guidelines for federal agencies' collection and use of personally identifiable information. Private sector entities are governed by a patchwork of narrower state and federal regulations that pertain to certain categories of information (e.g., educational or medical records) while leaving out others (e.g., behavioral profiling data). The general approach to privacy policy making in the United States has been "reactive rather than anticipatory, incremental rather than comprehensive, and fragmented rather than coherent," argues Colin Bennett. "There may be a lot of laws, but there is not much protection."[20]

Filling this void, the FTC became a somewhat misfit adjudicator of disputes between privacy activists and proponents of industry self-regulation. In June 1996, the FTC convened the first of what became a string of workshops at which a mix of industry, advocacy, and government representatives came together to discuss emerging issues in internet privacy.[21] In alignment with President Clinton's laissez-faire agenda for internet commercialization, the FTC adopted what the CME's Kathryn Montgomery called a "softball approach to prodding industry" to take privacy matters into its own hands.[22] In *Generation Digital*, Montgomery reports that the FTC chairman, Robert Pitofsky, opened the first privacy workshop by assuring the room that his agency was "not here to lay the groundwork for any government rules, guidelines, or otherwise."[23]

Nevertheless, workshop participants spent some time outlining a set of fair information practices that centered on the principles of notice and choice.[24] These guidelines drew on decades of precedent around intra-governmental privacy regulations.[25] The basic premise was that companies should uniformly disclose their data practices so that consumers could make informed choices about how their information was collected and used. The question became, how should such principles be applied? Industry's position was that fair information practices were best implemented through a system of self-regulation, voluntary guidelines, or accreditations that would ensure "consumer empowerment" while giving companies the freedom to innovate and drive economic growth. Civil liberties advocates argued that such a system would fail without a foundation of legally enforceable internet privacy rights.

The contours of the debate were summarized by an FTC staff report that recapped the 1996 workshop:

> Industry representatives and trade associations took the position that it would be both inappropriate and counterproductive to mandate particular privacy protections. According to these participants, regulation would stifle the creativity and innovation that have marked the development of interactive media to date, could infringe important First Amendment rights, and might force marketers off the internet entirely. Government should step back, it was argued, and permit industry to develop privacy protection models. Privacy advocates argued that the technologies demonstrated during the Workshop are not a substitute for an enforceable code of fair information practices, and that they are not likely to flourish without government enforcement of privacy rights.[26]

In making these arguments, industry representatives drew from what Chris Hoofnagle has described as the "denialist deck of cards," a series of "rhetorical techniques and predictable tactics" used by opponents of regulation to "erect barriers to debate and consideration of any type of reform, regardless of the facts."[27] Denialist talking points frame government action as not merely unnecessary but also as uniformly harmful to both social welfare and individual autonomy. Cycling through the rhetorical deck of cards, industry representatives argued that it was foolish to regulate the internet as it was still developing and that competition would naturally fix any problems that might arise. Trade association representatives claimed that the rapid advancement of internet technologies eliminated any need for privacy regulations.[28] They contended that any company that failed to respect consumers' privacy preferences would be punished by market forces. Others argued that government regulation was inherently harmful to innovation and risked slowing down the economy. As the president of the Direct Marketing Association put it, regulation would "easily disrupt the development of a very useful tool for consumers, and, indeed, a useful tool for business, which is going to have a significant impact on the United States and on global economies."[29]

The FTC agreed with industry arguments that self-regulation was the best option to address privacy concerns and that the private sector simply needed more time to formulate self-regulatory mechanisms. One such measure was a proposed privacy seal program called TRUSTe, wherein participating sites would display privacy badges verified by a third-party accreditor to indicate their data collection practices. Microsoft, Netscape, and others signed on to support the creation of a different system called the Open Profiling Standard (OPS), a web browser technology meant to enable "users to give their consent before their personal information is handed off to a website."[30] The OPS idea was part of a wider proposal called the Platform for Privacy Preferences (P3P), backed by a large group of tech companies, including AOL and IBM. The creator of the web himself, Tim Berners-Lee, traveled to Washington, D.C., to showcase a prototype of the P3P technology. The Clinton administration installed an early version of the system on the White House website as a show of good faith.[31] Still in a rough stage of development, the technology did not actually do much. But the message of political support was clear.

Despite the general disarray of industry self-regulation efforts, the FTC announced after a second round of workshops in 1997 that the commission would "give new industry initiatives more time to take effect."[32] The statement coincided with the Clinton administration's release of its *Framework for Global Electronic Commerce*, which strongly articulated that the private sector would lead internet development—a process that was already well under way.

The political winds began to shift when the FTC issued a ruling in support of CME's complaint against Kids.com. The FTC found that the site's data collection practices were deceptive, but it effectively dismissed the issue after the company pledged to disclose its surveillance practices in a privacy policy of some kind. The case highlighted what was becoming increasingly clear to observers: The internet advertising industry was not implementing meaningful self-regulation, even at the basic level of providing notice of data collection practices. In June 1998, the FTC released the results of an in-house study on the state of online privacy. Its examination of over 1,400 websites showed that while the majority (85 percent) of sites collected consumer information, few (14 percent) provided any notice whatsoever of such practices, and fewer still (2 percent) provided comprehensive privacy policies.[33] About half of sites directed at children disclosed their data collection practices, though less than 10 percent provided means for parental control over the collection and use of information from children.

The FTC study revealed that while industry leaders had been publicly trumpeting their commitment to privacy, the majority of commercial websites continued to collect consumer data with little regard for privacy concerns. Reporting to Congress, the FTC explained that though it had encouraged industry to address privacy through self-regulation, "the vast majority of online businesses have yet to adopt even the most fundamental fair information practices."[34] Underlining this point, the FTC brought charges against the popular home page community GeoCities for "misrepresent[ing] the purposes for which it was collecting personal information from children and adults."[35] In other words, roughly two years after CME filed its initial complaint about Kids.com, GeoCities, one of the largest websites in the world, was caught doing the exact same thing: lying to its users about consumer surveillance.

In what became a milestone for privacy activists and a warning shot across the bow of industry, the FTC attenuated its support for self-regulation and recommended that Congress pursue legislation to facilitate parental control over the collection and use of children's personal information online.[36] Shortly thereafter, Congress began to look into children's advertising and internet privacy more generally. Drawing on a staple argument from the denialist deck of cards, *Advertising Age* called proposed limits on children's advertising "a chilly prospect for responsible marketers who value the ability to innovate and experiment in this medium, free of detailed do's and don'ts," and warned that such restrictions would "stifle promising experiments" in internet advertising.[37]

Meanwhile, high-level trade negotiations between the United States and the European Union introduced an important international dynamic that further bolstered the case for congressional action on children's privacy. Although the White House officially supported industry self-regulation, a new E.U. data protection directive began to weigh heavily on the Clinton administration's approach to domestic privacy policy. As privacy activists organized at home, the White House was negotiating with the E.U. over the harmonization of international standards for data collection and privacy protection. In 1995, the E.U. enacted a Data Protection Directive containing a series of regulatory measures set to take effect in October 1998. Among the directive's stipulations were guidelines for E.U. member states that disallowed "data transfer" to countries that failed to provide an "adequate level of protection" for consumer information.[38] As it stood, the freewheeling internet advertising sector in the United States was far from meeting these impending requirements.

Looming in the not so distant future, the E.U. directive posed a hazard to intercontinental trade, which put stress on the Clinton administration's heretofore hands-off approach to advertising regulation. Specifically, the directive threatened to impede billions of dollars' worth of trade involving "personal information," a market that had long operated with few regulatory constraints.[39] To deal with this problem, Clinton deployed the Department of Commerce and the FTC to steward the development of more robust industry self-regulation in order to appease E.U. officials concerned about U.S. data practices. The Clinton administration's tentative support of legislation for children's internet privacy amid their otherwise staunch defense of self-regulation seemed to be a political accommodation meant to deflate the pressure stemming from the E.U. trade talks. As Montgomery notes, "By focusing on children, the government was able to demonstrate that it was taking decisive action to protect online privacy, while also buying additional time for industry to get its act together."[40]

Anticipating that Congress would not fully commit to legislation without buy-in from at least some of the powerful corporations in the children's media sector, privacy activists astutely partnered with the National PTA and other children's welfare groups to lobby Disney and other media companies directly.[41] Shortly thereafter, many in the marketing complex decided to cut their losses and work to shape the law that was likely coming.

These developments enabled the bipartisan passage of the Children's Online Privacy Protection Act (COPPA) in late 1998. The law created standards for the collection and use of children's data to be enforced by the FTC, and specifically required that websites obtain parental consent before collecting personal information from children under the age of thirteen. However, the law's opt-in provisions were undermined by vague language and poorly designed enforcement mechanisms. COPPA was a laudable activism effort but produced weak policy to support its stated goals of protecting children's privacy, to say nothing of adults. Privacy activists who initially supported the legislation have since criticized its implementation. The CME's Montgomery, who worked with the FTC to draft language for COPPA, has acknowledged that the bill contains loopholes and places an excessive burden on parents to maintain a haphazard system of privacy protection.[42]

Although the efficacy of COPPA's privacy protections are questionable, the bill's passage nevertheless produced a strong secondary effect of spurring the marketing complex to defensive action. Broader privacy legislation no longer seemed outside the realm of possibility. "It's a massive mistake to ignore Washington," said one industry consultant.[43] Wary of congressional action, the marketing complex began to view the threat of formal privacy rules as "a top barrier to the continued growth of e-commerce."[44] Companies and trade associations formed new partnerships to coordinate self-regulatory efforts and lobby government officials. Among the most prominent was the Online Privacy Alliance (OPA), a coalition of eighty-six organizations formed with the express purpose of securing industry self-regulation on internet data issues. The OPA's membership extended beyond the internet advertising industry proper to include the marketing complex at large. Reproducing its member list in full illustrates the breadth of companies and trade associations that found cause to rally around unrestrained internet data collection:[45]

3Com
Acxiom
AdForce
America Online
American Advertising Federation
American Electronics Association

American Institute of Certified Public Accountants
Ameritech
Apple Computer
Association of Online Professionals
AT&T
Bank of America
Bell Atlantic
Bell South
Business Software Alliance
Coalition for Advertising Supported Information and Entertainment
     (CASIE)
Centraal Corporation
Cisco
CommTouch Software
Compaq
Computer Systems Policy Project
Council of Growing Companies
Dell
Direct Marketing Association
Disney
DoubleClick Inc.
Dun & Bradstreet
Eastman Kodak
eBay
EDS
EDventure Holdings
E-LOAN
Engage Technologies (CMGI)
Equifax
Ernst and Young
European-American Business Council
Experian
Fast Forward/Interactive Advertising Bureau
Ford
Gateway
GeoCities
Hewlett-Packard
IBM
Individual Reference Services Group

Information Technology Association of America

Information Technology Industry Council

INSUREtrust.com

InsWeb Corporation

Intel

Interactive Digital Software Association

Interactive Travel Services Association

Internet Alliance

Intuit

KPMG

Lexis-Nexis

MatchLogic

MCI WorldCom

Microsoft

MindSpring Enterprises Inc.

Motion Picture Association of America

National Foundation for Consumer Credit

NCR

Nestlé

Netscape

NORTEL

Northpole.com

Novell

Oracle

Preview Travel

PricewaterhouseCoopers

PrivaSeek

Procter & Gamble

Rights Exchange

Software & Information Industry Association

Sun Microsystems

Time Warner

Unilever

The United States Chamber of Commerce

The United States Council for International Business

Viacom

ViewCall Canada

Virtual Vineyards

WebConnect

Women.com Networks

Xerox

Yahoo

The OPA achieved some success in propagating basic privacy disclosures among major websites and ad platforms. It helped that OPA members Microsoft and IBM, each among the net's largest advertisers, announced they would no longer advertise on any site that failed to give notice of data collection practices. Along these lines, the Direct Marketing Association instituted a rule requiring its members to create privacy policies.[46] Microsoft even developed a web-based "privacy wizard" tool to autogenerate privacy policies for website administrators. As a result of these nudges, more publishers and marketers began to disclose their data collection practices for the first time, but such information was often hard to find and written in impenetrable jargon. As one former FTC commissioner noted, "As a general rule, privacy policies are confusing, perhaps deliberately so."[47] Thus the internet privacy policy was born—not as a means to empower consumers but as a coordinated attempt to deflect the threat of enforceable data collection regulations.

Internet advertising companies, heretofore underrepresented in Washington, formed a trade association of their own called the Networking Advertising Initiative (NAI). Members included leading ad networks DoubleClick, 24/7 Media, and CMGI. The NAI intended to formalize a universal opt-out mechanism, whereby consumers could choose to withdraw from commercial data collection systems.[48] Together with the OPA, the NAI became a fixture among the private sector coalition dedicated to keeping substantive privacy legislation at bay.

Worlds Collide

The years of privacy activism leading up to the passage of COPPA produced a political struggle that tested the Clinton administration's commitment to self-regulation. COPPA seemed to put a stalemate in place, as did the Commerce Department's ongoing negotiations to carve out a "safe harbor" agreement to exempt U.S. companies from E.U. data oversight.[49] Then DoubleClick, hot off its recent IPO, announced its intention to merge with the data broker Abacus Direct. The deal was singularly important in that it represented the most sweeping attempt to date to link online profile information with personally identifiable information culled from everyday off-line consumption. Privacy activists were stridently opposed to merging online and off-line data and organized a campaign to block the merger.[50] Their efforts reinvigorated the privacy debate after COPPA and prompted a formal FTC investigation into DoubleClick's data collection practices. By generating news coverage, activists raised surveillance advertising to a new level of publicity and helped to clarify the limits of self-regulation, especially around the lack of enforcement mechanisms to ensure that companies actually followed their own privacy guidelines.

Already among the largest internet advertising platforms, DoubleClick was leveraging dot-com bubble finance capital for rapid expansion. Abacus, which maintained records on the spending habits of some 90 percent of U.S. households, was an attractive prospect for acquisition.[51] Although DoubleClick's 120 million consumer profiles were ostensibly anonymous, Abacus' 88 million profiles contained personally identifiable information such as names and addresses. As the *Wall Street Journal* explained: "If you've bought anything from a large department store or a catalog lately, Abacus probably has your name and address, what you bought, and how much you spent."[52] With the two of these data troves combined, Double-Click would possess incredibly granular information about consumer behavior, both online and off.

Beyond the sheer magnitude of the data stockpile that would result from the merger, privacy activists presciently worried that DoubleClick's move to combine anonymous online data with identifiable off-line data would become standard industry practice. Representatives from a collation of advocacy groups including CME, EPIC, and Junk Busters wrote an open letter to DoubleClick and Abacus executives, copying key members of Congress from both parties. The letter argued that the merger would "fundamentally change the internet from an anonymous space to one where consumers are silently identified."[53] Activists made similar pleas to the companies' shareholders and encouraged them to vote the merger down. DoubleClick responded by saying that not only was it against company policy to merge such information but also it was technically impossible to do so.[54] The technical anonymity of consumer profiles had become a standard rhetorical shield used by online data gatherers to deflect privacy-related criticism. As DoubleClick CEO Kevin O'Connor liked to say, "We can't invade anyone's privacy because we don't know who you are."[55]

Despite privacy advocates' efforts to discredit the merger, Wall Street loved the idea. Both companies' stock prices rose on news of the deal, which was successfully completed in late November 1999. The dot-com bubble was in a full-blown frenzy at this point, spiking DoubleClick's market capitalization to nearly $9 billion. A few months later, privacy activists' fears were validated as DoubleClick quietly modified its privacy policy, removing its pledge to keep consumer profiles anonymous. The change indirectly revealed DoubleClick's plans to merge Abacus' data with its own in order to build profiles that would include "name and address; retail, catalog and online purchase history; and demographic data."[56]

Press investigations indicated that DoubleClick had in fact begun working to combine the data almost immediately after the merger was finalized, a feat company executives had previously described as impossible.[57] Highlighting the limits of trade association-led self-regulation, DoubleClick and Abacus were both members of the OPA and Direct Marketing Association, organizations that nominally opposed such practices. Privacy activists filed a complaint with the FTC alleging that DoubleClick's merger of the online and off-line databases would violate prior assurances of anonymity and therefore constituted a deceptive business practice. As in previous FTC investigations, the complaint did not involve the legality of data collection or merging because there were no laws regulating those activities. Activists also organized a public letter-writing campaign to oppose the data merging. The CDT created an email application that enabled individuals to send complaints to DoubleClick and its business partners. Within three weeks, some 25,000 people had sent messages to DoubleClick, while "several thousand" had written to its marketer and publisher clients.[58]

The public relations fallout proved substantial. The *Washington Post* called DoubleClick "one of the most vilified companies in the online world," and *USA Today* reported that it had become "the media's poster boy for bad behavior on the web."[59] Responding to EPIC's complaint, the FTC opened a formal investigation into the matter, while a number of states' attorneys general initiated inquiries of their own.[60] Additionally, DoubleClick had been implicated in several civil lawsuits over its data collection practices.[61] Perhaps most damaging was the slippage of the company's stock price in a financial market that had already begun to show signs of impending collapse.[62]

At first DoubleClick dug in its heels, hiring a former congressional staffer as its new director of public policy and government affairs—that is, its "lead lobbyist."[63] The company also stepped up its own public relations efforts, announcing a consumer education campaign that included full-page advertisements in the *New York Times*, as well as 50 million banner impressions directing internet users to a newly created website, PrivacyChoices.org.[64] DoubleClick attempted to qualify the scope of its data collection, saying it did not use "highly sensitive information for profiling such as health information, detailed financial information, information of a sexual nature, and information on children."[65] It also maintained that it would "not link personally identifiable information about a user to online behavior without first giving that user notice and the choice not to participate."[66]

The rhetoric of notice and choice—of consumer empowerment—was a familiar refrain among defenders of online profiling. But in practice, DoubleClick's implementation of these ideals was far less empowering than the company claimed. DoubleClick's default practice was to link online profile data with off-line personally identifiable information whenever possible.[67] Further, DoubleClick essentially off-loaded the burden of disclosing its data collection practices to its massive network of publisher and marketer affiliates and clients. As a company executive explained, "Any site that we work with that provides us with personally identifiable information . . . must provide the user with the notice and choice."[68] The problem was that DoubleClick did not actually hold its network partners accountable for following its guidelines. As EPIC noted in its FTC complaint, AltaVista (DoubleClick's largest client) obliquely disclosed passing information to third parties but made no specific mention of Double-Click. Most web users were unaware that by "surfing the site of one of its affiliates, they had entered into an agreement to provide DoubleClick with their personal data."[69] Jason Catlett of the advocacy organization Junk Busters summarized the situation like this: "Thousands of sites are ratting on you, so as soon as one gives you away, you're exposed on all of them. If you don't like Yahoo's privacy policy, you don't have to use its site. But it's very difficult for consumers to avoid DoubleClick because most don't know when it is collecting information."[70]

DoubleClick made much of the fact that it provided an opt-out tool on its own website, noting that 50,000 people had elected to opt out of its tracking system.[71] Again, the catch was that the average web user was unaware of DoubleClick's existence, let alone its opt-out mechanism. As a third-party ad platform, DoubleClick's sprawling internet presence was largely behind the scenes. The company's access to consumers was mediated through web publishers and marketers, who were then responsible for disclosing DoubleClick's data practices. Fifty thousand people may have opted out of DoubleClick's profiling apparatus, but the company maintained a database of 120 million behavioral profiles.[72] The opt-outs were a drop in an ocean of surveillance.

A turning point came in March 2000, just as the dot-com bubble began to burst. DoubleClick had been battered in the media for months, and its stock price was falling fast.[73] Throwing a white flag, the company announced it would suspend its data merging program. CEO Kevin O'Connor left his position, saying that the plan to combine online and off-line data was a mistake "in the absence of government and industry standards."[74] The conflict surrounding the DoubleClick/Abacus merger subjected the growing surveillance advertising industry to its first bout of public scrutiny and forced one of its most powerful companies to halt its plans for expansion. Privacy activists had momentum, but the marketing complex was now on red alert.

Rich Lobby, Poor Regulation

A few months after DoubleClick walked back its data merging program, privacy activists achieved what appeared to be yet another important victory. After four years of waiting for industry to implement self-regulatory privacy protections on its own accord, the Federal Trade Commission reversed its opposition to federal privacy legislation. Frustrated by industry inaction and spurred on by activists, the commissioners recommended in a 3–2 vote that Congress "enact legislation that, in conjunction with continuing self-regulatory programs, will ensure adequate protection of consumer privacy online."[75] True to form, Chairman Pitofsky tempered the recommendation with a caveat that self-regulation had not failed entirely, "but in certain respects, it looks as if self-regulation would be more successful if there was some backup legislation."[76]

Due in no small part to the actions of activists, online privacy issues had "gone off the Richter scale in terms of public sensitivity."[77] One survey of internet users found that 87 percent of respondents were "somewhat or very concerned about threats to their privacy online."[78] With elections looming, the White House and both parties in Congress increased their focus on internet data collection. House Democrats convened a privacy task force, while the Senate created a bipartisan congressional privacy caucus.[79] "This year's campaign slogan could be: It's online privacy, stupid," wrote *BusinessWeek*.[80] Suddenly, legislators seemed eager to at least appear to be interested in getting a privacy law on the books. According to one account, "More than one hundred privacy bills had been introduced in the legislatures of 41 states."[81] At the national level, Congress held committee hearings on the subject, and several members began working on federal privacy bills.

Most congressional proposals hewed closely to the FTC's long-standing recommendations around the fair information practices of notice and choice. For example, Senator John McCain of Arizona introduced a bill that required companies to provide "conspicuous notice" of their data practices.[82] But other lawmakers went beyond the notice and choice framework. Democrats in both houses introduced plans containing a particular measure that some privacy activists had been requesting for years, but that industry universally reviled: an opt-in mandate for personal data collection. As summarized by the *Wall Street Journal:* "Beneath all the fuss about cookies and databases, the debate about internet privacy comes down to two very different approaches. In privacy jargon, the first is known as opt-in. Marketers agree not to collect or use personal data unless you affirm that you want to participate in their programs. Opt-out takes the opposite tack, assuming you want to participate unless the site hears otherwise."[83]

Most legislative proposals such as Senator McCain's were opt out. They required companies to post privacy policies but left data collection as the default practice from which consumers could opt out. The opposite was true for the Consumer Privacy Protection Act proposed by Senator Fritz Hollings of South Carolina.[84] This act was one of several opt-in bills that would have required all websites and ad platforms to obtain "affirmative consent in advance from consumers" before personal data could be collected or shared.[85] "Any bill that does not have the opt-in is just whistling Dixie," said Hollings at a committee hearing.[86] Though limited to data categorized as "personally identifying," these opt-in proposals nevertheless represented a significant legal challenge to the surveillance advertising status quo.

As Congress considered these opposing approaches, the *New York Times* reported of a "nervousness among internet marketers about the public relations and regulatory minefields" that lay ahead.[87] Marketers and ad platforms understood that a requirement to obtain affirmative consent in advance of data collection would severely impede the surveillance advertising economy they had been building, which relied on hidden data collection as the default setting. Shuffling again through the denialist deck of cards, industry groups foretold of apocalyptic consequences for economic growth and technological innovation should an opt-in framework be adopted. According to the Association of National Advertisers, "The whole question of target marketing [was] at risk."[88] Trade press editorial pages featured vitriolic defenses of data collection that accused privacy activists and government regulators of neo-Luddism. As Thornton May, a consultant and "corporate futurist," wrote in *Advertising Age:*

> Congratulations, interactive marketers: You have been anointed the new villains of the digital age. Like the chemical polluters of the 1960s, the napalm makers of the '70s, the oil companies of the '80s, and the HMOs of the '90s, interactive marketers are on the cusp of some very bad press. . . . These cyber-left-behinds, data privacy tree-huggers, and self-appointed guardians of digital rights for the bit-challenged, privacy-violated hoi polloi have targeted interactive marketers as the "digital satans" of the wired world. Privacy is their rallying cry. . . . Unless you mobilize a counteroffensive today . . . we will be forever branded the bad boys on the digital block.[89]

Mr. May was preaching to the choir. The marketing complex needed no convincing to ratchet up its lobbying and public relations efforts. The most powerful internet companies, including DoubleClick, Amazon, eBay, Yahoo, and Excite, "planted their corporate flags in the nation's capital," establishing "government affairs" offices to coordinate a unified industry response.[90] As one government relations practitioner noted, "Washington is no longer this great East Coast bogeyman, a place where you can trot out your CEO once or twice a year. Internet companies must include a policy component in their business model."[91] "If the industry moves aggressively," said an executive at CMGI's Engage, "there is still a shot to forestall legislation."[92]

DoubleClick hired New York City's former consumer affairs commissioner to serve in a newly created chief privacy officer role and assembled an external advisory board led by a former New York attorney general to consult on privacy issues.[93] Other internet marketers followed suit. Whatever their operative functions, the creation of these positions were highly symbolic, "as indicated by the fact that they worked more closely with internal marketing and public relations departments than management and operations."[94] Separately, trade groups floated the idea of launching a $25 million strategic communications campaign to pacify the public on privacy issues.[95] As critical scholars including Inger Stole and Molly Niesen have shown, public relations efforts such as these have a long history in media policy.[96] In this instance, aggressive industry campaigning simply overwhelmed the meager resources available to privacy activists.

In a classic example of Washington's revolving door, OPA hired as its director Christine Varney, a former FTC commissioner involved in the agency's early examinations of online privacy.[97] Under Varney's leadership, the OPA became a powerful voice for framing privacy self-regulation in terms of consumer empowerment. Varney testified twice on behalf of the OPA at congressional hearings, advancing a position that was uniformly against legislative action, opposed to giving the FTC increased authority to police privacy violations, and in full support of industry self-regulation.[98] The following quote from Varney's testimony before the Senate Committee on Commerce, Science, and Transportation in May 2000 is exemplary of broader industry arguments:

> What we do not need are sweeping regulations governing the collection and use of data [or] the conditions and methods under which that data use can be consented to . . . Whatever solutions Congress, industry, and consumers come to that will make privacy choices on the internet ubiquitous, the solutions must be technology neutral, market driven, and hospitable to the online [business] environment. [99]

Congress held no fewer than ten hearings on online privacy issues between 1998 and 2000. Responding to public concern and privacy activism, legislators introduced dozens of bills containing varying degrees of consumer data protections. Nevertheless, the only bill to make it out of committee, let alone be passed into law, was the Children's Online Privacy Protection Act (COPPA). The marketing complex was successful not only in defeating opt-in measures but also in preventing any privacy legislation outside of the narrowly targeted COPPA. Despite widespread public support for online privacy, federal legislation remained, as one observer noted, "a political football."[100] As Chris Hoofnagle notes, privacy activists waged an "uphill battle, as it is easier to defeat legislation than pass it."[101]

Facing an industry lobbying counteroffensive, legislation that contained opt-in provisions proved too far outside the neoliberal political consensus. Beyond the fact that, as White House advisor Ira Magaziner put it, "it is hard to underestimate the power of some of the groups who were lobbying for opt-out," the U.S. economy had been overtaken by the dot-com financial bubble.[102] Actions that were perceived as threats to economic growth, even if dubiously constructed as such, were seen as politically untenable. Privacy activists were not just fighting against

DoubleClick and other surveillance advertisers but also their clients and customers—effectively the full force of business enterprise. Moreover, both houses of Congress were controlled by the Republican Party, which was on the whole even more supportive of government deregulation and laissez-faire policies than neoliberal Democrats. As one journalist put it, "If you believe these [privacy] bills will pass, I have a can't-miss dot-com to sell you."[103]

By 2001, the issue of internet privacy had been substantively dropped by all branches of federal government. After George W. Bush's contested presidential victory in 2000, the already limited political capital of privacy activists dried up completely. The FTC abandoned its investigation into DoubleClick's data collection practices without saying whether or not deception or other violations had occurred. Many of the civil suits against the company were dropped as well. The "internet privacy debate is dead," declared *InternetWeek*.[104]

Privacy activists achieved certain successes, including stewarding the passage of the COPPA, pressuring DoubleClick to halt its plans to merge online and off-line data, and laboriously convincing the Federal Trade Commission to switch its stance from supporting industry self-regulation to recommending federal privacy legislation. Yet despite these victories, the marketing complex won the war. COPPA's passage was significant because it was the country's first internet privacy law, but its protections were limited. The DoubleClick/Abacus merger was completed as intended, expanding the company's market power and profiling capacities. Its plan to merge online and off-line data was postponed, but not for long. Most importantly, Congress never acted on the recommendations from activists and the FTC for federal internet privacy legislation, a "negative policy" silence that served as continuing support for a deeply flawed regime of industry self-regulation.[105]

In the absence of government privacy guidelines, commercial entities remained free to conduct surreptitious consumer surveillance on an increasing scale. Under the auspices of industry self-regulation, the "fair information principles" of notice and choice were implemented in such a way that they served the exact opposite purposes for which they were designed. As Joseph Turow argues, rather than providing genuine notice, privacy policies "let users know as little as possible about data collection activities, in as polite but complex a fashion as possible so that they wouldn't understand what was going on but could feel good about them."[106]

As I have argued in this book, disparate actors within the marketing complex broadly conceived came together to construct an advertising-supported internet. Smaller rivalries aside, these companies had a shared interest in creating the largest possible social canvas for surveillance advertising and sought to shape the development of the new internet medium accordingly. Activists' calls to rein in data collection obstructed these goals and needed to be neutralized. It was essential that unrestrained data collection be encoded into the legal structure of the developing internet, no matter that a growing number of people thought that they needed more—not less—privacy online.

The disappointing outcome of the privacy activists' challenge to surveillance advertising in the late 1990s reflected the extent to which the range of political debate had already been circumscribed in the preceding years. Discussion was largely restricted to issues of transparency, narrow notions of user empowerment, and the specific character of the data being collected. The controversy at the heart of the DoubleClick/Abacus merger was whether companies could combine anonymous online profile data with personally identifiable information obtained from off-line sources. These are legitimate issues, but they sidestep more foundational questions about the costs and benefits of pervasive internet surveillance. To what extent should companies be permitted to monitor people's behavior? What are the social costs of unrestrained surveillance? Who benefits from this system and who is harmed? To a significant degree, fundamental structural questions like these had already been pushed aside when the Clinton administration and lawmakers hitched their political wagons to unfettered internet commercialization at the beginning of the decade. From this baseline, the U.S. government approached privacy not as a public policy goal in its own right but as a means to an end. The real privacy policy objective was normalizing surveillance, making it palatable enough so that the internet's commercialization could proceed unabated. Mission accomplished.

7 THE LEGACY OF THE DOT-COM ERA

> We may or may not get the kind of advertising we deserve, but we most
> certainly get the kind of advertising corporations require.
>
> **DANIEL POPE, *THE MAKING OF MODERN ADVERTISING***
>
> The real winner in all of this will be the consumer.
>
> **KEVIN O'CONNOR, DOUBLECLICK CEO**

THE DOT-COM FINANCIAL BUBBLE imploded in the spring of 2000.
Within a year, the Nasdaq stock index had been cut in half, erasing tril-
lions of dollars' worth of inflated market value.[1] The internet advertising sector hit a stumbling block, halting five years of dramatic growth.[2]
Hundreds of dot-com companies—still an important source of internet
advertising demand—perished in the crash. Ad rates fell precipitously.[3]
Without the cushion of financial capital, many of the original surveillance advertising companies faltered. The holding company CMGI,
whose shares had once traded for hundreds of dollars apiece, became a
penny stock.[4] Its advertising subsidiaries were spun off or sold for parts.
Market leader DoubleClick fared better than most, but it was nevertheless weakened as two-thirds of its clients either went bankrupt or scaled
back their ad budgets.[5] To some observers, the future of online advertising looked bleak.

Others were more optimistic. Advertising trade press editorial boards
encouraged their readers to take a longer view of the situation. In the
midst of the crash, as dot-coms were shuttering their doors and laying
off workers, *Advertising Age* was notably sanguine:

> The dot-com debacle is in full force, but the future of the internet—of
> e-marketing, of e-commerce—has never been better. The marketing

community, far from mourning the loss of easy billings or writing off the field, should focus instead on the opportunity that lies ahead and the stronger surviving players that will lead the way. . . . The dot-com shakeout came as no surprise. But too much focus on its financial and marketing disasters misses the important point that the business-to-consumer internet market is wide open, with growth and profits ahead. There's never been a better time to be optimistic about opportunities in the consumer internet space. It's a good time to be a contrarian.[6]

This confidence proved to be well founded. The dot-com collapse was a setback, but the broader enterprise of internet advertising quickly resumed its precrash upward trajectory. By 2003, the sector had resumed strong growth, both in terms of aggregate revenues and as a percentage of total ad spending across all media. There are three reasons for this. While weaker online advertising companies went out of business, many of the biggest players survived, surveillance advertising infrastructures at the ready. Equally important, the cave-in of the new economy was not troublesome enough to ward off marketers, more and more of whom began to include the web in their advertising mix for the first time. Nearly 5,500 new companies tried internet advertising in the third quarter of 2000.[7] As an analyst with Forrester Research put it: "The dotcoms were the hare. Traditional companies have been the tortoise," plodding steadily along the path to become "the backbone of internet spending."[8]

The third contributing factor to internet advertising's revival was an expanding market for a different kind of ad product: keywords on web search engines. Although early web portals such as Yahoo, AOL, and AltaVista had run display ads in the years prior (often in partnerships with ad networks), companies like GoTo developed paid search advertising as an alternative to the prevailing ad network model of targeted banners. This kind of search advertising did not come into its own until the early 2000s, when a company called Google entered the market.

Founded in 1998, Google developed a search engine that was powerful, fast, and free. When the company's founders and financiers made the decision to monetize the business through advertising, Google's large and growing user base instantly made it a major player—and a formidable competitor to ad networks like DoubleClick. Google's search advertising business was in several important ways an antithesis to DoubleClick's surveillance advertising approach. It is useful to consider how these companies and their business models differed in the early 2000s because they represented a fork in the road for internet advertising's subsequent development.

DoubleClick grew out of the mania of the dot-com bubble as a pure business-to-business company, a boisterous and cutthroat deal maker. Google began as a consumer-facing company with a friendly brand, known for its technical chops and altruistic sensibility. Whereas Double-Click was a symbol of Silicon Alley finance capital, Google largely sat out the dot-com bubble, waiting until 2004 to go public after several years of profitability. DoubleClick pioneered the ad network model of targeted web advertising. Initially focused on providing data-driven ad services to web publishers, the company then expanded its purview to marketer clients when it adopted a strategy of platformization. By contrast, marketers comprised Google's original client base, and its ad inventory was not distributed across a network of partners but rather aggregated around the traffic of its own popular search engine.

The sharpest divergence between Google and DoubleClick was their approach to consumer surveillance. DoubleClick's leadership went all in on the notion that consumer data was the keystone for closing the loop between ads and sales, and in their bid for platform monopoly, they built out surveillance capacities to all of the company's marketer and publisher clients. Google's founders did exactly the opposite. Rather than collecting consumer information to target ads, Google relied instead on users' search keywords to display "contextual advertising."[9] For example, someone using Google's search engine to research a trip to Yellowstone National Park might see ads for nearby campsites alongside their search results. The ad targeting was based on the context of the user's activity rather than a composite of their IP address, browsing history, and department store purchases. In the contextual model, there was little point in capturing user data for ad-targeting purposes.

Contextual advertising was a new spin on a classic ad-targeting strategy used in print and broadcast media for many decades: assume people reading the sports section are into sports, and show them ads that reflect those affinities. The premise is that content—whether a web search, a TV show, or a magazine spread—can serve as a reasonable proxy for consumer interest. Google was neither the first nor the only internet advertising company to move in this direction, but it swiftly emerged as the market leader in contextual search advertising. As DoubleClick's surveillance advertising model grew more complex and multivariate, Google's search advertising emphasized simplicity and speed. Perhaps most importantly,

DoubleClick clung onto a pricing structure based on impressions, while Google developed a mechanism to sell ads via auctions on a cost-per-click basis.[10] This meant that marketers bid on advertising opportunities and only paid when an ad was clicked, a prospect that proved attractive to marketers obsessed with improving efficiency and return on investment.

With Google at the helm, search advertising took off in the early 2000s, quickly growing to account for more than 40 percent of all web advertising expenditures.[11] Surveillance advertising's targeted banners, formerly more than half of the market share, receded to around 30 percent. With many competitors still weakened by the dot-com fallout, the still privately held Google became web advertising's new king of the hill, capturing not only the largest share of the search advertising market but a significant chunk of the entire online ad sector.

By the mid 2000s, the two main thrusts in web advertising were key-word search, grounded in contextual placement, and targeted display, which relied on consumer monitoring. Together, these formats accounted for three quarters of industry revenues, but the fortunes of the archetypal companies of Google and DoubleClick were moving in opposite directions.[12] In 2005, DoubleClick was removed from the stock market after being acquired by a private equity firm for $1.1 billion, about one tenth of its market capitalization at the height of the dot-com bubble.[13] Google, on other hand, fresh off a successful IPO, was valued at over $100 billion.[14]

Google's incredible success demonstrated that web advertising could thrive without relying on consumer surveillance. Unlike the dot-coms of the 1990s, Google had achieved profitability soon after launching its ad business.[15] Ad sales were up 177 percent from the previous year, 2004, when Google went public. The company's founders, Sergey Brin and Larry Page, famously included "Don't be evil" among Google's official corporate objectives.[16] All of this was accomplished without surreptitiously collecting consumer data or building invasive profiles for targeted advertising. Was surveillance advertising a failed experiment, destined for history's dustbin of bad ideas?

The Discipline of the Market

In 2004, U.S. marketers spent nearly $10 billion on internet advertising, roughly equivalent to the amount spent on magazines.[17] Internet ad spending was once again growing at a rapid clip, but the proportion going to search had plateaued in just three years.[18] Google found itself in control of a saturated domestic search advertising market that accounted for nearly 100 percent of its revenues. Now subject to the uncompromising scrutiny of Wall Street, Google needed to find a way to maintain forward momentum. It was a classic case of what Douglas Rushkoff calls the "growth trap," where companies' operations become rigidly oriented toward expansion in order to meet shareholder expectations for increasing profits.[19] Simply maintaining a successful search advertising business was not sufficient. Google needed to move into new markets. One obvious place to look for growth was the second largest chunk of internet advertising: the adjacent market of targeted banner ads. "Google is a one-trick pony," declared a securities analyst. "It's a nice-looking pony. But they have to grab a bigger piece of the display advertising market."[20]

Google had already created a program called AdSense that enabled any web publisher to host Google's text ads, broadening the company's reach considerably. Lifted directly from the ad network playbook, AdSense was a distributed service that, in Ken Auletta's words, "turned the web into a giant Google billboard."[21] Still, Google remained distinct from surveillance advertising because these ads were targeted on the basis of the context provided by the surrounding web page rather than consumer data. Google began to move into display advertising with modest success, adding some graphical options to its text ads and striking partnerships with the likes of AOL to tap into its sales force in order to sell banners on Google's AdSense partner sites.[22] As broadband internet service diffused, online video emerged as a promising new ad format. In 2006, Google acquired YouTube, the hugely popular (and virtually advertising-free) video streaming platform. Enamored with prospects for "interactive television" since the early 1990s, marketers were eager to test out the format. Yet these efforts fell short of what was needed to maintain the company's upward trajectory. Online video remained a poor substitute for television advertising, and dabbling in display ads was not nearly enough to move the needle. To effectively exploit networked display and video formats, Google needed to get into the business of consumer surveillance, and it needed to do so quickly.

Competition was closing in. The other major companies in the search engine space, Yahoo and Microsoft, had also declared their intentions to move forcefully into targeted ads. Compounding the matter, social networks including MySpace, Twitter, and Facebook broke onto the scene in the mid-2000s and began to attract large numbers of users. Social networks offered novel experiences, giving people the ability to create their own unique profiles, share content, and connect with others. The fast-growing social networks began to capture firsthand a range of personal information that was otherwise difficult to obtain. Soon these companies began using data about user demographics, interests, and social connections—what Facebook CEO Mark Zuckerberg called the social graph—to inform targeted ad campaigns. The central business proposition of social networks stemmed from their arguably superior capacities to collect and operationalize personal information, not from any significant technical innovations in advertising practice. The stunning growth of Facebook, which amassed over a billion worldwide users in its first decade, brought strong competitive pressure to the entire internet advertising industry, and Google in particular, to build out—or acquire—capacities for consumer surveillance.

It was perhaps Google's good fortune that the leading purveyor of surveillance advertising was about to be put up for sale. Outflanked by search advertising and sorely missing its dot-com era market valuation, Double-Click was downsized in its private equity takeover. Still, the company's strong market position and technological prowess in targeted display put it in a better position than most to weather the bubble's collapse. And there was still an appetite among marketers for data-driven advertising. As one industry observer put it, "You're going to see online advertising is extremely targeted . . . because every cent has to count."[23] DoubleClick remained the industry's de facto standard for surveillance advertising, delivering more targeted banners annually in 2001 and 2002 than it did in any of the years leading up the crash, and for the first time ever, the company was profitable.[24]

In early 2007, Google, entered into a bidding war with Microsoft and Yahoo to buy DoubleClick from its private equity owners. Google emerged the victor but paid an estimated $1 billion premium.[25] The final cost was $3.1 billion (in stock), nearly double what Google had paid for YouTube the year before. Company leaders justified the expense as necessary not only to acquire DoubleClick but also to keep it out of the hands of Google's competitors. The acquisition instantly gave Google a major market position in display ads and yielded an extensive roster of DoubleClick clients from both the supply side (web publishers) and the demand side (marketers and ad agencies) of the online advertising market. "This shores up Google as the absolute leader," said an analyst with Forrester Research. With major positions in search, video, and targeted display, "there isn't anything they don't have."[26]

In addition to consolidating market power, the deal gave Google control over the surveillance advertising platform that DoubleClick had been building for over ten years.[27] Google's overarching objective was to integrate the companies' operations to offer an expanded range of targeted advertising services to publishers and marketers alike. According to *BusinessWeek*, Google saw DoubleClick as a way to "lock the interactive [advertising] agencies and media buyers deeper into their clutches, and . . . offer an integrated network that [was] easy to buy, easy to measure, and easy to manage."[28] Although its AdSense program had already made Google a multisided platform, DoubleClick added a host of new relationships with marketers and publishers that were grounded in the collection and exchange of consumer data. "Our goal is to create a single and complete advertising system," said Sergey Brin and Larry Page in a letter to shareholders.[29] It was clear that Google's founders were developing a platform monopoly strategy and that surveillance advertising would play a key part.

Before the ink was dry on the DoubleClick purchase contract, Google's biggest competitors went on a shopping spree to avoid drowning in its wake. Within four months, Microsoft, AOL, Yahoo, and the advertising holding giant WPP each announced plans to acquire one or more internet advertising companies with core competencies in consumer monitoring and networked ad distribution. In its largest acquisition to date, Microsoft paid $6 billion for aQuantive, a large ad-services provider built in part with the remnants of DoubleClick's former rival, CMGI.[30]

This cluster of mergers marked an inflection point where the differences among internet advertising formats and their respective data practices began to fall away. Propelled by market forces, the formerly distinct practices of contextual search advertising and targeted display converged on consumer surveillance. Google's acquisition of DoubleClick was finalized on March 11, 2008.[31] One year later to the day, Google announced a new service called interest-based advertising that would, for the first time, allow advertisers to target consumers on the basis of user profiles populated with behavioral data. As Susan Wojcicki, vice president of product management, explained:

> To date, we have shown ads based mainly on what your interests are at a specific moment. So if you search for [digital camera] on Google, you'll get ads related to digital cameras. . . . We think we can make online advertising even more relevant and useful by using additional information about the

websites people visit. Today we are launching "interest-based" advertising as a beta test on our partner sites and on YouTube. These ads will associate categories of interest—say sports, gardening, cars, pets—with your browser, based on the types of sites you visit and the pages you view. We may then use those interest categories to show you more relevant text and display ads.[32]

The new service would power targeted display ads across Google's publisher networks, thereby reincarnating the surveillance advertising campaigns pioneered by DoubleClick back in the dot-com heyday. Importantly, the new "interest-based ads" would be enabled by default for everyone.

Google's pivot toward surveillance turned out to be a smashing success. In 2009, the company sold display advertising to ninety-four of *Advertising Age*'s top hundred advertisers and earned $6.5 billion in profits, up 50 percent from the year before.[33] As its founders explained to shareholders, Google had "really benefited from a successful integration with Double-Click."[34] Over the course of the next decade, Google systematically incorporated surveillance advertising into its operations, profiling billions of people worldwide using data harvested from its own services, as well as a network of millions of web publisher and mobile partners. Charlie Warzel and Ash Ngu of the *New York Times* highlighted this dramatic expansion of surveillance with a detailed account of how Google has modified its privacy policy over time.[35] Google's first privacy policy, created in 1999, sparsely explained that the company did not collect data on individuals. Twenty years and thirty versions later, it now takes four thousand words to outline the company's extensive data collection practices across its array of websites, applications, and partners.

An important moment came in 2012 when Google announced that it would begin tracking users universally across its many services in order to further refine its ad-targeting capabilities. Before this, Google's data collection was more of a patchwork operation wherein information was kept in silos that were not connected to composite profiles. Critical observers argued that the move toward universal profiles undermined the ad industry's long-standing claim that online surveillance was anonymous. From this point forward, personally identifiable information gathered from Gmail, Maps, and the ill-fated Google Plus social network would be combined with Google's extensive histories of search, web browsing, and YouTube viewing habits. Although the company allowed users to modify certain settings via a renovated privacy manager tool and promised to keep targeting data anonymized, there was no option to opt out of the broader centralization of data. As Gizmodo put it in a piece subtitled "The End of Don't Be Evil," "If you want to use Google services, you have to agree to these rules."[36]

Google's appropriation of surveillance advertising plots the historical trajectory of the entire online advertising sector, and indeed the commercial internet at large. After a brief stall in the wake of the dot-com stock market collapse, surveillance advertising and its progenitors were summarily integrated into the rising central power structure of internet advertising. By the end of the 2000s, the five largest U.S. internet advertising companies—Google, Facebook, Microsoft, AOL, and Yahoo—all served profile-based targeted advertising and collected consumer data across expansive networks that included their own properties and millions of other websites and applications. Each also offered ad exchanges, software-powered markets for buying and selling access to individual consumers in real time, a process dependent on persistent transfer of identification data among any number of buyers and sellers.

This configuration is the realization of the platform monopoly that DoubleClick and its ilk sought to build in the dot-com era. By fusing consumer monitoring and ad distribution, the first generation of ad platforms created a technical prototype and provisional organizational model for web advertising that placed surveillance at the core. As the *New York Times* described in 2001, the business model advanced by DoubleClick "fundamentally altered the nature of surfing the web from being a relatively anonymous activity, like wandering the streets of a large city, to the kind of environment where records of one's transactions, movements and even desires could be sorted, mined and sold."[37]

Once surveillance advertising gained a foothold, competitive pressures made it increasingly difficult for organizations to abstain. This is the discipline of the market in action. When Susan Wojcicki announced Google's first behavioral profiling initiative in 2009, she acknowledged that "this kind of tailored advertising does raise questions about user choice and privacy." Pressed on the question of whether users should be able opt into targeted behavioral ads rather than have them turned on by default, a Google spokesperson simply said that "offering advertising on an opt-in basis goes against the economic model of the internet."[38] Wojcicki went on to explain that that such practices were already widespread and that advertisers had been "asking us for a long time to offer interest-based advertising."[39] Privacy concerns were signaled as legitimate, but they were "questions the whole online ad industry has a responsibility to answer." Wojcicki seemed to suggest that, as powerful as it was, Google had little choice in the matter. Surveillance advertising was not a Google problem. It was an internet problem.

If Google, after building a wildly successful advertising business free of consumer monitoring, was compelled to embrace surveillance advertising, then how much choice did individual publishers or marketers have? As Stacy Lynn Schulman, an executive at the advertising giant Interpublic argued in 2007, adopting data-driven advertising was "less about competitive advantage and more about survival."[40] Conducting consumer surveillance was not optional for marketers and ad agencies, explained Shulman. It was "simply the price of entry." Surveillance advertising stems from the instrumental desires of marketers and ad platforms to grow their businesses. However, it is also deeply rooted in structural factors: the competitive pressures and growth imperatives of the global capitalist economy.

Today, organizations of all kinds face such immense pressure to participate in consumer monitoring that nearly all components of the internet function as terminals of surveillance for platform hubs, sweeping data in and out of the systems of a handful of surveillance advertising's big winners. Although it has not been the focus of this book, it is important to note, as Yasha Levine argues, that this centralization of commercial surveillance capacity abets the data collection efforts of the national security state.[41] In important ways, commercial and state surveillance are two sides of the same coin. One need look no further than the 2013 revelations of whistle-blower Edward Snowden, which, among many other things, documented the National Security Agency's close partnerships with surveillance advertising's biggest players to conduct illegal mass surveillance on the American public.[42]

From banners to search to video, surveillance has been embedded in the internet to a greater extent than any other communications medium in history. Virtually all websites and digital applications now serve as gateways to cascading layers of data collection. Numerous studies show that the web's most popular sites and services not only overwhelmingly monitor their users but also share that user data with third-party ad platforms by giving them direct access to collect user information.[43] In recent years, it has become difficult to draw the lines demarcating where internet surveillance stops and off-line data collection begins. Aggregating online and off-line data, widely considered a bridge too far when DoubleClick attempted it in the late 1990s, is now standard industry practice. Mobile devices transmit precise location data to any number of companies thousands of times per day.[44] Data brokers and ad platforms combine this information with names, addresses, web browsing histories, brick-and-mortar retail purchases, and much more for use in targeted advertising campaigns. Contextual spillover is the norm, as data gathered for marketing purposes are used in myriad other applications, factoring into determinations about things like health insurance premiums, loan interest rates, college admissions, and housing applications.[45] As John Cheney-Lippold argues, these data are systematically constructed into identities that stand in and speak for us, "whether we know about, like it, or not."[46]

Internet users are now faced with the very situation that government analysts warned about in 1994. As I described in chapter 1, policy planners at the dawn of the internet's commercialization understood that a market-based system for internet data collection would create powerful pressures for companies to indiscriminately surveil internet users. They cautioned that if the internet were to become dominated by a handful of big companies, consumers would have few options to escape commercial surveillance. Whether this future would come to pass or not was less a question about markets than it was about politics.

Back to Politics

The history of surveillance advertising is not a story of disruption but rather one of continuity. This history reveals just how long the modern surveillance advertising apparatus has been under construction and how deeply it is entrenched in the capitalist political economy. The world's dominant internet companies pivoted toward consumer surveillance not with new technological innovations but by incorporating and building on the sociotechnical systems created in the dot-com era. Among the many interlocking components of surveillance advertising's construction addressed in this book, public policy played a foundational role.

In an op-ed entitled "What If We All Just Sold Non-creepy Advertising?," Gabriel Weinberg argues that marketers and publishers could do just fine without consumer surveillance.[47] Weinberg is the CEO of Duck Duck Go, a search engine that has managed to build a business doing purely contextual advertising and collecting no consumer data. Although Duck Duck Go is proof that the discipline of the market is not totalizing, the company nevertheless exists at the margins of the advertising industry. Duck Duck Go is a tiny fraction of the size of Google, operating entirely in the tech giant's shadow. Weinberg understands the difficulty of swimming against the current of surveillance as well as anyone but remains an advocate for internet privacy. Arguing that "people have a fundamental right to avoid being put under surveillance," Weinberg sails past the standard list of industry talking points about how to address privacy concerns. He does not suggest enhanced transparency in data collection, greater market competition, more responsible executives, or industry self-regulation. Instead, Weinberg points immediately to politics, advocating for "strong privacy laws" to "force the digital advertising industry to return to . . . contextual advertising" without consumer surveillance.[48]

As I have argued in this book, the history of surveillance advertising provides strong support for Weinberg's political instinct. Public policy is among the only levers of power capable of tempering capitalist digital enclosure and the relentless drive to commodify information. It is, after all, the exact set of tools that private and public actors used to set up the legal foundations of surveillance advertising in the first place. When Google bought DoubleClick back in 2007, the merger had to be cleared by the Federal Trade Commission. After a yearlong investigation into potential competitive ramifications, the deal was permitted by a 4–1 vote. Although privacy advocates filed objections with the FTC, concerns about consumer surveillance were not formally factored into the deliberations. Explaining the exclusion, the FTC noted that privacy concerns were "not unique to Google and DoubleClick," but rather "extend to the entire online advertising marketplace."[49] In other words, the FTC argued that surveillance advertising was already so well established that it did not make much sense to question the institutional buildup of surveillance capacity that would result from the merger. Equally significant, the commissioners admitted that even if they had wanted to consider data collection and privacy issues as part of the merger review, they simply had little jurisdiction over such matters. Consumer surveillance on the internet is industry's domain. The private sector is in charge. This is the political legacy of the dot-com era.

The surveillance advertising industry remains acutely aware of the importance of public policy. Google and Facebook have built empires on the proposition that the founding political principle of the internet—private sector leadership—can endure any techlash with enough lobbying and public relations maneuvering. Testifying before Congress in 2018, Facebook's Mark Zuckerberg told lawmakers he was "not opposed to regulation," as long as it was the "right regulation."[50] As Weinberg notes, surveillance advertising executives "may individually make public state-ments welcoming federal regulation, but in practice they are doing every-thing they can to weaken existing laws and shape new ones in their own interests."[51]

It is crystal clear to anyone paying attention that industry self-regulation and the "notice and choice" privacy paradigm are utter fail-ures.[52] That these policies remain intact reveals the antidemocratic nature of policy making in the United States, a feature that is unfortunately hardly limited to the domain of internet governance.[53] When pressed, surveil-lance advertising platforms will continue to roll out transparency tweaks, privacy dashboards, and other changes that fiddle at the margins of their enterprises. They will curb some of the more egregious uses of their sys-tems, while their public relations teams applaud a job well done. What these companies will not do, however, is anything that might undermine their core business model of unaccountable surveillance—that is, unless democratic society gives them no choice.

The only solution to a problem of this magnitude is a political program that confronts the surveillance advertising business model head on. There is no easy path forward, but the United States might look to the European Union as one source of inspiration. Over the howls of the digital advertis-ing industry, the E.U.'s 2018 data protection directive introduces a set of limitations on the collection and use of consumer data. Heeding ample evidence, regulators in Brussels have decided that free markets are simply not up to the task of protecting privacy.[54] It is not a perfect solution, but it points to a future in which people have a say over the communications technologies that structure so much of their lives.

In the United States, we now know what twenty-five years of neoliberal internet governance looks like. We are living with the outcome of letting the private sector lead. It is past time for an alternative political vision for the internet, one that includes greater democratic accountability, more equitable distribution of power, and far less subservience to the demands of the market.

ACKNOWLEDGMENTS

WRITING THIS BOOK has been at once a great challenge and immense privilege. Few people are fortunate enough to have the chance to make a career out of researching, writing, and teaching. I am grateful to a long list of colleagues, collaborators, mentors, editors, students, friends, and family for their support. The size of this group reflects the kindness and generosity I have experienced in writing this book and navigating academic life more generally. It also hints at just how long I have been working on this project.

Brooke Duffy, Mara Einstein, Ed Lamoureux, Rick Maxwell, Roopali Mukherjee, Tony Nadler, Dan Schiller, Chris Wendelin, and Shinjoung Yeo provided helpful comments on chapter drafts and proposals. Patrick Davison and Lee McGuigan read nearly the entire document and gave invaluable feedback. I cannot thank you all enough.

I have been lucky to work in two stellar academic departments, first at Queens College, City University of New York, and now at Miami University. I am grateful to many excellent colleagues at both of these institutions and for the support of my department chairs and area coordinators: Ron Becker, Richard Campbell, Bruce Drushel, and Rick Maxwell. danah boyd, Joan Donovan, and Tim Hwang at Data & Society provided wonderful opportunities to workshop ideas, collaborate, and bring my research to broader audiences. The team at the University of Minnesota Press was a pleasure to work with, as were the archivists at the Clinton Presidential Library in Little Rock.

I am grateful for the friendship and collegiality of a long list of folks, many of whom I've known since graduate school. Big thanks to Robert Bodle, Josh Braun, Mike Brown, Jonathan Buchsbaum, Ergin Bulut, Rob Carley, Nicole Cohen, T. C. Corrigan, Brian Dolber, J. V. Fuqua, Tarleton

Gillespie, Katie Day Good, Mack Hagood, Jay Hamilton, Carey Hardin, Kerry Hegarty, Aaron Heresco, Amy Herzog, Brian Hughes, Kathleen Kuehn, Chenjerai Kumanyika, Michael Lacy, Hongmei Li, Steve Macek, Christe McKittrick, Robert Mejia, Caroline Nappo, Molly Niesen, Andrew Peck, Rosemary Pennington, Victor Pickard, Jeff Pooley, Andy Rice, Aimee Rickman, Michelle Rodino-Colocino, Adam Rottinghaus, Douglas Rushkoff, Joe Sampson, Ellen Scott, John Stanislawski, Darren Stevenson, John Sullivan, John Tchernev, Mandy Tröger, Noah Tsika, Jing Wang, and Jud Wellington.

I am fortunate to have an extended group of mentors who have always been generous with their time and whom I still bother on occasion. Thanks to Ed Lamoureux, Bob McChesney, Lisa Nakamura, John Nerone, Rob Prescott, Christian Sandvig, Amit Schejter, Dan Schiller, Inger Stole, Anghy Valdivia, and the late Kevin Barnhurst. I am especially grateful to Rick Maxwell, who has helped me in more ways than I count, though he still may not have forgiven me for leaving New York!

I began writing this book while I was at the Institute of Communications Research at the University of Illinois, Urbana–Champaign, a hub of critical scholarship and community. At Illinois, I received helpful fellowship support from the Illinois Program for Research in the Humanities and the Graduate College. I also benefited from the labor activism of the tenacious Graduate Employees Organization. At Queens College, I obtained essential course releases and research funding from the Faculty Fellowship Publication Program and the Professional Staff Congress labor union, whose tireless organizing makes CUNY a far better place for teachers and students. The later stages of research and writing were supported by the National Endowment for the Humanities, the Miami University Senate Committee on Faculty Research, and Miami University's College of Arts and Science. My sincere thanks to all of these organizations.

Finally, I thank my wonderful family, without whom I would be lost. Special thanks to my parents and brothers, who always know how to bring me back to earth. Most of all, I am grateful to Cor, Cam, and Caroline. You make this book, and everything else, worthwhile.

NOTES

Introduction

1. Jasmine Enberg, "Global Digital Ad Spending 2019," eMarketer, March 28, 2019, https://www.emarketer.com.
2. Robert Bodle, "A Critical Theory of Advertising as Surveillance," in *Explorations in Critical Studies of Advertising*, ed. James F. Hamilton, Robert Bodle, and Ezequiel Korin (New York: Routledge, 2016), 138–51.
3. Thomas Streeter, *Selling the Air: A Critique of the Policy of Commercial Broadcasting in the United States* (Chicago: University of Chicago Press, 1996), 6.
4. "Internet Firms Face a Global Techlash," *Economist*, August 10, 2017, https://www.economist.com; Ben Zimmer, "Techlash: Whipping Up Criticism of the Top Tech Companies," *Wall Street Journal*, January 10, 2019, https://wsj.com.
5. Aaron Smith, "Public Attitudes Toward Technology Companies," Pew Research Center, June 28. 2018, https://www.pewresearch.org.
6. Ryan Mac, "Literally Just a Big List of Facebook's 2018 Scandals," BuzzFeed News, December 20, 2018, https://www.buzzfeednews.com.
7. Issie Lapowsky, "Facebook Exposed 87 Million Users to Cambridge Analytica," *Wired*, April 4, 2018, https://www.wired.com.
8. Alex Stamos, "An Update on Information Operations on Facebook," Facebook Newsroom (blog), September 6, 2017, https://newsroom.fb.com/news/2017/09/information-operations-update/.
9. United States of America v. Internet Research Agency LLC, No. 18 U.S.C. §§ 2, 371, 1349, 1028A (n.d.).
10. Scott Shane, "LinkedIn Co-founder Apologizes for Deception in Alabama Senate Race," *New York Times*, December 26, 2018, https://www.nytimes.com.
11. Young Mie Kim et al., "The Stealth Media? Groups and Targets behind Divisive Issue Campaigns on Facebook," *Political Communication* 35, no. 4 (2018): 515–41, https://doi.org/10.1080/10584609.2018.1476425.

12. "Protesters and 'Russian Troll' Demonstrate as Mark Zuckerberg Testifies before Congress," *Hollywood Reporter,* April 10, 2018, https://www.hollywood reporter.com.

13. Jon Evans, "The Techlash," TechCrunch, June 7, 2018, http://techcrunch .com.

14. Zeynep Tufekci, "Facebook's Surveillance Machine," *New York Times,* March 19, 2018, https://www.nytimes.com; Chris Gilliard and David Golumbia, "There Are No Guardrails on Our Privacy Dystopia," *Vice,* March 9, 2018, https://www.vice.com.

15. Nathalie Maréchal, "Targeted Advertising Is Ruining the Internet and Breaking the World," *Vice,* November 16, 2018, https://www.vice.com.

16. Rana Foroohar, "Big Tech's Unhealthy Obsession with Hyper-targeted Ads," *Financial Times,* October 28, 2018, https://www.ft.com.

17. Bruce Sterling, "Tech-Lash Galore," *Wired,* April 30, 2018, https://www.wired .com.

18. McKenzie Funk, "Cambridge Analytica and the Secret Agenda of a Facebook Quiz," *New York Times,* November 19, 2016, https://www.nytimes.com.

19. Jon Swartz, "Facebook's Sandberg: 'There Will Always Be Bad Actors,'" *Barron's,* March 22, 2018, https://www.barrons.com.

20. Sam Biddle, "Cambridge Analytica Might Have to Return Ad Award—But Industry Still Embraces Company's Goals," Intercept, March 27, 2018, https:// theintercept.com.

21. Dipayan Ghosh and Ben Scott, "Russia's Election Interference Is Digital Marketing 101," *Atlantic,* February 19, 2018, https://www.theatlantic.com.

22. George Slefo, "Desktop and Mobile Ad Revenue Surpasses TV for the First Time," *Advertising Age,* April 26, 2017.

23. Peter Kafka, "2017 Was the Year Digital Ad Spending Finally Beat TV," Recode (Vox), December 4, 2017, https://www.vox.com.

24. Julia Angwin, *Dragnet Nation: A Quest for Privacy, Security, and Freedom in a World of Relentless Surveillance* (New York: Times Books, 2014), 3.

25. Timothy Libert, "Exposing the Invisible Web: An Analysis of Third-Party HTTP Requests on 1 Million Websites," *International Journal of Communication* 9 (2015): 18.

26. Elena Maris, Timothy Libert, and Jennifer Henrichsen, "Tracking Sex: The Implications of Widespread Sexual Data Leakage and Tracking on Porn Websites," ArXiv, July 15, 2019, http://arxiv.org/abs/1907.06520.

27. Wolfie Christl, "Corporate Surveillance in Everyday Life: How Companies Collect, Combine, Analyze, Trade, and Use Personal Data on Billions" (Vienna: Cracked Labs, 2017).

28. Bruce Schneier, "The Internet Is a Surveillance State," CNN, March 16, 2013, https://www.cnn.com.

29. Edward Baig, "How Facebook Can Have Your Data Even If You're Not on Facebook," *USA Today*, April 13, 2018, https://www.usatoday.com.

30. Michal Kosinski, David Stillwell, and Thore Graepel, "Private Traits and Attributes Are Predictable from Digital Records of Human Behavior," *Proceedings of the National Academy of Sciences of the United States of America* 110, no. 15 (2013): 5802–5, https://doi.org/10.1073/pnas.1218772110.

31. Youyou Wu, Michal Kosinski, and David Stillwell, "Computer-Based Personality Judgments Are More Accurate than Those Made by Humans," *Proceedings of the National Academy of Sciences of the United States of America* 112, no. 4 (2015): 1036–40, https://doi.org/10.1073/pnas.1418680112.

32. Abigail Wise, "Research Says Facebook Knows You Better than Your Mom," Real Simple, January 15, 2013, https://www.realsimple.com.

33. Shoshana Zuboff, *The Age of Surveillance Capitalism: The Fight for the Future at the New Frontier of Power* (London: Profile Books, 2018), 352.

34. Christopher Graves and Sandra Matz, "What Marketers Should Know About Personality-Based Marketing," *Harvard Business Review,* May 2, 2018, https://hbr.org; Maurits Kaptein et al., "Personalizing Persuasive Technologies," *International Journal of Human-Computer Studies* 77, no. C (2015): 38–51, https://doi.org/10.1016/j.ijhcs.2015.01.004.

35. S. C. Matz et al., "Psychological Targeting as an Effective Approach to Digital Mass Persuasion," *Proceedings of the National Academy of Sciences of the United States of America* 114, no. 48 (2017): 12714–19, https://doi.org/10.1073/pnas.1710966114.

36. Michael Reilly, "Is Facebook Targeting Advertising at Depressed Teens?," *MIT Technology Review,* May 1, 2017, https://www.technologyreview.com.

37. Cory Doctorow, "How to Destroy Surveillance Capitalism," OneZero, August 26, 2020, https://onezero.medium.com.

38. For a well-rounded critique of digital advertising's effectiveness, see Tim Hwang, *Subprime Attention Crisis: Advertising and the Time Bomb at the Heart of the Internet* (New York: FSG Originals, 2020).

39. Robert W. McChesney, *Digital Disconnect: How Capitalism Is Turning the Internet against Democracy* (New York: New Press, 2013), 59.

40. Steven Morris, "British Army Ads Targeting 'Stressed and Vulnerable' Teenagers," *Guardian,* June 8, 2018, https://www.theguardian.com.

41. Zeninjor Enwemeka, "Under Agreement, Firm Won't Target Digital Ads Around Mass. Health Clinics," WBUR, April 4, 2017, https://www.wbur.org.

42. Ava Kofman and Ariana Tobin, "Facebook Ads Can Still Discriminate Against Women and Older Workers, Despite a Civil Rights Settlement," ProPublica, December 13, 2019, https://www.propublica.org; Safiya Umoja Noble, *Algorithms of Oppression: How Search Engines Reinforce Racism* (New York: New York University Press, 2018); Mary Madden et al., "Privacy, Poverty, and Big

Data: A Matrix of Vulnerabilities for Poor Americans," *Washington University Law Review* 95, no. 1 (2017): 53–125.

43. Timothy Carr and Craig Aaron, "Beyond Fixing Facebook" (New York: Free Press, 2019), 10.

44. Olivia Solon and Sabrina Siddiqui, "Forget Wall Street—Silicon Valley Is the New Political Power in Washington," *Guardian*, September 3, 2017, https://www.theguardian.com.

45. Ben Brody, "Google, Facebook Set 2018 Lobbying Records as Tech Scrutiny Intensifies," *Bloomberg*, January 22, 2019, https://bloomberg.com.

46. Solon and Siddiqui, "Forget Wall Street."

47. Carr and Aaron, "Beyond Fixing Facebook," 10.

48. "Newspapers Fact Sheet," State of the News Media, Pew Research Center, July 9, 2019, https://www.journalism.org.

49. Penelope Muse Abernathy, *The Expanding News Desert* (Chapel Hill: Center for Innovation and Sustainability in Local Media, University of North Carolina at Chapel Hill, 2018), 8.

50. Victor Pickard, "The Big Picture: Misinformation Society," Public Books, November 28, 2017, https://www.publicbooks.org.

51. "Newspapers Fact Sheet."

52. Hillary Hoffower and Shayanne Gal, "We Did the Math to Calculate Exactly How Much Money Billionaires and Celebrities like Jeff Bezos and Kylie Jenner Make an Hour," *Business Insider*, October 14, 2018, htts://www.businessinsider.com.

53. Tim Berners-Lee and Mark Fischetti, *Weaving the Web: The Original Design and Ultimate Destiny of the World Wide Web by Its Inventor* (New York: HarperCollins, 1999), 84.

54. Ben Zimmer, "Techlash: Whipping Up Criticism of the Top Tech Companies," *Wall Street Journal*, January 10, 2019, https://www.wsj.com.

55. Amy B. Wang, "Former Facebook V.P. Says Social Media Is Destroying Society with 'Dopamine-Driven Feedback Loops,'" *Washington Post*, December 12, 2017, https://www.washingtonpost.com.

56. Roger McNamee, "A Brief History of How Your Privacy Was Stolen," *New York Times*, June 3, 2019, https://www.nytimes.com.

57. McNamee, "A Brief History of How Your Privacy Was Stolen."

58. Andrew Granato and Scy Yoon, "A Look at the PayPal Mafia's Continued Impact on Silicon Valley," VentureBeat, January 13, 2019, https://venturebeat.com.

59. Paul Starr, *The Creation of the Media: Political Origins of Modern Communications* (New York: Basic Books, 2004).

60. Tim Wu, *The Master Switch: The Rise and Fall of Information Empires* (New York: Vintage, 2010), 83.

61. Robert W. McChesney, *Telecommunications, Mass Media, and Democracy:*

The Battle for Control of U.S. Broadcasting, 1928–35 (Oxford: Oxford University Press, 1993); Susan J. Douglas, *Inventing American Broadcasting, 1899–1922* (Baltimore, Md.: Johns Hopkins University Press, 1987).

62. Victor Pickard, *America's Battle for Media Democracy. The Triumph of Corporate Libertarianism and the Future of Media Reform* (Cambridge: Cambridge University Press, 2014).

63. *A Framework for Global Electronic Commerce* (Washington, D.C.: White House, 1997), Background section.

64. Zuboff, *Age of Surveillance Capitalism.*

65. Zuboff, *Age of Surveillance Capitalism,* 17.

66. For a critique of Zuboff's concept of surveillance capitalism along these lines, see Evgeny Morozov, "Capitalism's New Clothes," Baffler, February 4, 2019, https://thebaffler.com. See also Jathan Sadowski, *Too Smart: How Digital Capitalism Is Extracting Data, Controlling Our Lives, and Taking Over the World* (Cambridge, Mass.: MIT Press, 2020), 50.

67. David Harvey, *The Enigma of Capital and the Crises of Capitalism* (Oxford: Oxford University Press, 2010).

68. Douglas Rushkoff, *Throwing Rocks at the Google Bus: How Growth Became the Enemy of Prosperity* (New York: Portfolio/Penguin, 2016), 133.

69. Neil Postman, *Building a Bridge to the 18th Century: Ideas from the Past that Can Improve Our Future* (New York: Knopf, 1999), 42.

70. Raymond Williams, *Television: Technology and Cultural Form* (London: Routledge, 2008), 12.

71. John Sinclair, "Advertising and Media in the Age of the Algorithm," *International Journal of Communication* 10 (2016): 3523.

72. James Rorty, *Our Master's Voice: Advertising* (New York: John Day, 1934).

73. Vincent Mosco, *The Political Economy of Communication* (London: Sage, 1996); Robert W. McChesney, *Communication Revolution: Critical Junctures and the Future of Media* (New York: New Press, 2007); Dwayne Winseck and Dal Yong Jin, *The Political Economies of Media* (London: Bloomsbury Academic, 2011).

74. Jonathan Hardy, *Critical Political Economy of the Media: An Introduction* (London: Routledge, 2013), 112.

75. Susan Strasser, *Satisfaction Guaranteed: The Making of the American Mass Market* (New York: Pantheon, 1989).

76. Daniel Pope, *The Making of Modern Advertising* (New York: Basic Books, 1983) Pope also argues that mass advertising was a strategy developed by manufacturers to gain mercantile advantage over wholesalers and retailers.

77. Paul A. Baran and Paul M. Sweezy, *Monopoly Capital: An Essay on the American Economic and Social Order* (New York: Monthly Review Press, 1966).

78. Thorstein Veblen, *Absentee Ownership and Business Enterprise in Recent Times: The Case of America* (New York: Huebsch, 1923), 309.

79. Joseph Turow, *Breaking Up America: Advertisers and the New Media World* (Chicago: University of Chicago Press, 1996), 23.

80. A rich literature of critical media history chronicles the contested processes whereby marketing imperatives came to govern the structure and content of successive media systems. See Gerald J. Baldasty, *The Commercialization of News in the Nineteenth Century* (Madison: University of Wisconsin Press, 1992); Erik Barnouw, *The Sponsor: Notes on a Modern Potentate* (New York: Transaction, 1978); Strasser, *Satisfaction Guaranteed.*

81. Hannah Holleman et al., "The Sales Effort and Monopoly Capital," *Monthly Review,* April 1, 2009, https://monthlyreview.org.

82. Herbert I. Schiller, *Mass Communications and American Empire* (Boulder, Colo.: Westview Press, 1992), 13.

83. Robert Brenner, *The Boom and the Bubble* (London: Verso, 2001), 4. See also Nick Srnicek, *Platform Capitalism* (Cambridge, Mass.: Polity, 2017); David Hesmondhalgh, *The Cultural Industries* (Los Angeles: Sage, 2013).

84. Dan Schiller, *How to Think about Information* (Urbana: University of Illinois Press, 2007).

85. Dan Schiller, *Digital Capitalism: Networking the Global Market System* (Cambridge, Mass.: MIT Press, 1999).

86. David Harvey, *A Brief History of Neoliberalism* (Oxford: Oxford University Press, 2005).

87. Lee McGuigan, "Automating the Audience Commodity: The Unacknowledged Ancestry of Programmatic Advertising," *New Media and Society* 21, no. 11–12 (2019): 2366–85, https://doi.org/10.1177/1461444819846449.

88. Joseph Turow, *The Daily You: How the New Advertising Industry Is Defining Your Identity and Your Worth* (New Haven, Conn.: Yale University Press, 2011).

89. Don Peppers and Martha Rogers, *The One to One Future: Building Relationships One Customer at a Time* (New York: Currency Doubleday, 1993); Oscar H. Gandy, *The Panoptic Sort: A Political Economy of Personal Information* (Boulder, Colo.: Westview Press, 1993).

90. Josh Lauer, *Creditworthy: A History of Consumer Surveillance and Financial Identity in America* (New York: Columbia University Press, 2017).

91. Turow, *Breaking Up America.*

92. Raju Narisetti, "New and Improved: Ad Experts Talk about How Their Business Will Be Transformed by Technology," *Wall Street Journal,* November 16, 1998, https://www.wsj.com/.

93. Matthew P. McAllister, *The Commercialization of American Culture: New Advertising, Control, and Democracy* (Thousand Oaks, Calif.: Sage, 1995).

94. Joseph Turow, *Niche Envy: Marketing Discrimination in the Digital Age* (Cambridge, Mass.: MIT Press, 2006).

95. Howard Kurtz, *The Fortune Tellers Inside Wall Street's Game of Money, Media, and Manipulation* (New York: The Free Press, 2000), 179.

96. Thomas Hughes, *Networks of Power: Electrification in Western Society, 1880–1930* (Baltimore, Md.: Johns Hopkins University Press, 1983).

97. Naomi Klein, *No Logo: No Space, No Choice, No Jobs* (New York: Picador, 2010), xvii.

98. Bob Garfield, *The Chaos Scenario* (Nashville, Tenn.: Stielstra, 2009), 243.

1. The Revolution Will Be Commercialized

1. *Technology for America's Economic Growth: A New Direction to Build Economic Strength* (Washington, D.C.: White House, 1993).

2. *The National Information Infrastructure: Agenda for Action* (Washington, D.C.: Information Infrastructure Task Force, Department of Commerce, 1993), 7.

3. Judith Beth Prowda, "Privacy and Security of Data," *Fordham Law Review* 64, no. 3 (1995): 747.

4. *Privacy and the National Information Infrastructure: Principles for Providing and Using Personal Information* (Washington, D.C.: Privacy Working Group, Information Policy Committee, Information Infrastructure Task Force, 1995), 1–2.

5. *Privacy and the National Information Infrastructure*, 1–2.

6. *Privacy and the NII: Safeguarding Telecommunications-Related Personal Information* (Washington, D.C.: National Telecommunications and Information Administration, Department of Commerce, 1995).

7. *Privacy and the NII*, 7–8.

8. Edward Lee Lamoureux, *Privacy, Surveillance, and the New Media You* (New York: Peter Lang, 2016).

9. *Privacy and the NII*, 14.

10. *Privacy and the NII*, 14.

11. For a critique of the notice and choice approach to consumer privacy, see Matthew Crain, "The Limits of Transparency: Data Brokers and Commodification," *New Media and Society* 20, no. 1 (2018): 88–104, https://doi.org/10.1177/1461444816657096.

12. David Medine, "Public Workshop on Consumer Information Privacy, Session Two: Consumer Online Privacy" (Washington, D.C.: Federal Trade Commission, 1997); Christine Varney, "Online Privacy Protection Act of 1999," Pub. L. No. 106-1044, § Senate Committee on Commerce, Science, and Transportation (1999).

13. *Technology for America's Economic Growth*, 7.

14. John Markoff, "Building the Electronic Superhighway," *New York Times,* January 24, 1993, https://www.nytimes.com.

15. Markoff, "Building the Electronic Superhighway."

16. Brandon Keim, "June 29, 1956: Ike Signs Interstate Highway Act," *Wired*, June 29, 2010, https://www.wired.com.

17. *Framework for Global Electronic Commerce* (Washington, D.C.: White House, 1997), https://clintonwhitehouse4.archives.gov/WH/New/Commerce/index.html.

18. Raymond Williams, *Marxism and Literature* (Oxford: Oxford University Press, 1977), 85–86.

19. Robert Horowitz, *The Irony of Regulatory Reform: The Deregulation of American Telecommunications* (Oxford: Oxford University Press, 1988).

20. Holt, *Empires of Entertainment: Media Industries and the Politics of Deregulation, 1980–1996* (New Brunswick, N.J.: Rutgers University Press, 2011), 10.

21. Wendy Brown, *Undoing the Demos: Neoliberalism's Stealth Revolution* (Cambridge, Mass.: MIT Press, 2015); Harvey, *Brief History of Neoliberalism.*

22. The nickname references the consumer technology company Atari, a pioneer of video game consoles and personal computers that grew rapidly in the 1970s only to fail spectacularly in the early 1980s.

23. Thomas B. Edsall, "'Atari Democrats' Join Party Conflicts Revived by Gains," *Washington Post*, November 7, 1982, https://www.washingtonpost.com.

24. Christopher Wright, "The National Cooperative Research Act of 1984: A New Antitrust Regime for Joint Research and Development Ventures," *Berkeley Technology Law Journal* 1, no. 1 (1986): 133, https://doi.org/10.15779/Z38KQ18.

25. Earl Foell, "A Modern Marshall Plan to Help U.S. in R&D Battle," *Christian Science Monitor*, October 3, 1983, https://www.csmonitor.com.

26. Jerrold E. Schneider, *Campaign Finance Reform and the Future of the Democratic Party* (New York: Routledge, 2002), 2–3.

27. Leslie David Simon, *NetPolicy.com: Public Agenda for a Digital World* (Washington, D.C.: Woodrow Wilson Center Press, 2000), 369.

28. Paul M. Hallacher, *Why Policy Issue Networks Matter: The Advanced Technology Program and the Manufacturing Extension Partnership* (Lanham, Md.: Rowman & Littlefield, 2005).

29. Lily Geismer, "Atari Democrats," Jacobin, February 8, 2016, https://www.jacobinmag.com. See also Lily Geismer, *Don't Blame Us: Suburban Liberals and the Transformation of the Democratic Party* (Princeton, N.J.: Princeton University Press, 2014).

30. Jeff Faux, "Industrial Policy: Will Clinton Find the High Wage Path?," in *Toward a Global Civil Society*, ed. Michael Walzer (Providence, R.I.: Berghahn, 1994), 159–73.

31. Leslie Wayne, "Designing a New Economics for the 'Atari Democrats,'" *New York Times*, September 26, 1982, https://www.nytimes.com.

32. Al From, *New Democrats and the Return to Power* (New York: Palgrave Macmillan, 2013).

33. Jacob S. Hacker and Paul Pierson, *Winner-Take-All Politics: How Washington Made the Rich Richer and Turned Its Back on the Middle Class* (New York: Simon & Schuster, 2010), 181.

34. Matthew Stoller, "Why the Democratic Party Acts The Way It Does," Naked Capitalism (blog), November 9, 2014, https://www.nakedcapitalism.com.

35. Stoller, "Why the Democratic Party Acts The Way It Does."

36. Jon F. Hale, "The Making of the New Democrats," *Political Science Quarterly* 110, no. 2 (1995): 218–24, https://doi.org/10.2307/2152360. See also Ryan Grim, *We've Got People: From Jesse Jackson to Alexandria Ocasio-Cortez, the End of Big Money and the Rise of a Movement* (Washington, D.C.: Strong Arm Press, 2019).

37. Joseph Stiglitz, *The Roaring Nineties: Seeds of Destruction* (London: Allen Lane, 2003), 26.

38. From, *New Democrats and the Return to Power.*

39. William Clinton, "Address Accepting the Presidential Nomination at the Democratic National Convention in New York," July 16, 1992, https://www.presidency.ucsb.edu/documents/address-accepting-the-presidential-nomination-the-democratic-national-convention-new-york.

40. *Technology for America's Economic Growth*, 3.

41. Janet Abbate, *Inventing the Internet* (Cambridge, Mass.: MIT Press, 1999); Shane Greenstein, *How the Internet Became Commercial: Innovation, Privatization, and the Birth of a New Network* (Princeton, N.J.: Princeton University Press, 2015).

42. Greenstein, *How the Internet Became Commercial*, 13. For more on the public roots of the internet, see Janet Abbate, "Government, Business, and the Making of the Internet," *Business History Review* 75, no. 1 (2001): 147–76, https://doi.org/10.2307/3116559.

43. Daniel Burstein and David Kline, *Road Warriors: Dreams and Nightmares along the Information Highway* (New York: Dutton, 1995), 338.

44. Matt Bai, "The Clinton Referendum," *New York Times*, December 23, 2007, sec. Magazine, https://www.nytimes.com.

45. *Technology for America's Economic Growth*, 21.

46. *Technology for America's Economic Growth*, 1.

47. *National Information Infrastructure: Agenda for Action*, 5.

48. *National Information Infrastructure: Agenda for Action*, 5–8.

49. Horowitz, *Irony of Regulatory Reform*, 4–7.

50. Robert W. McChesney, *Digital Disconnect: How Capitalism Is Turning the Internet against Democracy* (New York: The New Press, 2013), 107.

51. Hesmondhalgh, *Cultural Industries*, 127; Vincent Mosco, *Pushbutton*

Fantasies: Critical Perspectives on Videotext and Information Technology (Norwood, N.J.: Ablex, 1982), 45.

52. *Framework for Global Electronic Commerce,* n.p.
53. Stiglitz, *Roaring Nineties,* xviii.
54. Stiglitz, *Roaring Nineties,* 17.
55. Stiglitz, *Roaring Nineties,* 90.
56. Rick Perlstein, "From and Friends," *Nation,* February 11, 2014, https://www .thenation.com.
57. Gwen Ifill, "The 1992 Campaign; Clinton's Standard Campaign Speech: A Call for Responsibility," *New York Times,* April 26, 1992, https://www.nytimes .com.
58. Justin Fox, "The Mostly Forgotten Tax Increases of 1982–1993," Bloomberg. com, December 15, 2017, https://www.bloomberg.com.
59. Michelle Alexander, *The New Jim Crow* (New York: New Press, 2012).
60. Peter Baker, "Bill Clinton Concedes His Crime Law Jailed Too Many for Too Long," *New York Times,* July 15, 2015, https://www.nytimes.com.
61. Baker, "Bill Clinton Concedes."
62. Jean-Christophe Plantin et al., "Infrastructure Studies Meet Platform Studies in the Age of Google and Facebook," *New Media and Society* 20, no. 1 (2018): 293–310, https://doi.org/10.1177/1461444816661553.
63. Stiglitz, *Roaring Nineties,* 91.
64. Quoted in Stiglitz, *Roaring Nineties,* 91.
65. Simon, *NetPolicy.com,* 370.
66. Stiglitz, *Roaring Nineties,* 90–91.
67. Jill Lepore, "The Hacking of America," *New York Times,* September 14, 2018, https://www.nytimes.com.
68. "Communications/Electronics: Money to Congress," Open Secrets, n.d., https://www.opensecrets.org.
69. "History of the Office of the Vice President and Clinton Administration History Project, 'OVP—Gore Tech/Tech Outreach [1],'" August 20, 1996, Box 59, Clinton Digital Library, https://clinton.presidentiallibraries.us/items/show/ 5066.
70. "History of the Office of the Vice President and Clinton Administration History Project, 'OVP—Gore Tech/Tech Outreach [1],'" January 16, 1997, Box 59, Clinton Digital Library, https://clinton.presidentiallibraries.us/items/ show/5066.
71. Simon, *NetPolicy.com,* 371.
72. Simon, *NetPolicy.com,* 373.
73. Simon, *NetPolicy.com,* 371.
74. Michael Kinsley, "Let Them Eat Laptops," *New Yorker,* January 16, 1995, https://www.newyorker.com.
75. Lepore, "Hacking of America."

76. Hesmondhalgh, *Cultural Industries,* 125.
77. Markoff, "Building the Electronic Superhighway."
78. "Clinton Economic Conference" (Little Rock, Ark.: C-SPAN, December 14, 1992), https://www.c-span.org/video/?36064-1/clinton-economic-conference.
79. David Bank, "Shaping the Info Highway," *San Jose Mercury News,* April 4, 1994.
80. Lee Gomes, "Superhighway Has Social Curves," *San Jose Mercury News,* January 12, 1994; Simon, *NetPolicy.com,* 171.
81. For a discussion of the methodology of reading the trade press see Thomas F. Corrigan, "Making Implicit Methods Explicit: Trade Press Analysis in the Political Economy of Communication," *International Journal of Communication* 12 (2018): 2751–72.
82. Gary Levin, "Interactive Makes a Splash," *Advertising Age,* April 5, 1993.
83. Mosco, *Pushbutton Fantasies.*
84. Scott Donaton, "Prodigy Cuts In-House Ad Sales Team," *Advertising Age,* May 9, 1994.
85. Marcy Magiera, "Map to Superhighway Beset by Uncertainty," *Advertising Age,* January 17, 1994.
86. "The Revolution Is Now," *Advertising Age,* May 31, 1993.
87. Debra Aho Williamson, "Building a New Industry. There Is a Business, but Defining It Is Like Lassoing Jell-O," *Advertising Age,* March 13, 1995.
88. Christopher Anderson, "Net Profits," *Economist,* July 1, 1995.
89. Turow, *Niche Envy,* 22.
90. Turow, *Daily You,* 38.
91. Scott Donaton, "Agencies Being Left Behind by Technology," *Advertising Age,* April 26, 1993.
92. Donaton, "Agencies Being Left Behind."
93. John Motavalli, *Bamboozled at the Revolution: How Big Media Lost Billions in the Battle for the Internet* (New York: Viking, 2002), 9.
94. Magiera, "Map to Superhighway Beset by Uncertainty."
95. Motavalli, *Bamboozled at the Revolution,* 19.
96. "Revolution Is Now."
97. Schiller, *Digital Capitalism.*
98. Edwin L. Artzt, "P&G's Artzt: TV Advertising in Danger," *Advertising Age,* May 23, 1994.
99. Jay Matthews, "Are the Ads Infinitum? Madison Avenue Fears the Day May Come When Television Won't Carry Commercials," *Washington Post,* July 31, 1994, https://www.washingtonpost.com.
100. Artzt, "P&G's Artzt." On the subject of radio, it is worth noting that Lee de Forest, one of the principal inventors of broadcasting technology, called commercials "stains" rather than "spots," and he rejected the idea that advertising was a necessary component of media. De Forest even worked toward

developing a mechanism for consumer radios that could automatically mute the volume during advertising messages and raise it again once programming returned. See Vincent Mosco, *The Pay-Per Society: Computers and Communication in the Information Age* (Toronto: Garamond, 1989), 32; McChesney, *Digital Disconnect*, 146.

101. McAllister, *Commercialization of American Culture*.
102. McAllister, *Commercialization of American Culture*, 225–26.
103. Artzt, "P&G's Artzt."
104. Scott Donaton and Jennifer Lawrence, "New-Media Summit Called," *Advertising Age*, September 26, 1994.
105. Steven W. Colford, "Mr. Herbold Goes to Washington," *Advertising Age*, July 18, 1994.
106. Colford, "Mr. Herbold Goes to Washington."
107. "Inquiry on Universal Service and Open Access Issues; Notice Department of Commerce," *Federal Register* 59, no. 80 (1994), https://www.gpo.gov/fdsys/pkg/FR-1994-09-19/html/94-23033.htm.
108. Colford, "Mr. Herbold Goes to Washington."

2. A Framework for Global Electronic Commerce

1. Hesmondhalgh, *Cultural Industries*, 40, 99.
2. William Clinton, "Remarks Announcing the Electronic Commerce Initiative," *Weekly Compilation of Presidential Documents* 33, no. 27 (1997): 1003–7.
3. Schmidt later went on to become CEO of Google.
4. Eric Schmidt, "Letter to Ira Magaziner on Behalf of Novell," July 3, 1997, Box 1, Folder 6, Domestic Policy Council, Ira Magaziner Electronic Commerce Series, William J. Clinton Presidential Library, Little Rock, Ark.
5. Ken Wasch, "Re: Software Industry Comments on Proposed Administration Strategy (Letter to Ira Magaziner on Behalf of Software Publishers Association)," January 31, 1997, Domestic Policy Council, Ira Magaziner Electronic Commerce Series, William J. Clinton Presidential Library.
6. Joseph Dionne, "Letter to Ira Magaziner on Behalf of McGraw-Hill," January 23, 1997, Box 11, Folder 1, Domestic Policy Council, Ira Magaziner Electronic Commerce Series, William J. Clinton Presidential Library.
7. Marilyn Cade, "Letter to Ira Magaziner on Behalf of AT&T," January 31, 1997, Box 10, Folder 3, Domestic Policy Council, Ira Magaziner Electronic Commerce Series, William J. Clinton Presidential Library; Christopher Caine, "Letter to Ira Magaziner on Behalf of IBM," January 30, 1997, Box 10, Folder 3, Domestic Policy Council, Ira Magaziner Electronic Commerce Series, William J. Clinton Presidential Library.
8. Stiglitz, *Roaring Nineties*, 106.

9. *Framework for Global Electronic Commerce* (Washington, D.C.: White House, 1997), https://clintonwhitehouse4.archives.gov/WH/New/Commerce/index.html.

10. Carla Michelotti, "Re: Information Infrastructure Task Force Framework for Global Electronic Commerce (Letter to Ira Magaziner on Behalf of Leo Burnett)," January 24, 1997, 2, Box 11, Folder 1, Domestic Policy Council, Ira Magaziner Electronic Commerce Series, William J. Clinton Presidential Library.

11. Dallas Smythe, *Dependency Road: Communications, Capitalism, Consciousness, and Canada* (Norwood, N.J.: Ablex, 1981), 37.

12. *Framework for Global Electronic Commerce,* n.p.

13. Michelotti, "Re: Information Infrastructure Task Force Framework for Global Electronic Commerce (Letter to Ira Magaziner on Behalf of Leo Burnett)," January 24, 1997, 7.

14. "Comments on the Principles and Positions Set Forth in 'A Framework for Global Electronic Commerce' (Letter to Ira Magaziner on Behalf of The Direct Marketing Association)," January 31, 1997, 6, Box 10, Folder 2, Domestic Policy Council, Ira Magaziner Electronic Commerce Series, William J. Clinton Presidential Library.

15. "Letter to Ira Magaziner on Behalf of the Cato Institute," January 23, 1997, Box 27, Folder 5, Domestic Policy Council, Ira Magaziner Electronic Commerce Series, William J. Clinton Presidential Library.

16. *Framework for Global Electronic Commerce,* n.p.

17. Charles Piller, "Net Regulation: How Much Is Enough?," *PC World,* May 1997, https://www.pcworld.com.

18. Piller, "Net Regulation."

19. "Letter to Ira Magaziner on Behalf of Information Technology Industry Council," January 31, 1997, Box 10, Folder 4, Domestic Policy Council, Ira Magaziner Electronic Commerce Series, William J. Clinton Presidential Library.

20. William Burrington and Jill Lesser, "Letter to Ira Magaziner on Behalf of America Online," January 31, 1997, Box 10, Folder 4, Domestic Policy Council, Ira Magaziner Electronic Commerce Series, William J. Clinton Presidential Library.

21. Cade, "Letter to Ira Magaziner on Behalf of AT&T," January 31, 1997; K. McGee, "Re: Interagency Task Force Paper on Global Electronic Commerce (Letter to Ira Magaziner on Behalf of Oracle)," January 31, 1997, Box 10, Folder 3, Domestic Policy Council, Ira Magaziner Electronic Commerce Series, William J. Clinton Presidential Library.

22. Daniel J. Weitzner, "Letter to Jonathan Greenblatt on Behalf of Center for Democracy and Technology," December 4, 1996, Box 10, Folder 6, Domestic Policy Council, Ira Magaziner Electronic Commerce Series, William J. Clinton Presidential Library.

23. Jeff Chester, "Letter to Ira Magaziner on Behalf of Center for Media Education," January 9, 1997, Box 10, Folder 6, Domestic Policy Council, Ira Magaziner Electronic Commerce Series, William J. Clinton Presidential Library.

24. Bill Poulos, "EDS Applauds E-Com White Paper (Letter to Ira Magaziner on Behalf of Electronic Data Systems)," May 20, 1997, Domestic Policy Council, Ira Magaziner Electronic Commerce Series, William J. Clinton Presidential Library.

25. Poulos, "EDS Applauds E-Com White Paper."

26. Ellen Messmer, "White House Backs Global Internet Free Trade in Electronic Commerce Report Event," *Network World*, July 7, 1997.

27. "Electronic Commerce Report Takes Information Superhighway from 55 mph to Autobahn," *PR Newswire*, June 30, 1997.

28. Patricia Aufderheide, *Communications Policy and the Public Interest* (New York: Guilford, 1999); Holt, *Empires of Entertainment*; Robert W. McChesney, *Rich Media, Poor Democracy: Communication Politics in Dubious Times* (Urbana: University of Illinois Press, 1999).

29. McChesney, *Digital Disconnect*, 91.

30. Aufderheide, *Communications Policy*, 5.

31. Ann G. Cutter and Len A. Costa, "The Framework for Global Electronic Commerce: A Policy Perspective," *Journal of International Affairs* 51, no. 2 (1998): 527.

32. Cutter and Costa, "Framework for Global Electronic Commerce," 536.

33. Cutter and Costa, "Framework for Global Electronic Commerce," 536.

34. Matthew Petrillo, "Administration Moving to Coordinate Electronic Commerce, Internet Policies," *Telecommunication Reports* 63, no. 5 (1997): 9–10; "Whitehouse Seeks Input on Electronic Commerce Policy," *Phillips Business Information's Internet Week*, December 23, 1996.

35. NTIA held public hearings in 1995, but they were limited to telecommunications access issues.

36. Mara Liasson, "Conservative Advocate," Morning Edition, NPR, May 25, 2001, http://www.npr.org.

37. *Framework for Global Electronic Commerce*, n.p.

38. Hesmondhalgh, *Cultural Industries*, 127.

39. Herbert I. Schiller, "Computer Systems: Power for Whom and for What?," *Journal of Communication* 28, no. 4 (1978): 184–93.

40. Cutter and Costa, "Framework for Global Electronic Commerce," 527.

41. Molly Niesen, "Crisis of Consumerism: Advertising, Activism, and the Battle over the U.S. Federal Trade Commission, 1969–1980" (PhD diss., University of Illinois, Urbana–Champaign, 2013).

42. Tarleton Gillespie, *Wired Shut: Copyright and the Shape of Digital Culture* (Cambridge, Mass.: MIT Press, 2007).

43. Burrington and Lesser, "Letter to Ira Magaziner on Behalf of America Online," January 31, 1997.

44. Mosco, *Pushbutton Fantasies,* 23.

45. Mosco, *Pushbutton Fantasies,* 23.

46. Mosco, *Pushbutton Fantasies,* 38.

47. Brenner, *The Boom and the Bubble.*

48. Dan Schiller, *Digital Depression: Information Technology and Economic Crisis* (Urbana: University of Illinois Press, 2014).

49. Edsall, "'Atari Democrats' Join Party Conflicts Revived by Gains."

50. Harvey, *Brief History of Neoliberalism.*

51. Gabriel Zucman, "Global Wealth Inequality," *Annual Review of Economics* 11 (2019): 120–21.

52. Lawrence Mishel and Jori Kandra, "CEO Compensation Surged 14% in 2019 to $21.3 million," Economic Policy Institute, August 18, 2020, https://www.epi.org/publication/ceo-compensation-surged-14-in-2019-to-21-3-million-ceos-now-earn-320-times-as-much-as-a-typical-worker/.

53. Drew Desilver, "For Most Americans, Real Wages Have Barely Budged for Decades," Pew Research Center (blog), August 7, 2018, https://www.pewresearch.org.

54. Elise Gould, *State of Working America Wages 2018: Wage Inequality Marches On—And Is Even Threatening Data Reliability* (Washington, D.C.: Economic Policy Institute, 2019).

55. McChesney, *Digital Disconnect,* 29–57.

56. Hesmondhalgh, *Cultural Industries,* 124–25.

57. David A. Carter, Betty J. Simkins, and W. Gary Simpson, "Corporate Governance, Board Diversity, and Firm Value," *Financial Review* 38 (2003): 33–53, https://doi.org/10.1111/1540-6288.00034.

58. Charles B. Shrader, Virginia B. Blackburn, and Paul Iles, "Women in Management and Firm Financial Performance: An Exploratory Study," *Journal of Managerial Issues* 9, no. 3 (1997): 358.

59. Victor Pickard, *America's Battle for Media Democracy: The Triumph of Corporate Libertarianism and the Future of Media Reform* (Cambridge: Cambridge University Press, 2014), 218.

60. Marc Rotenberg, "Privacy and the Second Term (Letter to Ira Magaziner on Behalf of Electronic Privacy Information Center)," November 1, 1996, 2, Box 1, Folder 5, Domestic Policy Council, Ira Magaziner Electronic Commerce Series, William J. Clinton Presidential Library.

61. Sally Katzen and Tom Kalil, "Memorandum for NEC/DPC Deputies Re: Privacy in the Information Age," April 7, 1998, 5, Box 22, Folder 3, Domestic Policy Council, Ira Magaziner Electronic Commerce Series, William J. Clinton Presidential Library.

62. Katzen and Kalil, "Memorandum for NEC/DPC Deputies," 6.

63. Bruce McConnell and Becky Burr, "Memorandum for Privacy Contacts, Privacy Functions for Your Consideration," April 7, 1998, 3, Box 22, Folder 3, Domestic Policy Council, Ira Magaziner Electronic Commerce Series, William J. Clinton Presidential Library.

64. McConnell and Burr, "Memorandum for Privacy Contacts," 4.

65. Des Freedman, *The Contradictions of Media Power* (London: Bloomsbury Academic, 2014), 62.

66. Freedman, *Contradictions of Media Power,* 64.

67. Freedman, *Contradictions of Media Power,* 74.

3. The Web Gets a Memory

1. Debra Aho Williamson, "Turning On the PC Turns Off Pay TV," *Advertising Age,* September 19, 1994; Motavalli, *Bamboozled at the Revolution,* 9–33.

2. For a history of the World Wide Web, see William Aspray and Paul E. Ceruzzi, eds., *The Internet and American Business* (Cambridge, Mass.: MIT Press, 2008); and Niels Brügger and Ian Milligan, *The Sage Handbook of Web History* (Los Angeles: Sage, 2019).

3. John Cassidy, *Dot.con: The Greatest Story Ever Sold* (London: Allen Lane, 2001), 77.

4. Michelle Rafter Reuter, "Internet Advertising Is Hippest '90s Trend," *Financial Post,* December 22, 1995.

5. Reuter, "Internet Advertising Is Hippest '90s Trend."

6. Marc Andreessen, "Netscape: Portal to the Web," in *Architects of the Web: 1,000 Days that Built the Future of Business,* ed. Robert Reid (New York: Wiley, 1997), 5.

7. Debra Aho Williamson, "Privacy Is a Very Public Issue," *Advertising Age,* October 17, 1994.

8. Garett Sloane, "Love It or Hate It, the Banner Ad Turns 25," *Advertising Age,* October 27, 2019.

9. Lawrence Aragon, "The Real Thing?," *PC Week,* December 16, 1995.

10. Magiera, "Map to Superhighway Beset by Uncertainty."

11. Reuter, "Internet Advertising Is Hippest '90s Trend."

12. Cathy Taylor, "The Repping of the Web," *MediaWeek,* February 26, 1996.

13. Turow, *Daily You,* 36.

14. Richard Karpinski, "Ad Sales Go Real-Time," *InternetWeek,* December 1, 1997.

15. David Shen, *Takeover! The Inside Story of the Yahoo! Ad Revolution* (Palo Alto, Calif.: VTDS, 2017), 39.

16. Taylor, "Repping of the Web."

17. Sally Goll Beatty, "Poppe Tyson Leads the Charge of Agencies Signing on the Internet," *Wall Street Journal,* February 2, 1996.

18. Kim Cleland, "Poppe Creates Web Net," *Advertising Age,* October 30, 1995.

19. Kim Cleland, "Rep Firms Stake out Web Territory," *Advertising Age*, February 19, 1996.
20. Debra Aho Williamson, "CBS to Outsource Web Ad Sales," *Advertising Age*, January 29, 1996.
21. Taylor, "Repping of the Web."
22. Richard M. Ohmann, *Selling Culture: Magazines, Markets, and Class at the Turn of the Century* (New York: Verso, 1996).
23. "80% of the Advertising in the U.S. Is . . . through . . . J. Walter Thompson," 1889, J0101, John W. Hartman Center for Sales, Advertising, and Marketing History, Emergence of Advertising in America: 1850–1920, Duke University David M. Rubenstein Rare Book and Manuscript Library, Durham, N.C., https://idn.duke.edu/ark:/87924/r4tq5t42b.
24. Ohmann, *Selling Culture*, 94–95.
25. Daniel Pope, *The Making of Modern Advertising* (New York: Basic Books, 1983).
26. Kevin O'Connor, *The Map of Innovation: Creating Something out of Nothing* (New York: Crown Business, 2003), 190.
27. Patricia Riedman, "Digital Media Masters," *Advertising Age*, September 23, 1996.
28. Ethan Zuckerman, "The Internet's Original. Sin," *Atlantic*, August 14, 2014, https://www.theatlantic.com.
29. Zuckerman, "Internet's Original Sin."
30. Randall Rothenberg, "An Advertising Power, but Just What Does DoubleClick Do?," *New York Times*, September 22, 1999, https://www.nytimes.com.
31. Karpinski, "Ad Sales Go Real-Time."
32. Kim Cleland, "New Tools Make It Easier to Buy Web Ads," *Advertising Age*, May 20, 1996.
33. Taylor, "Repping of the Web."
34. Jeffrey M. O'Brien, "Feeling like a Number?," *MC: Marketing Computers*, April 1996.
35. "DoubleClick Short Term Buy," *Standard & Poor's Emerging and Special Situation*, January 15, 1998.
36. Charles Waltner, "Going Beyond the Banner with Web Ads," *Advertising Age*, March 4, 1996; Debra Aho Williamson, "Breaking Free from Boring Banners," *Advertising Age*, April 1, 1996. See also Ramon Lobato and Julian Thomas, "Formats and Formalization in Internet Advertising," in *Format Matters: Standards, Practices, and Politics in Media Cultures*, ed. Marek Jancovic, Axel Volmar, and Alexandra Schneider (Lüneburg, Germany: Meson, 2020), 65–79.
37. Turow, *Niche Envy*.
38. David M. Kristol, "HTTP Cookies: Standards, Privacy, and Politics," *Communications of the ACM* 1, no. 2 (2001): 155–56, https://doi.org/10.1145/502152.502153.

39. Thomas Weber, "The Man Who Baked the First Web Cookies Chews Over Their Fate," *Wall Street Journal*, February 28, 2000.

40. Weber, "Man Who Baked the First Web Cookies."

41. Rajiv C. Shah and Jay P. Kesan, "Recipes for Cookies: How Institutions Shape Communication Technologies," *New Media and Society* 11, no. 3 (2009): 324, https://doi.org/10.1177/1461444808101614.

42. Mark Gibbs, "Cookies: Feeding Session Information from Web Servers to Clients, and Back," *Network World*, January 20, 1997.

43. Ariel Poler, "Advertising on the Web," in *Architects of the Web: 1,000 Days that Built the Future of Business*, ed. Robert Reid (New York: Wiley, 1997), 217.

44. Turow, *Daily You*, 47.

45. "Internet Advertising Bureau Backs Cookies," press release, Internet Advertising Bureau, June 9, 1997, http://www.iab.net/about_the_iab/recent_press_releases/press_release_archive/press_release/4234.

46. Technically, this created a link between DoubleClick's ad servers and users' Web browsers. The advertising industry goes to great lengths to use this fact to claim that surveillance is anonymous. Numerous studies have shown that it is trivial to deanonymize many kinds of so-called anonymous advertising data sets. See Arvind Narayanan and Vitaly Shmatikov, "Myths and Fallacies of 'Personally Identifiable Information,'" *Communications of the ACM* 53, no. 6 (2010): 24–26, https://doi.org/10.1145/1743546.1743558.

47. *FTC Staff Report: Self Regulatory Principles for Online Behavioral Advertising* (Washington, D.C.: Federal Trade Commission, February 2009).

48. Zina Moukheiber, "DoubleClick Is Watching You," *Forbes*, November 4, 1996.

49. Kristi Coale, "DoubleClick Tries to Force Hand into Cookie Jar," *Wired*, March 17, 1997, https://www.wired.com.

50. "America Online 1996 Annual Report," 10-K (America Online, 1996).

51. "The Burger King of Internet Advertising," *Interactive PR*, August 12, 1996.

52. Judith Messina, "New Media's Hot Play: DoubleClick Infusion Largest Ever in City," *Crain's New York Business*, June 16, 1997.

53. "Ads Find Strength in Numbers," CNET, November 4, 1996, http://news.cnet.com.

54. Kate Maddox, "Internet Ad Sales Approach $1 Billion," *Advertising Age*, April 6, 1998.

55. Quoted in Peter Golding, "World Wide Wedge: Division and Contradiction in the Global Information Infrastructure," *Monthly Review* 48, no. 3 (1996): 70, https://monthlyreview.org.

56. John Schwartz, "Giving Web a Memory Cost Its Users Privacy," *New York Times*, September 4, 2001, https://www.nytimes.com.

57. David M. Kristol and Lou Montulli, "HTTP State Management Mechanism," request for comments, 2109, Network Working Group, Internet Engineering Task Force, February 1997, http://tools.ietf.org.

58. Schwartz, "Giving Web a Memory Cost Its Users Privacy."
59. David M. Kristol, e-mail message to the author, August 4, 2012.
60. Tim Jackson, "This Bug in Your PC Is a Smart Cookie," *Financial Times*, February 12, 1996, https://www.ft.com; Shah and Kesan, "Recipes for Cookies."
61. Rick E. Bruner, "Cookie Proposal Could Hinder Online Advertising," *Advertising Age*, March 31, 1997.
62. Kristol, "HTTP Cookies," 178–81.
63. The IETF's mailing list (titled ietf-http-wg-old) is archived by the World Wide Web Consortium, "Mailing List Search Service," https://www.w3.org/Search/Mail/Public/. I reviewed correspondence from February to April 1997.
64. Mark Hedlund, "RE: Issues with the Cookie Draft," March 22, 1997, https://lists.w3.org/Archives/Public/ietf-http-wg-old/1997JanApr/0588.html.
65. David Stein, "RE: Unverifiable Transactions/Cookie Draft," March 14, 1997, https://lists.w3.org/Archives/Public/ietf-http-wg-old/1997JanApr/0507.html.
66. Kristol, "HTTP Cookies," 160.
67. Yaron Goland, "RE: Issues with the Cookie Draft," March 22, 1997, https://lists.w3.org/Archives/Public/ietf-http-wg-old/1997JanApr/0594.html.
68. Yaron Goland, "RE: Unverifiable Transactions/Cookie Draft," March 18, 1997, https://lists.w3.org/Archives/Public/ietf-http-wg-old/1997JanApr/0507.html.
69. Helen Nissenbaum, "From Preemption to Circumvention: If Technology Regulates, Why Do We Need Regulation (and Vice Versa)?," *Berkeley Technology Law Journal* 26, no. 3 (2011): 1367–86.
70. Bruner, "Cookie Proposal Could Hinder Online Advertising."
71. Kristol, "HTTP Cookies," 161.
72. Bruner, "Cookie Proposal Could Hinder Online Advertising."
73. "User Complaints Sour Cookie Technology," *Phillips Business Information's Internet Week*, February 19, 1996.
74. Kristol, "HTTP Cookies," 169–70.
75. Shah and Kesan, "Recipes for Cookies," 329.
76. Shah and Kesan, "Recipes for Cookies," 329.
77. Joshua Piven, "Outsmarting the Cookie Monster," *Computer Technology Review* 16, no. 11 (1996).
78. Dwight Merriman, "Unverifiable Transactions/Cookie Draft," March 13, 1997, https://lists.w3.org/Archives/Public/ietf-http-wg-old/1997JanApr/0416.html.
79. Mark Hedlund, "RE: Unverifiable Transactions/Cookie Draft," March 14, 1997, https://lists.w3.org/Archives/Public/ietf-http-wg-old/1997JanApr/0419.html.
80. Bruner, "Cookie Proposal Could Hinder Online Advertising."
81. Rajiv C. Shah and Christian Sandvig, "Software Defaults as De Facto Regulation

the Case of the Wireless Internet," *Information, Communication and Society* 11, no. 1 (2008): 25–46, https://doi.org/10.1080/13691180701858836.

82. Gillespie, *Wired Shut*, xiv.

83. Paul Judge, "Internet Evangelist," *BusinessWeek*, October 25, 1999.

4. The Dot-com Bubble

1. David Kirsch and Brent Goldfarb, "Small Ideas, Big Ideas, Good Ideas: Get Big Fast and Dot-Com Venture Creation," in *The Internet and American Business*, ed. William Aspray and Paul E. Ceruzzi (Cambridge, Mass.: MIT Press, 2008), 261.

2. Kirsch and Goldfarb, "Small Ideas, Big Ideas, Good Ideas," 261.

3. Michael Peltz, "High Tech's Premier Venture Capitalist," *Institutional Investor* 30, no. 6 (1996): 89–98.

4. Joshua Quittner and Lawrence Mondi, "Browser Madness," *Time*, August 21, 1995.

5. Marc Andreessen, "Netscape: Portal to the Web," in *Architects of the Web: 1,000 Days that Built the Future of Business*, ed. Robert Reid (New York: Wiley, 1997), 31.

6. Adam Lashinsky, "Remembering Netscape," CNN Money, July 25, 2005, https://money.cnn.com.

7. "Dot Con," *Frontline*, PBS, January 24, 2002, http://www.pbs.org.

8. Kirsch and Goldfarb, "Small Ideas, Big Ideas, Good Ideas," 261.

9. Between 1990 and 2000, the number of VC firms in the U.S. more than doubled, while the number of start-ups funded grew sixfold, from 1,050 to 6,420. See *National Venture Capital Association Yearbook 2011* (Arlington, Va.: National Venture Capital Association, 2011); and *Venture Impact: The Economic Importance of Venture Capital–Backed Companies to the U.S. Economy* (Arlington, Va.: National Venture Capital Association, 2011).

10. Matthew Zook, *The Geography of the Internet Industry: Venture Capital, Dot-Coms, and Local Knowledge* (Oxford: Blackwell, 2005).

11. Debra Aho Williamson and Alice Z. Cuneo, "Flexing VC Influence," *Advertising Age*, November 1, 1999.

12. Brent Goldfarb, Michael Pfarrer, and David Kirsch, "Searching for Ghosts: Business Survival, Unmeasured Entrepreneurial Activity and Private Equity Investment in the Dot-Com Era," *Robert H. Smith School Research Paper No. RHS*, October 12, 2005, 6–27.

13. Robert J. Shiller, *Irrational Exuberance* (Princeton, N.J.: Princeton University Press, 2000), 105.

14. Gretchen Morgenson, "How Did They Value Stocks? Count the Absurd Ways," *New York Times*, March 18, 2001, https://www.nytimes.com.

15. For more on how informational practices create economic realities, see

Micky Lee, "What Can Political Economists Learn from Economic Sociologists? A Case Study of NASDAQ," *Communication, Culture, and Critique* 7, no. 2 (2014): 246–63, https://doi.org/10.1111/cccr.12043.

16. Kurtz, *Fortune Tellers.*

17. Geert Lovink, "After the Dotcom Crash: Recent Literature on Internet, Business and Society," *Australian Humanities Review* 27 (2002), http://australian humanitiesreview.org/2002/09/01/after-the-dotcom-crash-recent-literature -on-internet-business-and-society/.

18. Nigel Thrift, "'It's the Romance, Not the Finance, that Makes the Business Worth Pursuing': Disclosing a New Market Culture," *Economy and Society* 30, no. 4 (2001): 425, https://doi.org/10.1080/03085140120089045.

19. Brett Trueman, M. H. Franco Wong, and Xiao-Jun Zhang, "The Eyeballs Have It: Searching for the Value in Internet Stocks," *Journal of Accounting Research* 38 (2000): 137–62, https://doi.org/10.2307/2672912.

20. Jim Clark and Owen Edwards, *Netscape Time: The Making of the Billion-Dollar Start-up that Took on Microsoft* (New York: St. Martin's Press, 1999), 98.

21. Mary Meeker and Chris DuPuy, *The Internet Report* (New York: Morgan Stanley, 1996), 1–20.

22. Beth Snyder, "GSD&M Swaps Work for Equity in Net Start-ups," *Advertising Age,* November 15, 1999.

23. Michael Wolff, *Burn Rate: How I Survived the Gold Rush Years on the Internet* (New York: Simon & Schuster, 1998), 51.

24. Wolff, *Burn Rate,* 54.

25. Laurie Freeman, "Net Slashes Time from Hello to Adios," *Advertising Age,* October 4, 1999; Suein Hwang, "Growing Pains on the Web: In Web Firms' Ad Blitz, an Eye on Wall Street," *Wall Street Journal,* August 19, 1999, https://www.wsj.com/.

26. Bradley Johnson, "Boom or Bust?," *Advertising Age,* November 1, 1999.

27. "Breaking News," *Advertising Age,* October 25, 1999.

28. David Goetzl, "Spokesman Reeve Stars in Effort for Disability Insurer," *Advertising Age,* February 21, 2000.

29. Hwang, "Growing Pains on the Web."

30. Bradley Johnson, "Out-of-Sight Spending Collides with Reality," *Advertising Age,* August 7, 2000.

31. Catharine P. Taylor, "E-Business Falls Back to Earth," *Advertising Age,* May 21, 2001.

32. Chuck Ross, "The Race to TV Creates Pain and Gain for Buyers," *Advertising Age,* November 1, 1999; Wayne Friedman and Kate Fitzgerald, "Dot-Coms Give Commercials a Break," *Advertising Age,* August 7, 2000.

33. WebVan, Value America, HomeGrocer, CNET, AltaVista, and E*Trade each launched $100 million–plus ad campaigns in 1999. See Dawn Kawamoto, "Dot-Commercials," CNET, February 21, 2000, http://news.cnet.com; Alice C.

Cuneo, "Milkman of Cyberspace," *Advertising Age,* November 2, 1999; Jennifer Gilbert et al., "Dot-com Doubt," *Advertising Age,* April 10, 2000.

34. "100 Leading National Advertisers: 1997 Edition," top advertisers by media (Advertising Age, September 29, 1997), Advertising Age Data Center, http://adage.com.

35. Galen Svanas, "Out of the Box," *BrandWeek,* June 9, 1997; "Yahoo 1996 Annual Report," 10-K (Yahoo, 1996).

36. Peter Elsworth, "Internet Advertising Growing Slowly," *New York Times,* February 24, 1997, https://www.nytimes.com; Bradley Johnson, "Advertising Jumps 80% to $359 Mil," *Advertising Age,* October 18, 1999.

37. Kevin Featherly, "Traditional Firms Flock to Online Advertising," *NewsBytes,* November 20, 2000.

38. "100 Leading National Advertisers: 2001 Edition," domestic ad spending by medium (September 24, 2001), Advertising Age Data Center, http://adage.com; "2000 IAB Internet Advertising Revenue Report" (New York: Interactive Advertising Bureau, April 2001); "2010 IAB Internet Advertising Revenue Report" (New York: Interactive Advertising Bureau, April 2011).

39. "2000 IAB Internet Advertising Revenue Report."

40. "Net Results," *Advertising Age,* November 1, 1999.

41. Stefanie Olsen, "If You Post It, Will They Pay?," CNET, March 29, 2001, http://news.cnet.com.

42. Zuckerman, "Internet's Original Sin."

43. Patrice Flichy, *The Internet Imaginaire* (Cambridge, Mass.: MIT Press, 2007), 1–2.

44. Lovink, "After the Dotcom Crash."

45. Vincent Mosco, *The Digital Sublime: Myth, Power, and Cyberspace* (Cambridge, Mass.: MIT Press, 2004), 3–4.

46. Kevin Kelly, *New Rules for the New Economy: 10 Ways the Network Economy Is Changing Everything* (New York: Viking, 1998), 1.

47. Judith Messina, "Double-Time DoubleClick Acquisition Strategy," *Crain's New York Business,* July 19, 1999.

48. Justin Fox, "Net Stock Rules: Masters of a Parallel Universe," *Fortune,* June 7, 1999.

49. Cassidy, *Dot.con,* 241.

50. Colin Barrow, "Internet Firms: What Strategic Changes Have to Be Managed?," *Strategic Change* 10, no. 2 (2001): 79, https://doi.org/10.1002/jsc.530.

51. *National Venture Capital Association Yearbook 2011,* 11.

52. Suein Hwang, "Who's in Charge? The Dot-Com Blur," *Wall Street Journal,* February 16, 2000, https://www.wsj.com/.

53. Williamson and Cuneo, "Flexing VC Influence."

54. Michael Indergaard, *Silicon Alley: The Rise and Fall of a New Media District* (New York: Routledge, 2004), 51.

55. O'Connor, *Map of Innovation.*

56. Messina, "New Media's Hot Play."

57. John Mulqueen, "DoubleClick Wants to Hit Big Button," *InternetWeek,* December 22, 1997.

58. Messina, "New Media's Hot Play."

59. Judith Messina, "Kevin O'Connor and the Mouse That Roared," *Crain's New York Business,* May 15, 2000.

60. Messina, "Kevin O'Connor and the Mouse That Roared."

61. Mark Walsh, "DoubleClick Clique Expands as Internet's Appeal Boosts IPO," *Crain's New York Business,* February 23, 1998.

62. Michael Schrange, "Kevin O'Connor," *Adweek,* January 18, 1999.

63. "DoubleClick, Inc. 2000 Annual Report," 10-K (DoubleClick Inc., 2000), 48; cash flow data from CapitalIQ financial database.

64. CapitalIQ financial database.

65. Messina, "Double-Time DoubleClick Acquisition Strategy."

66. "DoubleClick, Inc. 1997 Annual Report," 10-K (DoubleClick Inc., 1997), 4. This language also appears verbatim in the 1998, 1999, and 2000 reports.

67. Judith Dobrzynski, "CEO Round Table; Online Pioneers: The Buzz Never Stops," *New York Times,* November 21, 1999, https://www.nytimes.com.

68. Steven Vonder Haar, "Data Chase," *Adweek,* September 6, 1999.

69. "Distinguished Achievement Citation: David S. Wetherell," Ohio Wesleyan University, May 19, 2001; Judge, "Internet Evangelist."

70. Dennis Callaghan, "CGMI's Excellence @ Venture," *MC: Technology Marketing Intelligence,* August 1999.

71. Judge, "Internet Evangelist"; Fox, "Net Stock Rules"; Kimberly Weisul, "Net Investor CMGI Readies Raft of New Offerings," *Inter@ctive Week,* March 8, 1999.

72. Stewart Deck, "Alta Vista Stake Sold to CMGI for $2.3B," *Computerworld,* July 5, 1999.

73. John R. Wilke and George Anders, "Microsoft Sets a New Strategy for Investments," *Wall Street Journal,* December 11, 1998, https://www.wsj.com/; "Intel to Buy 4.9% Stake in CMG," *Wall Street Journal,* December 9, 1997.

74. Judge, "Internet Evangelist."

75. Beth Snyder, "Pre-IPO Branding Essential for Web Companies," *Advertising Age,* August 24, 1998.

76. Kurtz, *Fortune Tellers,* 118–19.

77. The deal with the Patriots was later canceled in the wake of the crash. Judge, "Internet Evangelist."

78. Callaghan, "CGMI's Excellence @ Venture."

79. McChesney, *Rich Media, Poor Democracy.*

80. Peltz, "High Tech's Premier Venture Capitalist."

81. Mark Walter, "DoubleClick Merges with NetGravity," *Seybold Report on Internet Publishing* 4, no. 1 (1999).

82. Messina, "Double-Time DoubleClick Acquisition Strategy."

83. Messina, "Double-Time DoubleClick Acquisition Strategy."

84. Courtney Macavinta, "DoubleClick, Abacus Merge in $1.7 Billion Deal," *CNET*, November 24, 1999, http://news.cnet.com.

85. Randall Rothenberg, "An Advertising Power, but Just What Does DoubleClick Do?," *New York Times*, September 22, 1999, https://www.nytimes.com.

86. Fox, "Net Stock Rules."

87. "DoubleClick Takes 30% Stake in ValueClick," *Advertising Age's Business Marketing*, February 2000.

88. Judge, "Internet Evangelist."

89. The deals included the FlyCast media buying platform; the AdForce ad network; Yesmail, an email marketer; and AdKnowledge, a provider of ad targeting systems. Jennifer Gilbert, "CMGI's Web Dealmaking Hits Big-Time," *Advertising Age*, October 4, 1999; Stephen Lacey, "In the Net Ad Wars, CMGI Squares Off," *Mergers and Acquisitions Report*, December 20, 1999.

90. Judge, "Internet Evangelist."

91. Norm Alster, "Can CMGI Stop the Bleeding?," *BusinessWeek*, September 25, 2000.

92. Mitch Wagner, "Ad Agency DoubleClick Heads Off Downtime with Redundant Systems," *InternetWeek*, June 13, 1999.

93. "DoubleClick, Inc. 1997 Annual Report."

94. Messina, "New Media's Hot Play."

95. David P. Baron, "DoubleClick and Internet Privacy," Stanford Graduate School of Business, August 2000, https://www.gsb.stanford.edu; Judith Messina, "On-line Networks Confront Survival of the Clickest," *Crain's New York Business*, January 12, 1998.

96. "DoubleClick, Inc. 2000 Annual Report," 12.

97. "CMGI 1996 Annual Report," 10-K (CMGI, 1996), 13; "CMGI 1998 Annual Report," 10-K (CMGI, 1998), 12; "CMGI 2000 Annual Report," 10-K (CMGI, 2000), 4.

98. DoubleClick Inc., "Dynamically Targeted Advertising," advertisement, *Adweek*, March 6, 1997.

99. "DoubleClick, Inc. 1998 Annual Report," 10-K (DoubleClick Inc., 1998), 1–2.

100. "DoubleClick, Inc. 2000 Annual Report," 4.

101. "CMGI 1998 Annual Report," 3.

102. Federal Trade Commission (FTC), *Online Profiling: A Report to Congress* (Washington, D.C.: Federal Trade Commission, June 3, 2000), 2.

103. Gina Neff, *Venture Labor: Work and the Burden of Risk in Innovative Industries* (Cambridge, Mass.: MIT Press, 2012), 53; Indergaard, *Silicon Alley*, 78.

104. DoubleClick took a 30 percent stake in ValueClick, while FlyCast and AdForce were purchased outright by CMGI.

105. Matthew Goldstein, "Web Agency Uses Its New Bulk to Make On-line Strat-

egy Click," *Crain's New York Business,* April 13, 1998; "Company News: Excite Agrees to Buy Matchlogic for $120 Million," *New York Times,* January 16, 1998, https://www.nytimes.com; Kate Maddox, "Dave Morgan," *Advertising Age,* June 1, 1998.

106. Debra Aho Williamson, "Targeting Distinguishes AdForce from the Pack," *Advertising Age,* March 1, 1999; "24/7 Media, Inc. Reports Year-End and Fourth Quarter Revenues That Exceed Expectations," *Business Wire,* March 2, 1999, 7; "ValueClick Serves More than One Billion Impressions per Month," *PR Newswire,* November 1, 1999; "High Availability and Scalable Capacity for Internet Servers Cited as Top Issues Driving the Integration of New Web Switching Technology," *PR Newswire,* July 12, 1999; FTC, *Online Profiling,* 2; "Christopher D. Neimeth Leaving New York Times Company to Become President, CEO of Real Media," *PR Newswire,* December 8, 1999.
107. Rothenberg, "Advertising Power."
108. FTC, *Online Profiling,* 3.
109. "Ads Find Strength in Numbers," CNET, November 4, 1996, http://news.cnet.com.
110. Messina, "New Media's Hot Play."
111. Vonder Haar, "Data Chase."
112. "DoubleClick Takes 30% Stake in ValueClick."
113. Messina, "On-line Networks Confront Survival of the Clickest."
114. Jennifer Gilbert, "Weathering the I-Storm," *Advertising Age,* November 1, 1999.
115. Gilbert, "Weathering the I-Storm."
116. Judge, "Internet Evangelist."
117. Norm Alster, "CMGI: Cashing in on Internet Jackpot," *Upside,* June 1999.
118. Alster, "Can CMGI Stop the Bleeding?"
119. "CMGI 2000 Annual Report," 2.
120. "DoubleClick," in *Gale Encyclopedia of E-commerce* (Detroit, Mich.: Gale, 2002); "DoubleClick, Inc. 2000 Annual Report," 8.
121. "DoubleClick, Inc. 2001 Annual Report," 10-K (DoubleClick Inc., 2001), 26.
122. Alster, "Can CMGI Stop the Bleeding?"
123. Wolff, *Burn Rate,* 15.
124. Fox, "Net Stock Rules."
125. "DoubleClick, Inc. 1999 Annual Report," 10-K (DoubleClick Inc., 1999), 31.
126. "DoubleClick, Inc. 1997 Annual Report," 4.
127. Judge, "Internet Evangelist."
128. Judge, "Internet Evangelist."
129. Judge, "Internet Evangelist."
130. Alster, "Can CMGI Stop the Bleeding?"
131. "DoubleClick, Inc. 1999 Annual Report," 31.
132. Cassidy, *Dot.con,* 135.

5. Surveillance Advertising Takes Shape

1. "Toward a More Responsible Future for Advertising," P&G Signal 360 (blog), February 6, 2020, https://pgsignal.com.
2. Artzt, "P&G's Artzt."
3. Dylan Tweney, "Online Advertising: A $3 Billion Industry Limping on Its Last Legs," *InfoWorld,* October 4, 1999.
4. Rothenberg, "Advertising Power."
5. This quote is possibly the most hackneyed in all of advertising scholarship. I consider it a rite of passage to include it in this book. See Turow, *Niche Envy,* 21.
6. Peppers and Rogers, *One to One Future.*
7. Turow, *Daily You,* 90.
8. Judith Mottl, "The Trouble with Online Ads," *Information Week,* October 11, 1999.
9. Debra Aho Williamson, "Sony Seeks Big-Bucks Sponsors for Web Site," *Advertising Age,* March 18, 1996.
10. Sally Beatty, "P&G, Rivals and Agencies Begin Attempt to Set On-line Standards," *Wall Street Journal,* August 24, 1998, https://www.wsj.com/.
11. Martin Nisenholtz, "Public Workshop on Consumer Information Privacy, Session Two: Consumer Online Privacy," Federal Trade Commission (1997), 224, 227.
12. Jim Clark and Owen Edwards, *Netscape Time: The Making of the Billion-Dollar Start-up that Took on Microsoft* (New York: St. Martin's Press, 1999), 3.
13. Beatty, "P&G, Rivals and Agencies"; "2000 IAB Internet Advertising Revenue Report" (New York: Interactive Advertising Bureau, April 2001), 6.
14. Beatty, "P&G, Rivals and Agencies"
15. Nick Srnicek, *Platform Capitalism* (Cambridge, Mass.: Polity, 2017), 103.
16. Sean Silverthorne, "New Research Explores Multi-sided Markets," HBS Working Knowledge, March 12, 2006, http://hbswk.hbs.edu. For a useful discussion of platformization, see Anne Helmond, David B. Nieborg, and Fernando N. van der Vlist, "Facebook's Evolution: Development of a Platform-as-Infrastructure," *Internet Histories* 3, no. 2 (2019): 123–46, https://doi.org/10.1080/24701475.2019.1593667.
17. O'Connor, *Map of Innovation,* 61.
18. Schrange, "Kevin O'Connor."
19. Tina Grant, ed., "DoubleClick, Inc.," in *International Directory of Company Histories* (Detroit, Mich.: St. James Press, 2002).
20. Kurtz, *Fortune Tellers,* 179.
21. Seth Fineberg, "Dot-com Sea Change Forces Ad Networks to Rethink Strategies," *Advertising Age,* October 30, 2000.
22. Kevin O'Connor, "I Am Kevin O'Connor, the Co-founder and Former CEO of

DoubleClick, and Now CEO of FindTheBest-AMA," Reddit, October 9, 2012, http://www.reddit.com.

23. "DoubleClick," in *Gale Encyclopedia of E-commerce*.

24. "DoubleClick, Inc. 1998 Annual Report," 10-K (DoubleClick Inc., 1998), 1–2; Beth Snyder, "DoubleClick Forms Consumer-Tracking Unit," *Advertising Age,* October 5, 1998.

25. Judge, "Internet Evangelist."

26. Rick E. Bruner, "Engage and AdSmart Team up to Offer Improved Ad Targeting," *Advertising Age,* January 19, 1998.

27. "Engage.Knowledge (TM)," Engage Technologies, Internet Archive Wayback Machine, February 13, 1998, http://web.archive.org/web/19980213153314/http://www.engagetech.com/text/knowledge.htm.

28. "Microsoft Acquires LinkExchange to Greatly Expand Small-Business Services from MSN," *PR Newswire,* November 5, 1998.

29. Jennifer Owens, "DoubleClick Debuts Web-Ad Exchange Program," *Adweek,* August 14, 2000.

30. O'Connor, *Map of Innovation,* 206.

31. Jennifer Gilbert, "Flycast MediaNet Tracks Online Ads," *Advertising Age,* June 14, 1999.

32. "Bulletin Board," *Advertising Age,* January 19, 1998.

33. David Wamsley, "Online Ad Auctions Offer Sites More than Bargains," *Advertising Age,* March 29, 1999.

34. "Ad Info/Products," DoubleClick, Internet Archive Wayback Machine, February 5, 1998, http://web.archive.org/web/19980205040958/http://www.doubleclick.net/nf/adinfo/spotlset.htm.

35. "Boomerang," DoubleClick, Internet Archive Wayback Machine, August 15, 2000, http://web.archive.org/web/20000815064513/http://www.doubleclick.net:8080/advertisers/network/boomerang/.

36. Kim M. Bayne, "AdKnowledge Rolls out Web Ad Evaluation Tool," *Advertising Age,* June 8, 1998.

37. Debra Aho Williamson, "Targeting Distinguishes AdForce from the Pack," *Advertising Age,* March 1, 1999.

38. Nigel Watson, "A Brief History of Experian: Our Story" (Dublin: Experian, 2013), https://www.experianplc.com/media/1323/8151-exp-experian-history-book_abridged_final.pdf.

39. Rothenberg, "Advertising Power."

40. Rothenberg, "Advertising Power."

41. Gandy, *Panoptic Sort,* 1.

42. Gandy, *Panoptic Sort,* 2.

43. Gandy, *Panoptic Sort,* 18.

44. David Lyon, *Surveillance and Social Sorting: Privacy, Risk and Digital Discrimination* (New York: Routledge, 2002).

45. Turow, *Daily You,* 88.
46. Turow, *Niche Envy,* 186.
47. Philip M. Napoli, *Audience Evolution: New Technologies and the Transformation of Media Audiences* (New York: Columbia University Press, 2010).
48. Kipp Cheng, "Engage Technology Plays Follow the User," *Adweek,* October 11, 1999.
49. "Engage.Knowledge (TM)."
50. Lori Andrews, "Facebook Is Using You," *New York Times,* February 4, 2012, https://www.nytimes.com.
51. Turow, *Breaking Up America;* Turow, *Daily You,* 194.
52. Marcia Stepankek, "Weblining," *BusinessWeek,* April 3, 2000.
53. Stepankek, "Weblining."
54. Noble, *Algorithms of Oppression;* Jathan Sadowski, *Too Smart: How Digital Capitalism Is Extracting Data, Controlling Our Lives, and Taking Over the World* (Cambridge, Mass.: MIT Press, 2020).
55. Tamara Shepherd, "Desperation and Datalogix: Facebook Six Months after Its IPO," Culture Digitally (blog), November 12, 2012, http://culturedigitally.org.
56. Virginia Eubanks, *Automating Inequality: How High-Tech Tools Profile, Police, and Punish the Poor* (New York: St. Martin's Press, 2017).
57. Mark Andrejevic, *ISpy: Surveillance and Power in the Interactive Era* (Lawrence: University Press of Kansas, 2007), 2–4.
58. Andrejevic, *ISpy,* 7.
59. Vincent Mosco, *The Political Economy of Communication* (London: Sage, 1996); Dan Schiller, *How to Think about Information* (Urbana: University of Illinois Press, 2007); Matthew Crain, "The Limits of Transparency: Data Brokers and Commodification," *New Media and Society* 20, no. 1 (2018): 88–104, https://doi.org/10.1177/1461444816657096.
60. "100 Leading National Advertisers: 1999 Edition," domestic ad spending by medium, September 27, 1999, and "100 Leading National Advertisers: 2000 Edition," domestic ad spending by medium, September 25, 2000, Advertising Age Data Center, http://adage.com.
61. Stefanie Olsen, "Advertisers Flock to the Web," CNET, December 3, 2000, http://news.cnet.com.
62. Stuart Elliott, "A Study Says Many Traditional Marketers Are Quickly Becoming Devotees of Cyberspace," *New York Times,* May 9, 2000, https://www.nytimes.com.
63. "Net Results," *Advertising Age,* November 1, 1999; "Net Results," *Advertising Age,* February 26, 2001; "2000 IAB Internet Advertising Revenue Report," 6. The 1999 totals are annualized.
64. Jennifer Gilbert, "Agencies Centralize Web Serving," *Advertising Age,* March 1, 1999.

65. Gilbert, "Agencies Centralize Web Serving."

66. "DoubleClick Short Term Buy," *Standard & Poor's Emerging and Special Situation,* January 15, 1998.

67. "DoubleClick, Inc. 2000 Annual Report," 10-K (DoubleClick Inc., 2000), 6.

68. Schrange, "Kevin O'Connor."

69. "The Burger King of Internet Advertising," *Interactive PR,* August 12, 1996.

70. George Anders, "Wide Open Space: Internet Advertising, Just Like Its Medium, Is Pushing Boundaries," *Wall Street Journal,* November 30, 1998, https://www.wsj.com/.

71. "Tech Firms Promise New Era of Interactive Selling," *Interactive Marketing News,* December 20, 1996.

72. Thomas Weber, "The Man Who Baked the First Web Cookies Chews Over Their Fate," *Wall Street Journal,* February 28, 2000.

73. FTC, *Online Profiling,* 6.

74. Federal Trade Commission (FTC), *Privacy Online: Fair Information Practices in the Electronic Marketplace* (Washington, D.C.: Federal Trade Commission, 2000), 9.

75. Fineberg, "Dot-Com Sea Change."

76. Vonder Haar, "Data Chase."

77. Schiller, *Digital Capitalism,* 99–101.

78. "100 Leading National Advertisers: 1999 Edition."

79. Kate Maddox, "Net Gains Credibility as Ad Medium," *Advertising Age,* April 26, 1999.

80. Kate Maddox, "P&G: Interactive Marketer of the Year," *Advertising Age,* May 3, 1999.

81. Maddox, "P&G: Interactive Marketer of the Year."

82. Kate Maddox, "Marketers Debate FAST's Outcome," *Advertising Age,* September 7, 1998.

83. "DoubleClick, Inc. 2003 Annual Report," 10-K (DoubleClick Inc., 2003), iii.

84. Dana Blankenhorn, "NetGravity Puts Emphasis on Solutions," *Advertising Age,* March 1, 1999.

85. Blankenhorn, "NetGravity Puts Emphasis on Solutions."

86. Vonder Haar, "Data Chase."

87. Vonder Haar, "Data Chase."

88. "DoubleClick, Inc. 2000 Annual Report."

89. "DoubleClick, Inc. 2000 Annual Report," 8; Alster, "Can CMGI Stop the Bleeding?"; FTC, *Online Profiling,* 6.

90. Rick Whiting, "Web Data Piles Up," *Information Week,* May 8, 2000.

91. Patricia Riedman, "AOL Taps Offline Databases in Ad Targeting Quest," *Advertising Age,* October 20, 1997.

6. The Privacy Challenge

1. Federal Trade Commission (FTC), *Privacy Online: A Report to Congress* (Washington, D.C.: Federal Trade Commission, 1998).

2. Marc Rotenberg, "Public Workshop on Consumer Information Privacy, Session Four: Database Study," Federal Trade Commission (1997), 237–39.

3. Freedman, *Contradictions of Media Power.*

4. Lauer, *Creditworthy;* Jason Pridmore and Detlev Zwick, "Marketing and the Rise of Commercial Consumer Surveillance," *Surveillance and Society* 8, no. 3 (2011): 269–77, https://doi.org/10.24908/ss.v8i3.4163.

5. Colin J. Bennett, *The Privacy Advocates: Resisting the Spread of Surveillance* (Cambridge, Mass.: MIT Press, 2008).

6. Center for Media Education, Internet Archive Wayback Machine, February 23, 1999, http://web.archive.org/web/19990223194220/http://tap.epn.org/cme/.

7. Other participating organizations included the Electronic Frontier Foundation, Junk Busters, Privacy International, Privacy Rights Clearinghouse, Consumer Federation of America, and the National Parent Teacher Association.

8. McChesney, *Rich Media, Poor Democracy,* 126; Streeter, *Selling the Air.*

9. Kathryn C. Montgomery, *Generation Digital: Politics, Commerce, and Childhood in the Age of the Internet* (Cambridge, Mass.: MIT Press, 2007), 68.

10. Jeff Chester, telephone interview with the author, December 14, 2012.

11. Lee Gomes, "Leading Web Browsers May Violate Privacy of Users' Computers, Activities," *San Jose Mercury News,* February 13, 1996.

12. Federal Trade Commission (FTC), *Staff Report: Public Workshop on Consumer Privacy on the Global Information Infrastructure* (Washington, D.C.: Federal Trade Commission, 1996), 8.

13. Janlori Goldman, "Public Workshop on Consumer Information Privacy, Session Two: Consumer Online Privacy," Federal Trade Commission (1997), 335.

14. Ira Teinowitz, "Privacy Groups Ready to Seek FTC Regs for Online Biz," *Advertising Age,* June 9, 1997.

15. David P. Baron, "DoubleClick and Internet Privacy," Stanford Graduate School of Business, August 2000, 5, https://www.gsb.stanford.edu.

16. Evan Hendricks, "Public Workshop on Consumer Information Privacy, Session Two: Consumer Online Privacy," Federal Trade Commission (1997), 325.

17. *Web of Deception: Threats to Children from Online Marketing* (Washington, D.C.: Center for Media Education, 1996).

18. These concerns led to the controversial Communications Decency Act of 1996 (Title V of the Telecommunications Act of 1996), the anti-indecency provisions of which were struck down by the Supreme Court in 1997.

19. Montgomery, *Generation Digital,* 76.

20. Colin J. Bennett, "Convergence Revisited: Toward a Global Policy for the Pro-

tection of Personal Data," in *Technology and Privacy: The New Landscape*, ed. Philip E. Agre and Marc Rotenberg (Cambridge, Mass.: MIT Press, 1997), 113.

21. Industry representatives included Netscape, Prodigy, and trade associations including CASIE, ANA, AAAA, and DMA. The privacy advocates included representatives from CME, EPIC, and CDT.

22. Montgomery, *Generation Digital*, 79.

23. Montgomery, *Generation Digital*, 80.

24. FTC, *Privacy Online*, 36–37.

25. Edward Lee Lamoureux, *Privacy, Surveillance, and the New Media You* (New York: Peter Lang, 2016); Chris Jay Hoofnagle, *Federal Trade Commission Privacy Law and Policy* (Cambridge: Cambridge University Press, 2016).

26. FTC, *Staff Report*, 27–28.

27. Chris Jay Hoofnagle, "Denialists' Deck of Cards: An Illustrated Taxonomy of Rhetoric Used to Frustrate Consumer Protection Efforts," Social Science Research Network (SSRN) Scholarly Paper, February 9, 2007.

28. Ira Teinowitz, "Internet Privacy Concerns Addressed," *Advertising Age*, June 16, 1997.

29. Medine, "Public Workshop on Consumer Information Privacy," 88.

30. Gregory Dalton, "OPS: Answer to Cookies?," *Information Week*, October 13, 1997, 3.

31. Baron, "DoubleClick and Internet Privacy," 8.

32. Teinowitz, "Privacy Groups Ready to Seek FTC Regs for Online Biz."

33. FTC, *Privacy Online*, ii–iii.

34. FTC, *Privacy Online*, 41.

35. "Internet Site Agrees to Settle FTC Charges of Deceptively Collecting Personal Information in Agency's First Internet Privacy Case," Federal Trade Commission, August 13, 1998, https://www.ftc.gov.

36. FTC, *Privacy Online*, 42.

37. "Editorial: Help Hold Off Online Rules," *Advertising Age*, April 8, 1996.

38. Simon, *NetPolicy.com*, 143.

39. Robert Schriver, "You Cheated, You Lied: The Safe Harbor Agreement and Its Enforcement by the Federal Trade Commission," *Fordham Law Review* 70, no. 6 (2002): 2279.

40. Montgomery, *Generation Digital*, 95.

41. Montgomery, *Generation Digital*, 93–94.

42. Montgomery, *Generation Digital*, 102.

43. Judith Messina, "Companies Idling as Beltway Maps Plans for I-Way," *Crain's New York Business*, March 9, 1998.

44. "Microsoft Wants Net Privacy," *Philadelphia Inquirer*, June 24, 1999.

45. "Online Privacy Alliance Says Web Sweeps Confirm Significant Progress in Privacy Self-Regulation," Online Privacy Alliance, Internet Archive Wayback

Machine, February 29, 2000, https://web.archive.org/web/20000229083227/ http://www.privacyalliance.org/news/05121999.shtml.

46. Ira Teinowitz, "FTC Chief Asks Congress to Ensure Privacy on Web," *Advertising Age,* June 8, 1998.

47. Sheila F. Anthony, "The Case for Standardization of Privacy Policy Formats," July 1, 2001, https://www.ftc.gov/public-statements/2001/07/case-standardization-privacy-policy-formats. Draper and Turow argue persuasively that opaque privacy policies are part of a tool kit for the deliberate corporate cultivation of resignation among Internet users. See Nora A. Draper and Joseph Turow, "The Corporate Cultivation of Digital Resignation," *New Media and Society* 21, no. 8 (2019): 1824–39, https://doi.org/10.1177/1461444819833331.

48. Beth Cox, "Profiling Firms Defend Themselves," ClickZ, November 10, 1999.

49. Simon, *NetPolicy.com.*

50. Courtney Macavinta, "Consumer Group to Fight DoubleClick Deal," CNET, June 8, 1998, http://news.cnet.com/.

51. "The Internet's Chastened Child," *Economist,* November 9, 2000, http://www.economist.com.

52. Andrea Petersen and Jon G. Auerbach, "Online Ad Titans Bet Big in Race to Trace Consumers' Web Tracks," *Wall Street Journal,* November 8, 1999, https://www.wsj.com/.

53. David J. A. Todd, "Politicizing Privacy: 'Focussing Events' and the Dynamics of Conflict" (master's thesis, University of Victoria, 2001).

54. Evan Hansen, "DoubleClick under Email Attack for Consumer Profiling Plans," CNET, February 2, 2000, http://news.cnet.com; Jennifer Gilbert, "D'Click Says Merging Abacus Data Impossible," *Advertising Age,* November 15, 1999.

55. Schrange, "Kevin O'Connor."

56. Hansen, "DoubleClick under Email Attack."

57. "Internet's Chastened Child."

58. Todd, "Politicizing Privacy," 121.

59. Kurtz, *Fortune Tellers,* 273–74.

60. Greg Sandoval, "Probes Are Latest Headache in E-Commerce," CNET, February 16, 2000, https://www.cnet.com.

61. Evan Hansen, "DoubleClick Postpones Data-Merging Plan," CNET, March 2, 2000, https://www.cnet.com.

62. "Internet's Chastened Child."

63. Hansen, "DoubleClick Postpones Data-Merging Plan."

64. Todd, "Politicizing Privacy," 119–20.

65. Hansen, "DoubleClick under Email Attack."

66. Hansen, "DoubleClick under Email Attack."

67. Jennifer Gilbert and Ira Teinowitz, "Privacy Debate Continues to Rage," *Advertising Age,* February 7, 2000.

68. Jennifer Gilbert and Ira Teinowitz, "Online Privacy Disputes Reach FTC Panel," *Advertising Age,* January 31, 2000.
69. Ross McGhie, "Internet Advertising: The Internet as a Commercial Mass Medium" (master's thesis, Carleton University, 2003), 199.
70. Baron, "DoubleClick and Internet Privacy," 6.
71. Baron, "DoubleClick and Internet Privacy," 6.
72. "DoubleClick, Inc. 2000 Annual Report," 10-K (DoubleClick Inc., 2000), 8.
73. Bennett, *Privacy Advocates,* 155.
74. Messina, "Kevin O'Connor and the Mouse That Roared."
75. FTC, *Privacy Online,* iii.
76. Baron, "DoubleClick and Internet Privacy," 8.
77. Heather Green, "Privacy: Outrage on the Web," *BusinessWeek,* February 14, 2000.
78. Federal Trade Commission, *Self-Regulation and Privacy Online: A Report to Congress* (Washington, D.C.: Federal Trade Commission, 1999), 2.
79. Simon, *NetPolicy.com,* 145.
80. Green, "Privacy."
81. Simon, *NetPolicy.com,* 143.
82. Greg Sandoval, "McCain-Led Group Introduces Net Privacy Bill," CNET, July 26, 2000, https://www.cnet.com.
83. Weber, Thomas, "To Opt In or Opt Out: That Is the Question When Mulling Privacy," *Wall Street Journal,* October 23, 2000, https://www.wsj.com/.
84. Other proposed bills of note were the Electronic Privacy Bill of Rights Act of 1999 and the Secure Online Communication Enforcement Act of 2000.
85. L. Scott Tillett, "Pressure Builds for Privacy Laws," *InternetWeek,* June 5, 2000.
86. Ernest Hollings, "Internet Privacy Concerns," Pub. L. No. 106-1147, § Senate Committee on Commerce, Science, and Transportation (2000), 6.
87. Rothenberg, "Advertising Power."
88. Wendy Melillo, "Getting Personal," *Adweek,* March 27, 2000.
89. Thornton May, "Privacy's Pariahs; If Interactive Marketers Aren't Careful, We Will Be Branded the Bad Boys on the Digital Block," *Advertising Age,* April 17, 2000.
90. W. John Moore, "Invasion of the Internet Industry," *National Journal,* March 18, 2000.
91. Moore, "Invasion."
92. Wendy Melillo, "Private Matters," *Adweek,* June 19, 2000.
93. Messina, "Kevin O'Connor and the Mouse That Roared."
94. McGhie, "Internet Advertising: The Internet as a Commercial Mass Medium," 204.
95. Melillo, "Getting Personal."
96. Inger Stole, *Advertising on Trial: Consumer Activism and Corporate Public Relations in the 1930s* (Urbana: University of Illinois Press, 2005); Molly

Niesen, "The Little Old Lady Has Teeth: The U.S. Federal Trade Commission and the Advertising Industry, 1970–1973," *Advertising and Society Review* 12, no. 4 (2012), https://doi.org/10.1353/asr.2012.0000.

97. Steve Lohr, "Seizing the Initiative on Privacy," *New York Times*, October 11, 1999, https://www.nytimes.com.

98. Varney, "Online Privacy Protection Act of 1999."

99. Christine Varney, "To Review the Federal Trade Commission's Survey of Privacy Policies Posted by Commercial Web Sites," Pub. L. No. 106-1116, § Senate Committee on Commerce, Science, and Transportation (2000).

100. Patricia Jacobus, "Cookies Targeted as Congress, Advocates Address Net Privacy," CNET, February 11, 2000, http://news.cnet.com.

101. Hoofnagle, *Federal Trade Commission Privacy Law and Policy*, 158.

102. Ira Magaziner, telephone interview with the author, February 22, 2013.

103. David Joachim, "Internet Privacy Debate Is Dead," *InternetWeek*, April 16, 2001.

104. Joachim, "Internet Privacy Debate Is Dead."

105. Freedman, *Contradictions of Media Power*.

106. Turow, *Niche Envy*, 83.

7. The Legacy of the Dot-com Era

1. Gretchen Morgenson, "How Did They Value Stocks? Count the Absurd Ways," *New York Times*, March 18, 2001, https://www.nytimes.com.

2. "2003 IAB Internet Advertising Revenue Report" (New York: Interactive Advertising Bureau, April 2004), 7.

3. Normandy Madden, "Economy Hampering Yahoo's Global Goals," *Advertising Age*, March 12, 2001.

4. Dawn Kawamoto, "CMGI Severs Engage Ties," CNET, September 9, 2002, http://news.cnet.com.

5. "Gilt's Kevin Ryan: It Is All in the Presentation," Tech Crunch: Founder Stories, 2011, http://techcrunch.com.

6. "Brighter Days for Net Plays," *Advertising Age*, August 7, 2000.

7. Kevin Featherly, "Traditional Firms Flock to Online Advertising," *NewsBytes*, November 20, 2000.

8. Patricia Riedman, "Net Loss; Flat Online Ad Spending Forces i-Shops to Pare Down," *Advertising Age*, September 18, 2000.

9. Ken Auletta, *Googled: The End of the World as We Know It* (New York: Penguin Books, 2010), 61.

10. Google actually "borrowed" the idea for auction-based pay-per-click ads from a rival search engine called GoTo.com. See Will Oremus, "Google's Big Break," Slate, October 13, 2013, https://slate.com.

11. "2002 IAB Internet Advertising Revenue Report" (New York: Interactive Ad-

vertising Bureau, June 2003); "2003 IAB Internet Advertising Revenue Report."

12. "2004 IAB Internet Advertising Revenue Report" (New York: Interactive Advertising Bureau, April 2005), 3.

13. Brian Morrissey, "Private Equity Firm to Buy DoubleClick," *Adweek*, April 25, 2005.

14. Paul La Monica, "Google Surges above $400," CNN Money, November 17, 2005, https://money.cnn.com.

15. Alex Wilhelm, "A Look Back in IPO: Google, the Profit Machine," TechCrunch, July 31, 2017, https://techcrunch.com.

16. Paul La Monica, "Google Files for Its Long Awaited IPO," CNN Money, April 30, 2004, https://money.cnn.com.

17. "2006 IAB Internet Advertising Revenue Report" (New York: Interactive Advertising Bureau, May 2007).

18. By 2004, the keyword format accounted for around 40 percent of internet advertising, where it has hovered ever since. See "2018 IAB Internet Advertising Revenue Report" (New York: Interactive Advertising Bureau, May 2019).

19. Douglas Rushkoff, *Throwing Rocks at the Google Bus: How Growth Became the Enemy of Prosperity* (New York: Portfolio/Penguin, 2016), 68.

20. Chris Gaither, "Google Aspires beyond Text Ads," *Los Angeles Times*, April 25, 2005.

21. Auletta, *Googled*, 91.

22. Saul Hansell, "Google to Sell Type of Ad It Once Shunned," *New York Times*, May 13, 2004, https://www.nytimes.com.

23. Stefanie Olsen, "Dot-Coms Paring Down Ad Spending Ahead of Holidays," CNET, January 2, 2002, http://news.cnet.com.

24. David C. Churbuck, "Google and the Rebirth of Banner Ads," Bloomberg. com, April 27, 2007, https://www.bloomberg.com; "DoubleClick, Inc. 2000 Annual Report," 10-K (DoubleClick Inc., 2000), 4; "DoubleClick, Inc. 2001 Annual Report," 10-K (DoubleClick Inc., 2001), ii; "DoubleClick, Inc. 2002 Annual Report," 10-K (DoubleClick Inc., 2002), iv.

25. Auletta, *Googled*, 174.

26. Eric Auchard, "Google to Pay $3.1 bln for DoubleClick Ad Business," Reuters, April 13, 2007, https://www.reuters.com.

27. Auletta, *Googled*, 174.

28. Churbuck, "Google and the Rebirth of Banner Ads."

29. "2006 Founders' Letter," Alphabet Investor Relations, https://abc.xyz/investor/founders-letters/2006/.

30. Chris Isidore, "Microsoft Buys AQuantive for $6 Billion," CNN Money, May 18, 2007, https://money.cnn.com.

31. Eric Schmidt, "We've Officially Acquired DoubleClick," Official Google Blog, March 11, 2008, https://googleblog.blogspot.com.

32. Susan Wojcicki, "Making Ads More Interesting," Official Google Blog, March 11, 2009, https://googleblog.blogspot.com. Google's rollout of behavioral advertising was an abrupt turnaround. As late as July 2007, Wojcicki told a reporter that Google was averse to collecting data for behavioral ads. See Eric Auchard, "Google Wary of Behavioral Targeting in Online Ads," Reuters, July 31, 2007, https://www.reuters.com.

33. "Google, Inc. 2009 Annual Report," 10-K (Google Inc., 2009), 6.

34. "Google, Inc. 2009 Annual Report," 6.

35. Charlie Warzel and Ash Ngu, "Google's 4,000-Word Privacy Policy Is a Secret History of the Internet," *New York Times,* July 10, 2019, https://www.nytimes.com.

36. Mat Honan, "Google's Broken Promise: The End of 'Don't Be Evil,'" Gizmodo, January 24, 2012, https://gizmodo.com.

37. Schwartz, "Giving Web a Memory Cost Its Users Privacy."

38. J. R. Raphael, "Google's Behavioral Ad Targeting: How to Reclaim Control," *PC World,* March 11, 2009, https://www.pcworld.com.

39. Wojcicki, "Making Ads More Interesting."

40. Stacey Lynn Schulman, "Hyperlinks and Marketing Insight," in *The Hyperlinked Society,* ed. Joseph Turow and Lokman Tsui (Ann Arbor: University of Michigan Press, 2011), 145.

41. Yasha Levine, *Surveillance Valley: The Rise of the Military-Digital Complex* (New York: Public Affairs, 2018).

42. "Six Months of Revelations on the NSA," *Washington Post,* December 24, 2013, https://www.washingtonpost.com.

43. Timothy Libert, "Exposing the Invisible Web: An Analysis of Third-Party HTTP Requests on 1 Million Websites," *International Journal of Communication* 9 (2015): 18; Julia Angwin, "The Web's New Gold Mine: Your Secrets," *Wall Street Journal,* July 30, 2010, https://www.wsj.com/; "Cross Device Tracking: An FTC Staff Report," United States Federal Trade Commission, January 2017, https://www.ftc.gov.

44. Jennifer Valentino-DeVries et al., "Your Apps Know Where You Were Last Night, and They're Not Keeping It Secret," *New York Times,* December 10, 2018, https://www.nytimes.com.

45. "Stat Oil," *Economist,* February 9, 2013, http://www.economist.com.

46. John Cheney-Lippold, *We Are Data: Algorithms and the Making of Our Digital Selves* (New York: New York University Press, 2017), xiii.

47. Gabriel Weinberg, "What If We All Just Sold Non-creepy Advertising?," *New York Times,* June 19, 2019, https://www.nytimes.com.

48. Weinberg, "What If We All Just Sold Non-creepy Advertising?"

49. "Federal Trade Commission Closes Google/DoubleClick Investigation," Federal Trade Commission, December 20, 2007, https://www.ftc.gov.

50. Mark Zuckerberg, "Facebook, Social Media Privacy, and the Use and Abuse

of Data," § Senate Committee on the Judiciary, Senate Committee on Commerce, Science, and Transportation (2018), 132, https://www.judiciary.senate.gov/meetings/facebook-social-media-privacy-and-the-use-and-abuse-of-data.

51. Weinberg, "What If We All Just Sold Non-creepy Advertising?"

52. Woodrow Hartzog, "Policy Principles for a Federal Data Privacy Framework in the United States," § U.S. Senate Committee on Commerce, Science and Transportation (2019).

53. Hacker and Pierson, *Winner-Take-All Politics*.

54. Much of the current debate hinges upon the GDPR's implementation and whether rules will be enforced by privacy regulators. See Adam Satariano, "Europe's Privacy Law Hasn't Shown Its Teeth, Frustrating Advocates," *New York Times,* April 27, 2020, https://www.nytimes.com.

INDEX

Abacus (data broker), merger with DoubleClick, 87, 102, 113, 125–27, 129, 133, 134

Abernathy, Penelope Muse, 7

Accipter, turnkey ad servers of, 64

Acxiom (data broker), Info-Base Ethnicity System, 104

Adauction, sale of remnants, 99

Adbot, sale of remnants, 99

AdForce (CMGI): ad serving capacity of, 89; CMGI's purchase of, 174n104; partnership with Experian, 102. *See also* CMGI

advertising: brand, 12; mass, 61, 155n76; print, 11, 37, 62; regulatory environment for, 33; ROI problem, 94; spending data on, 81; waste in, 94, 176n5. *See also* digital advertising; internet advertising; marketing; radio advertising; surveillance advertising; television advertising; web advertising

Advertising Age (periodical): on children's advertising, 120–21; on dot-com collapse, 135–36; on FAST Summit, 110; on intellectual property, 111; on interactive media, 34, 36; on Procter & Gamble, 109; on SME ratios, 81; on web advertising, 107

advertising agencies: advertising networks' services to, 96; partnering with ad networks, 107

advertising campaigns: dot-coms', 80; negotiations for, 60–61; proof of effectiveness, 107; speed of execution, 64

advertising industry: in dot-com boom, 80–81; freedom from censorship, 39; funding models of, 36–37, 38; interest in *Framework for Global Electronic Commerce*, 45; in internet commercialization, 39; inventory swapping in, 99; lobbying efforts, 6, 38, 121, 122, 132; opposition to legislation, 131; opposition to regulation, 118–19; outsourcing of sales, 61, 62; reorganization in late twentieth century, 13; response to interactive media, 36–39; self-regulation by, 16, 46–47, 48, 55, 114, 119, 147; strategic communications campaign, 131; subsidization of internet, 38–39; support of commercial mass media, 45; warnings on opt-in framework, 131. *See also* marketing complex

advertising networks: business model of, 57–58, 61; centralized ad serving, 63; centralized surveillance systems, 101; cookie use, 57–58, 67–68; courting of national marketers, 96; data aggregation capacity of, 111; discount, 99;

embrace of platformization, 108; growth of, 64, 75, 83–90; infrastructure of, 61; logistical improvements of, 65; mimicry of broadcasting, 62; nonexclusive contracts of, 99; partnering with ad agencies, 107; platformization of, 100, 101; provision of marketer ROI, 107; as publisher/marketer intermediary, 61, 64, 111; publisher partners of, 100; purchase of competitors, 96; service to ad agencies, 96; site-to-site connections, 67; standardization of practices for, 60–66; supply-to-demand transition, 96; targeting algorithms of, 103; as third-party advertising, 64; tracking technologies of, 57; use of bundling, 62; web publishers' outsourcing to, 63, 64

advertising trade press: on dot-com collapse, 135; on interactive media, 34, 35

Adweek (periodical), on tracking, 112

Alexander, Michelle, 29

Allen, Robert, 33

AltaVista (web portal): CMGI investment in, 90; disclosure practices of, 128; user base of, 85

America Online (AOL), 34–35; banner ads of, 139; on market-driven internet, 51; on private sector interests, 47; subscriber base of, 68

Anderson, Chris, 35

Andreessen, Marc, 31; anticommercialism of, 58; on market share, 77

Andrejevic, Mark, 106

Andrews, Lori, 104

Angwin, Julia, 4

Artzt, Edwin, 37; CASIE leadership, 38; on technological change, 93

asset valuation: dot-coms', 78–79, 110; marketing-based, 79

Association of National Advertisers:

on internet advertising, 95, 107; on privacy activism, 131

AT&T: banner ads of, 59; on *Framework for Global Electronic Commerce*, 47

Atari company, failure of, 25, 158n22

Aufderheide, Patricia, 49

Auletta, Ken, 139

Bain Capital, investment in DoubleClick, 89

banner advertisements: consumer avoidance of, 65; cookies in, 67; dot-coms' use of, 82; enhancements for, 65; hyperlinked, 59; measurement of value for, 60; as measure of advertising development, 107; mouse click-through for, 60, 65, 94; networked model, 57; return on investment (ROI) from, 93–94, 100; sale of, 61; standardization of, 62; static, 59; traditional marketers on, 93–94

Beausejour, Denis, 109–10

Bennett, Colin, 115, 117

Berners-Lee, Tim: on consumer manipulation, 3; goals for World Wide Web, 7; on P3P technology, 119

Bezos, Jeff, 31, 92

BPA Interactive, audit data from, 101

Brenner, Robert, 12

Brewster's Millions (film), 86

Brin, Sergey, 138, 141

British army, Facebook recruitment campaign, 6

broadcasting: advertising networks' mimicry of, 62; versus internet advertising, 95. *See also* radio; television

broadcasting, commercial: advertising-supported, 9; federal regulation of, 8–9

broadcasting, public: licensing of, 8–9

Brown, Wendy, 24

Burnett, Leo, 45, 46

Bush, George H. W.: internet policy of, 26

Bush Administration (George W.),
   internet policy during, 133
Business Week: on Google/DoubleClick
   merger, 141; on internet investing, 91

Cambridge Analytica, 4; data harvesting
   scandal, 2
capital, risk: in dot-com bubble, 76,
   82–84, 96; DoubleClick's use of, 83–84,
   88, 91; through IPOs, 78; in technology development, 88
capitalism: assimilation of internet into,
   18; coercive power of, 109; digital
   transformation of, 8; expansion of,
   51; influence on internet, 12; political
   economy of, 18; sites of expansion,
   17; social division and, 106; social
   needs in, 10; surveillance, 10, 155n66
capitalism, global: neoliberal, 55; surveillance advertising in, 17
Carpenter, Candice, 91
Carter, Jimmy, 29
Cassidy, John, 83
Catlett, Jason, 128
Cato Institute, on civil liberties, 46
CD-ROMs, advertising on, 35
Center for Democracy and Technology
   (CDT), 115; campaign against
   DoubleClick, 127; on *Framework for
   Global Electronic Commerce,* 47
Center for Media Education (CME),
   115–16; on *Framework for Global
   Electronic Commerce,* 48; Kids.com
   complaint, 116, 117, 120; *Web of
   Deception,* 116–17
Center for Media Legislation, lobbying of
   Magaziner, 46
Chester, Jeff, 115, 116
children: data collection from, 116, 117,
   120–22; privacy activism for, 121–22,
   132
Children's Online Privacy Protection Act
   (COPPA, 1998), 122, 132

Clark, Jim, 80, 95–96
class rule, instrumental power of, 52–54
Clinton, Bill: conservatism of, 29;
   DLC chairmanship, 26; economic
   roundtable (1992), 32–33; market
   orientation of, 26; on private sector
   leadership, 31; reelection of, 31; as
   reformer, 27; on tech sector support,
   31
Clinton administration: bipartisanship
   during, 30; Council of Economic
   Advisors, 28; Information Infrastructure Task Force of, 19; on information
   superhighway, 22–26, 49; internet
   advertising and, 34, 41, 45, 69–70;
   internet commercialization during,
   41, 52, 134; internet policy of, 14,
   22–34, 41–42, 52; laissez-faire internet
   agenda, 14, 23–26; marketing trade
   groups and, 114; negative policy of,
   55, 73; neoliberalism of, 24, 32, 42, 52;
   policy agenda of, 43; privacy issues
   and, 34, 41, 45–46, 129; private sector
   development during, 113–14, 119;
   public/private partnerships during,
   31; relationship with tech sector,
   27, 31–32; response to economic
   stagnation, 52–53; self-regulation
   policy, 46–47, 55, 121, 125; support
   for children's privacy, 121; tax hike on
   wealthy, 29; on transnational capitalism, 42; use of P3P technology, 119
CMGI: acquisitions of, 87–88, 90,
   174n104; AdKnowledge service,
   101; AdSmart network of, 88–89, 90;
   audience aggregator investment, 85;
   competitors of, 85, 86; expansion of
   capacity, 88–89; following dot-com
   collapse, 135, 141; fundraising by,
   91; interlocking subsidiaries of, 85;
   investment in AltaVista, 90; investment portfolio of, 85–86; market
   capitalizations, 86; money-losing

operations, 91; online advertising revenues, 90; public relations of, 86; risk capital use, 83, 84, 91; speculative investments of, 91; staff of, 88; strategic partnerships of, 86; unprofitability of, 90, 91; valuation of, 86, 87–88. *See also* Engage Technologies

Coalition for Advertising Supported Information and Entertainment (CASIE), 38, 60

commerce, electronic, 28; moratorium on taxation for, 51

Commerce Department, U.S.: data oversight negotiations, 125

commercialization, versus privatization, 26–27. *See also* internet commercialization

commodification: expansion of, 106; of information, 13, 17, 106; of interactive media, 42

communications: antidemocratic policy in, 49; insincere, 6; political economy of, 11

Communications Decency Act (1996), 180n18

communications revolution, effect on privacy, 19–20

compensation, CEO-to-worker ratio, 53

CompuServe (online service), 34–35

computers, personal: as gateways to interactive media, 58; limited power of, 58–59

Computer Systems Policy Project (CSPP), 32

Congress, U.S.: laissez-faire policies of, 133; online privacy investigations, 120, 129–30, 132

consumer data: ease of compiling, 20; European Union regulation of, 147; harvesting for, 55; marketers' control over, 37–38; networked, 20; online/off-line merger of, 112, 113, 126–28, 133, 134, 144–45; private sector, 19;

storage for, 112; threat to civil liberties, 46; transfer of, 143

consumer data collection, 4; affirmative consent for, 130; capture and exchange of, 17, 97, 112, 141; choices in, 21; contractual model of, 21; discursive capture of, 54; by DoubleClick, 68, 115, 98, 112, 129; Facebook's, 17; Google's, 17; infrastructure of, 4, 21; integration into ad delivery, 67; lack of regulation for, 9; manipulation of behavior, 3, 5, 10; from mobile devices, 145; NTIA on, 20–21, 46; opt-in, 16, 70, 114, 130, 143; opting out of, 114, 116, 125, 130, 132; partnerships among brokers, 101; without permission, 66–67, 113; private sector, 46; for targeted advertising, 57, 68, 95; transaction information in, 102; unification with ad delivery, 101. *See also* cookies, HTTP; surveillance, internet

consumer empowerment, 46; self-regulation and, 47

consumerism, global, 12

consumer profiles, 5; behavioral data in, 102–6, 126, 141–44, 186n32; on commercial internet, 20; discriminatory, 104–5, 111; ethnic data in, 104; generation of commercial messages, 104; integration of off-line information into, 112, 113, 126–28, 133, 134, 144–45; lack of precision in, 109; merger with ad serving, 89; passive collection of, 101–2; social opportunities and, 104; technical anonymity of, 126; unique IDs for, 102

consumers: classification of, 102–6; free market protection for, 70; grouping of, 103; information gathering on, 12; low value, 105; manipulation through data collection, 3; personalized ads for, 65; privacy decisions of, 21–22;

profiles of, 5; sale of access to, 11; social worth of, 102–6; web's recognition of, 65–66

consumer surveillance: abstention from, 106; awareness of, 112; centralization of, 144; costs and benefits of, 134; default status for, 113, 114, 115, 143; ease of participation in, 108; Google's use of, 4, 16, 139, 140, 142–44; improved technologies for, 73; increasing scale of, 133; legalization of, 114; in mainstream advertising, 13; markets' fostering of, 54; maximized returns for, 111; monetization of, 1; normalization of, 2, 134; private sector control over, 146; for ROI, 110; social costs of, 104, 105, 111; unchecked, 114. *See also* surveillance

cookies, HTTP, 67–69; in advertising networks, 57–58, 67–68; in banner ads, 67; in building user profiles, 67; default, 115; disabling of, 69–73; DoubleClick's use of, 67, 68; flexibility of, 67; hidden, 115; identification of browsers, 66; IETF review of, 69–72; infrastructural, 72; integration into communication protocols, 73; Internet Advertising Bureau's endorsement of, 66–67; media coverage of, 116; native deployment of, 73; normalization of surveillance, 73; privacy issues concerning, 69–73; public awareness of, 115; revised standards for, 69–71; user consent for, 69. *See also* consumer data collection; tracking technologies

Crain's New York Business, on Double-Click, 68

customer relationships, data analysis for, 94–95

DART (Dynamic Advertising, Reporting, and Targeting) system, 68

data, expansion of aggregation, 103. *See also* consumer data

data collection, children's, 116, 117, 120–22; parental consent for, 122

De Forest, Lee: on radio advertising, 161n100

Deloitte & Touche, on commercial internet, 33

Democratic Leadership Council (DLC), neoliberal platform of, 25

Democratic Party: communications sector donations to, 30; election meddling strategies, 3; free market ideology of, 29; internet agenda of, 22–26; neoliberalism of, 25–26, 29, 30–31, 133; New Deal, 25; technological orientation of, 22–26; working-class base of, 25

Democrats, Atari: internet agenda of, 24–25; successors to, 26

Democrats, New: on commercial technology, 30; compliance with instrumental power, 52; conservatism of, 29; information superhighway of, 22–26; internet policy under, 30; Old Republicans and, 30; politics of growth, 53; on public–private partnerships, 48; on role of government, 50; technology sector's support for, 30–32

Department of Commerce, privacy working group of, 55

deregulation: government supported, 51; for information superhighway, 33–34; of telecommunications, 28–29

digital advertising: in disinformation operations, 4; effectiveness of, 153n38; effect on democratic society, 1; erosion of autonomy, 1, 70; in global economy, 10–11; internet surveillance surge in, 113; microtargets of, 3; psychological profiles in, 4; technologies of, 1. *See also* internet advertising; web advertising digital enclosures: restraints on, 146; surveillance advertising as, 106

digital networks: influence capacities of, 2; techlash against, 2–4. *See also* advertising networks; social media

digital sublime, myth of, 82

Direct Marketing Association: on consumer empowerment, 46; privacy policies of, 125

Disney company, children's privacy work, 121

Doctorow, Cory, 5

Doerr, John, 30–31, 86

dot-com bubble, 16; advertising industry during, 80–81; collapse of, 75, 95–96, 129, 135, 143; competitive pressures of, 111; domination of U.S. economy, 132; investor losses in, 91; new economy discourse of, 82; political legacy of, 146; profit versus growth in, 83; risk capital in, 76, 82–84, 96; sociotechnical systems of, 145; surveillance advertising in, 15, 73, 75–76, 78, 92, 98, 113; unprofitability of, 90–92; volatility of, 95–96; Wall Street's driving of, 92; web advertising during, 107, 108–9

dot-coms: advertising by, 78, 80, 81; asset valuation for, 78–79, 110; data storage needs, 112; follow-on stock offerings, 77; funding of marketing communications, 81; "get big fast" strategy of, 76, 96; IPOs for, 76, 80, 81, 83; market capitalization of, 84–85, 86; media publicity for, 80; mimicry of Microsoft, 97; number of start-ups, 170n9; profitability standards of, 79; public relations of, 78–79, 80; SME ratios of, 81; television advertising, 81; use of banner ads, 82; use of marketing communications, 79; VC investment in, 76–77, 79–80

DoubleClick (firm): accountability of partners, 128; acquisitions of, 87–88, 90; ad sale representation, 63; ad serving / consumer profiling merger, 89, 129; advertising network model of, 98; banner ad sales, 61, 63, 107; behavioral profiling by, 103, 126; behind-the-scenes presence of, 128–29; Boomerang application, 100; business model of, 143; as business-to-business company, 137; capitalization of, 75; civil suits against, 133; client roster of, 98, 99; "Closed Loop Marketing Solutions," 100; competitors, 85, 86; cookie use, 67, 68, 72; on cooperative business practices, 110; customer base of, 87; DART technology of, 68, 98–99, 100; data collection by, 68, 115, 98, 112, 129; in Direct Marketing Association, 127; downsizing of, 140; exclusive partnerships of, 98; expansion of capacity, 88; external advisory board, 131; following dot-com collapse, 135, 137; follow-up ads of, 100; FTC complaint against, 127, 133; fundraising by, 91; Google's acquisition of, 16, 111, 140–42; growth of, 64, 75, 83; identifiable information of, 128; international operations of, 88, 89; invisible tracking codes of, 101; IPO of, 84, 88, 91, 125; linking of online/off-line data, 128, 133; link to web browsers, 67, 168n46; market capitalizations, 86; market power of, 68, 98; market share of, 85; merger with Abacus, 87, 102, 113, 125–27, 129, 133, 134; merger with IAN, 63; mimicry of broadcasting, 62; money-losing operations, 91–92; negative publicity for, 127–28; NetGravity subsidiary of, 87, 111; Netscape's contract with, 62; notice and choice rhetoric of, 128; OPA membership, 127; opt-out tool of, 128–29; outsourcing to, 64; political challengers for, 112; post-click functionality of, 100–101; pricing structure of, 98, 138; privacy activists on, 126; privacy officer of, 131; private financing of, 84; profile database of, 68; protoplatformization of, 97–98, 111; public complaints to, 128; public relations efforts, 127–28; public relations of, 73, 84, 86; publishers' network, 68; remarketing application, 100; removal from stock market, 138; reorganization of, 97; rivals of, 71; sale of surveillance advertising, 108; SEC filings, 91; server architecture investment, 88; service to web publishers, 97; speculative investment in, 83, 92; stand-alone services of, 99; stock-based transactions of, 87; strategic partnerships of, 86; surveillance advertising of, 15, 16, 108, 136–37, 140–41; suspension of data merging, 129; unprofitability of, 90–91; use of risk capital, 83–84, 88, 91; web browsing data collection, 115

Draper, Nora A., 182n47

Duck Duck Go, contextual advertising of, 145–46

economy, global: digital advertising in, 10–11

economy, U.S.: dot-coms' dominance in, 132; effect of informational practices on, 170n15; industrial, 12; "long downturn" of, 12–13; mass production in, 12; "new," 82–83; recession of 1990s, 14

Edgar Online (website), 6

Eisenhower, Dwight: interstate highway system of, 23

Electronic Data Systems, on *Framework for Global Electronic Commerce*, 48

Electronic Privacy Bill of Rights Act (1999, proposed), 183n84

Electronic Privacy Information Center (EPIC), 54, 115, 116; complaint against DoubleClick, 128

Engage Technologies (CMGI): client roster of, 99; consumer databases of, 90; consumer interest profiles of, 103–4, 112; on cookie privacy issues, 71; creation of, 85; innovation for marketers, 98; international operations of, 89; Next-Generation Profiling service, 104; Real-Time Visitor Intelligent service, 99. *See also* CMGI

E-Stamp (retailer), IPO of, 80

European Union, Data Protection Directives, 121, 125, 147, 187n54

Experian, partnership with AdForce (CMGI), 102

Facebook: advertising spending of, 6; data collection by, 17; exploitation of vulnerabilities, 5; growth of, 140; "likes," 5; non-user profiles of, 5; platform monopoly of, 96; public relations crisis of, 2–3; socially destructive aspects of, 7–8; surveillance networks of, 4; techlash management, 146; Trump campaign's use of, 2–3

Fair Information Practices, 21; of *Framework for Global Electronic Commerce*, 45; FTC recommendations, 130; in marketing, 47; notice and choice in, 128, 147

FAST alliance, 110; ad-buying power of, 96. *See also* Future of Advertising Stakeholders (FAST) Summit

Fast Company, web hosting by, 63

Federal Radio Commission, 8–9

Federal Trade Commission (FTC), 146; adjudication of privacy disputes, 117–18; authority over privacy violations, 132; charges against GeoCities, 120; complaint against DoubleClick, 127, 133; on consumer surveillance, 108; European data protection and, 121; fair information recommendations, 130; on internet advertising, 22; online privacy study, 120; privacy complaints to, 115, 117; privacy workshops of, 117–19; support for privacy legislation, 129; support for self-regulation, 119; on web privacy, 69

Flichy, Patrice, 82

FlyCast (media buying platform), 174n89; ad serving capacity of, 89; auctioning of advertising inventory, 99; CMGI's purchase of, 174n104

Forbes, on cookies, 68

Foroohar, Rana, 3

Fortune magazine, on dot-com advertising, 83

Fortune 1000 companies, lack of diversity in, 54

Fourth Amendment, search and seizure restrictions of, 117

Framework for Global Electronic Commerce (Clinton administration, 1997), 14, 28, 41–55; access to policy making in, 53; advertising interests in, 45; antidemocratic policy-making for, 47–52; civil interests on, 47–48; corporate input into, 43–44; drafting of, 42–47; fair information practices of, 45; final version of, 55; free market policies of, 42; global capitalism in, 55; instrumental power in, 52–55; intellectual property interests in, 44; market-led approach of, 47; multinationals input for, 44; neoliberalism of, 41–42, 50, 55; policy formation processes, 53–54; privacy issues in, 45–46; private sector comments on, 47; private sector dominance in, 46, 48, 51–52, 119; public/private sector roles in, 43, 47–48, 51; public release of, 48; structural imperatives of, 52–55; technology CEOs on, 48–49; trade association input, 44

Freedman, Des, 55

From, Al, 25

Future of Advertising Stakeholders

(FAST) Summit (Cincinnati, 1998), 93, 94, 95, 109; ad industry representation at, 96; cooperation following, 110. *See also* FAST alliance

Gandy, Oscar, 105; *The Panoptic Sort,* 102–3

Garfield, Bob, 18

Gates, Bill: on *Framework for Global Electronic Commerce,* 48–49

Geismer, Lily, 25

gender, in access to policy making, 53, 54

General Foods, children's privacy concerns of, 117

GeoCities network, 85; FTC charges against, 120

geofencing, mobile: antiabortion groups' use of, 6

Ghosh, Dipyan, 4

Gillespie, Tarleton, 72

Gingrich, Newt, 30; technology policy of, 32

Gizmodo, on Google surveillance, 142

Gmail, personal information gathering from, 142

Goldberg Moser O'Neill (ad agency), dot-com clients of, 80–81

Goldfarb, Brent, 76

Goldman, Janlori, 116

Google: acquisition of DoubleClick, 16, 111, 140–42; acquisition of YouTube, 139, 140; Adsense program of, 139, 141; advertising spending of, 6; behavior profiling initiative of, 143–44, 186n32; collection/exchange of consumer data, 17, 141; competitors of, 139, 141; consumer surveillance by, 4, 16, 139, 140, 142–44; contextual search advertising by, 137–38; cost-per-click pricing, 138, 184n10; default advertising service of, 142; "Don't be evil" objective, 138, 143; "growth trap" for, 139; interest-based advertising service, 141–42; IPO of, 137, 138; lobbying by, 6; market leadership, 140–41; platform monopoly of, 96; privacy policies of, 142; profitability of, 138; search engine of, 136, 137; supply/demand side clients, 140; techlash management, 146; universal user tracking, 142; use of keyword searches, 137; user base of, 136; web advertising leadership, 138

Google Maps, personal information gathering from, 142

Google Plus social network, 142

Gore, Al, 19; advocacy of public internet, 32–33; as Atari Democrat, 24; information technology advocacy, 22; neoliberalism of, 25; as reformer, 27; support for deregulation, 33–34; on universal internet service, 39

GoTo.com (search engine), 184n10; paid search advertising model, 136

Greenstein, Shane, 27

Greylock Partners, investment in Double-Click, 89

Grove, Andy, 48–49

Hacker, Jacob, 25

Hardy, Jonathan, 12

Harvey, David, 24

HealthExtra, IPO of, 80

Herbold, Robert, 39

Hesmondhalgh, David, 32

Hollings, Fritz: Consumer Privacy Protection Act proposal, 130

Holt, Jennifer, 24; on antidemocratic policy, 49

Hoofnagle, Chris, 118, 132

Horowitz, David, 28

incarceration, in U.S., 29

influence peddling, data-driven, 4

information: commodification of, 13, 17, 106, 146; fair practices of, 21; free flow of, 20; global infrastructure for, 42–43; media control over, 5

information, networked: early failures in, 34–35

Information Infrastructure Task Force (IITF), 19–20; on consumer surveillance, 54; on data collection, 20–21; privacy issues in, 46; privatization/commercialization policy of, 27–28

information superhighway: ad-free, 39; Clinton administration on, 22–26, 49; deregulation for, 33–34; economic/cultural opportunities in, 23; lack of understanding about, 38; non-profit threats to, 33

information technology: in Clinton campaign (1992), 22; social benefits of, 23

Information Technology Industry Council: on *Framework for Global Electronic Commerce*, 47; lobbying by, 31–32

intellectual property, sharing of, 111

Interactive Advertising Network (IAN), merger with DoubleClick, 63

internet: advertising industry's subsidization of, 38–39; broadband diffusion of, 139; capitalism's influence on, 12, 18; democratic accountability for, 147; free market orthodoxy for, 52, 86; indecent content on, 32; market-oriented approach to, 28; mergers in, 86; political foundations of, 10; popularity of, 109; private sector development of, 9, 23, 113–14; public–private partnerships in, 14, 24; socialism of, 58; speculative investment in, 77, 83, 91, 92; universal, 39; VC investment in, 76–77. *See also* World Wide Web

internet, public: business opposition to, 33; noncommercial, 17, 109

internet advertising: ad exchanges in, 143; versus broadcasting, 95; Clinton administration and, 34, 41,

45, 69–70; closed-loop, 100, 110; contextual, 145–46; cost per thousand ad impressions (CPM), 94; critical mass in, 89–90; delivery services for, 15; denialist rhetoric of, 118, 120, 130; dot-coms', 78; early demand for, 75; FAST Summit on, 93; following dot-com collapse, 135–36; formative movements of, 17; government inaction on, 21–22; increases in capacity, 88; investment capital in, 75; IPOs of, 89; logistical solutions of, 15; market discipline in, 138–45; marketers' expectations for, 95; versus mass marketing, 95; mergers in, 141; micro-targeting in, 89; opposition to regulation, 118–19; percentage of U.S. spending, 81; performance-based pricing, 94; privacy policies of, 133; regulatory environment for, 33, 113; remnant auction market, 99–100; speculative investment in, 75, 83, 95; technical capacity for, 57; traditional marketers' use of, 82; venture capital in, 15; video, 139; web funding and, 70

Internet Advertising Bureau, endorsement of cookies, 66–67

Internet Archive, Wayback Machine, 104

internet commercialization, 1, 26–28, 34; advertising industry in, 39; capital investment in, 24; during Clinton administration, 41, 52, 134; competition in, 27–28; consumer profiling in, 20; instrumental power in, 53; market-based data collection in, 145; neoliberal ideology of, 53, 54, 55, 115; NII on, 26; politics of, 39; private sector control of, 23

internet development: advertising industry in, 36; business models of, 15; exclusion of civil society from, 14; industry/government partnership in, 42; marketing complex's influence

on, 60; neoliberal capitalism and, 55; power in, 51; private-sector, 113–14; public funding for, 33

Internet Engineering Task Force (IETF): cookie review of, 69–72; deliberative process of, 71; mailing list of, 169n63; "social engineering" complaints against, 70; on user privacy, 70

internet policy: antidemocratic, 14, 47–52; business influence in, 33; Clinton administration's, 26–34; corporate interests in, 42; discursive capture of, 54; federal, 19–22; neoliberal, 53, 54, 55, 115, 147; under New Democrats, 30; of 1990s, 19–22; third way, 26–34

interstate highway system, 23

IP addresses, user analysis using, 66

I/PRO (ad metrics company), information gathering by, 66

Jackson, Jesse, 26

Jim Crow, "new," 29

Jobs, Steve, 31

journalism: evisceration of, 7; revenue crisis of, 1

Junk Busters (advocacy group), 128

J. Walter Thompson Company, sale of ad space, 62

Kamp, John, 39

Katzenberg, Jeffrey, 59

Kelly, Kevin, 82

Kesan, Jay, 71

keyword searches, 136, 138, 185n18; Google's use of, 137

Kids.com, CME complaint against, 116, 117, 120

Kim, Young Mie, 3

Kirsch, David, 76

Klein, Naomi: *No Logo*, 17

Kleiner Perkins Caufield & Byers (venture capital firm), investment in Netscape, 76–77

Kristol, David: cookie development specifications, 69–70, 72

land enclosure, in transition to capitalism, 106
Leonsis, Ted, 58
Lepore, Jill, 30
Levin, Gerald, 36
Levine, Yasha, 144
LinkExchange, small-traffic websites of, 99
Lycos (search portal), 85

Madison Avenue, ad industry of, 59
Magaziner, Ira: on capitalist expansion, 51; citizen correspondence to, 50; draft of *Framework for Global Electronic Commerce,* 41–55; engagement with corporations, 43; interaction with civil organizations, 43; lobbying of, 44–45, 46, 47; on opt-out lobbying, 132; on release of *Framework* draft, 49
magazines, market segmentation in, 12
Malone, John, 36
marketers: ad agency proxies of, 96; advertising problems facing, 37; branding by, 95; control over consumer information, 37–38; direct consumer engagement, 65; First Amendment rights of, 118; increased web advertising, 107; interest in interactive media, 45; online data collection by, 92; political mobilization of, 38; privacy officers of, 131; use of remarketing, 100–101; on web shortcomings, 109. *See also* marketing complex
marketers, traditional: on banner ads, 93–94; use of internet advertising, 82
marketing: brand, 12; contested processes of, 156n80; customer relationships, 13; fair information practices in, 47; feedback loop with finance, 75; in industrial economy,

12; sales-to-marketing (SME) ratio, 81; trade groups, 16, 70, 114. *See also* advertising; internet advertising
marketing, mass: and dissolution of mass audience, 105; versus internet advertising, 95; origins of, 12
marketing complex, 10–11; advertising funding model, 59, 134; anti-regulation lobbying, 122; competition within, 11; copyright protection for, 51; defeat of opt-in measures, 132; discriminatory profiling by, 105; at FAST summit, 93; federal support for, 13, 14; generation of consumption, 106; influence on internet development, 60; interactive media and, 34–35, 38; on internet utility, 110; lobbying efforts, 131; mass production in, 12; media changes and, 13; media lobbying campaign, 38; neutralization of privacy activism, 134; online advertising norms for, 57; political mobilization of, 59, 71; private sector institutions of, 11; public relations efforts, 131; reorganization of, 13; self-regulating, 51, 114, 122; shaping of public policy, 114; shared internet surveillance by, 97. *See also* advertising industry
marketing research, consumer information in, 20
markets: fostering of consumer surveillance, 54; multi-sided, 96; neoliberal mechanisms of, 50–51; self-regulation of, 47; supply and demand sides of, 98
Markoff, John, 23
MatchLogic, profile cache of, 112
May, Thornton, 131
McCain, John: internet privacy bill of, 130
McChesney, Robert, 6; on antidemocratic policy, 49; on government regulation, 28
McNamee, Roger, 9; "A Brief History of How Your Privacy Was Stolen," 8

media: advertising-funded, 51; anti-democratic policy in, 49; autonomy of, 13; free market orthodoxy for, 52; market imperatives of, 156n80; role in stock market, 78; state policy on, 8–10

media, interactive: access through personal computers, 58; advertiser–audience relationship in, 35; advertising industry's response to, 36–39; advertising trade press on, 34, 35; commodification of, 42; consumer control of, 35; consumer persuasion in, 35–36; global audience of, 45; household ads in, 35; marketers' interest in, 45; marketing complex and, 34–35, 38; as opportunity, 34–39; print publishers' use of, 59; as threat, 34–39; user tracking in, 58; web browsers in, 58

MediaMetrix (online ratings service), 101

MediaWeek, on web advertising, 61

metadata, user analysis using, 66

Microsoft: acquisition of aQuantive, 141; control of ad market, 71; in-house ad service of, 68; platform monopoly of, 97; "privacy wizard" tool, 125; product ubiquity of, 77; search engine of, 139; software design decisions, 71

mobile devices, location data from, 145

Montgomery, Kathryn, 115; on children's internet privacy, 121; on COPPA, 122; on FTC, 118

Montulli, Lou, 71; cookie development specifications, 69–70, 72

Morgan Stanley (firm), on dot-com economy, 79, 80

Mosco, Vincent, 82

mouse click-throughs, for banner advertisements, 60, 65, 94

NAFTA, neoliberal agenda of, 52

"nanny state," 51

Napoli, Phillip, 103

National Economic Council, on privacy regulation, 55

National Information Infrastructure (NII), 19–20, 35; advisory council for, 31; on internet commercialization, 26

National Information Infrastructure: Agenda for Action (IITF, 1993), 27–28; on role of government, 51

National PTA, children's privacy work of, 121

National Security Agency, mass surveillance by, 144

National Telecommunications and Information Administration (NTIA): on consumer surveillance, 54; on data collection, 20–21, 46; on privacy protection, 21; telecommunications hearings (1995), 164n35; universal service hearing, 39

neoliberalism, 13; antidemocratic policies of, 14; of Clinton administration, 24, 32, 42, 52; of Democratic Party, 25–26, 29, 30–31, 133; of *Framework for Global Electronic Commerce*, 41–42, 50, 55; of internet commercialization, 53; in internet policy, 53, 54, 55, 115, 147; market mechanisms of, 50–51; political economy of, 51; state/private sector relationships of, 42

Neptune Capital Management, 83

NetGravity: DoubleClick's acquisition of, 87; integrated services of, 111; turnkey ad servers of, 64

NetRatings (online ratings service), 101

Netscape: contract with DoubleClick, 62; control of ad market, 71; cookie use, 69, 71–72; financial market successes, 78; *Frontline* on, 77; "get big fast" strategy of, 76–77; IPO of, 77, 79, 80; media acumen of, 80; Navigator graphical browser, 58, 71–72, 76–77; software design decisions, 71; VC investment in, 76–77; web browser market, 77

networking, computer: consumer information in, 20; free market approaches to, 29; of 1990s, 23. *See also* advertising networks; digital networks

Networking Advertising Initiative, 125

Network World, on cookies, 66

newspapers, decline of, 6–7

New York City, "Silicon Alley" district, 84, 89

New York Times: on banner ads, 94; DoubleClick advertising in, 128; in-house ad service of, 68; on online privacy, 130

Ngu, Ash, 142

Niesen, Molly, 131

Nisenholtz, Martin, 36, 95

O'Connor, Kevin, 68; on banner advertising, 107–8; on data merging, 129; on market share, 85; on micro-targeting, 89; on privacy, 126; on public relations, 84, 86; on reintermediation, 97; on stand-alone services, 99

Ohmann, Richard, 62

Online Privacy Alliance (OPA): member list, 122–25; privacy disclosures of, 125; self-regulation efforts of, 132

online services, computer-based, 34–35; anticommercialization mythos of, 58; web browser functionality in, 58

Open Profiling Standard (OPS), user consent in, 119

Oracle (systems provider): on data storage, 112; on *Framework for Global Electronic Commerce*, 47

Page, Larry, 138, 141

Palihapitiya, Chamath, 7–8

"PayPal mafia," 8

Perlstein, Rick, 29

Perot, Ross, 48

personal information: commercialized, 21; private sector use of, 20. *See also* consumer profiles

personality traits, data prediction of, 5

Pickard, Victor, 7, 54

Pierson, Paul, 25

Pitofsky, Robert, 118; on self-regulation, 129

Platform for Privacy Preferences (P3P), user consent in, 119

platformization: advertising networks', 100, 101, 108; centralized monitoring in, 108; in surveillance advertising, 16. *See also* protoplatformization

platform monopolies, 97, 111, 143; Google's, 96

political economy: of communications, 11–12; of surveillance advertising, 10

Pope, Daniel, 12, 155n76

Postman, Neil, 10

power, accountability for, 1

power, instrumental: of class rule, 52–54; in *Framework for Global Electronic Commerce*, 52–55; in internet commercialization, 53; New Democrats and, 52; of private sector, 42

print advertising in, 11, 37, 62

print publishers, use of interactive media, 59

privacy: broad legislation on, 122; U.S. policy on, 117

privacy, online: advocacy network for, 115, 117, 180n7; asymmetrical loss of, 106; Clinton administration and, 34, 41, 45–46, 129; congressional investigation of, 120, 129–30; cookie issues concerning, 69–73; developers' opposition to, 69–73; discursive capture of, 54; effect of communications revolution on, 19–20; erosion of, 1, 4; federal agency for (proposed), 54–55; Federal Trade Commission on, 69, 120, 133; *Framework for Global*

Electronic Commerce's treatment of, 45–46; fundamental right to, 146; jurisdiction over, 117; laissez-faire approach to, 9; legally enforceable rights to, 116; legislation for, 129–30; market-based controls of, 22, 125, 182n47; negative policy approach to, 55, 73, 114, 133; notice and choice paradigm of, 128, 147; NTIA on, 22; opt-in/opt-out measures for, 130; politicization of, 114–19; private sector defeat of, 114; public awareness of, 115, 129; public debates over, 16, 114; risks on commercial internet, 20; self-regulation guidelines, 118; social goods of, 20; universal regulatory framework for, 54; web configurations of, 58

privacy activism, 9; for children, 121–22; on DoubleClick, 126; failures of, 134; fight against business enterprise, 132–33; marketing complex's neutralization of, 134; marketing lobbyists and, 113; opposition to data mergers, 126; partnership with children's welfare groups, 121; pleas to shareholders, 126; successes of, 133

PrivacyChoices.org, 128

private sector: consumer data collection, 19, 46; control of internet commercialization, 23; control over consumer surveillance, 146; defeat of online privacy, 114; development during Clinton administration, 113–14, 119; development of internet, 9, 23, 113–14; on *Framework for Global Electronic Commerce*, 47; instrumental power of, 42; leadership in surveillance advertising, 14; use of personal information, 20

privatization, versus commercialization, 26–27

Procter & Gamble, online advertising budget of, 109

Prodigy (online service), 34; use of advertising, 58

profiling. *See* consumer profiles

Progressive Policy Institute, 25

protoplatformization, 92, 95–98, 111; digital enclosure in, 106; of Double-Click, 97–98, 111; sociotechnical infrastructure of, 96–97. *See also* platformization

public policy: concerning surveillance advertising, 8–10, 145–47; market-based, 23; marketing complex's shaping of, 114; negative policy, 55, 73. *See also* Clinton administration; Federal Trade Commission

race, in access to policy making, 53

radio, commercial: citizen opposition to, 9

radio advertising, 11, 37; market segmentation in, 12; muting mechanism for, 162n100

Raging Bull (financial information site), 90

Reagan, Ronald: supply-side tax cuts of, 23

RealMedia, ad serving capacity of, 89

redlining, 104–5

Republican revolution (1994), 29–30

resignation, culture of, 182n47

ROI (return on investment): ad networks' services for, 107; consumer surveillance for, 110; enhanced, 96; from internet advertising, 93–94, 100; internet shortcomings concerning, 109

Rorty, James: *Our Master's Voice*, 11

Rotenberg, Marc, 54, 114

Rushkoff, Douglas, 10, 139

Russia, election manipulation by, 3

Ryan, Kevin, 84, 90; on transaction information, 102

Sand Hill Road (Silicon Valley), venture capitalist enclave of, 83

Sandvig, Christian, 72

San Jose Mercury News, on cookies, 116

Schaut, Paul, 109

Schiller, Dan, 13, 109

Schiller, Herbert, 51

Schmidt, Eric, 162n3; input into *Framework for Global Electronic Commerce,* 44

Schneider, Jerrold, 24

Schneier, Bruce, 4

Schulman, Stacy Lynn, 144

Scott, Ben, 4

Secure Online Communications Enforcement Act (2000, proposed), 183n84

Shah, Rajiv, 71, 72

Shen, David, 61

Shepherd, Tamara, 105

Shiller, Robert, 78

Silicon Valley: Clinton's meetings with, 30–31; moral failures of, 8, 9–10; ownership class of, 1; scandals of, 2

Simon, Leslie David, 30, 31; on CSPP, 32

Sinclair, John, 11

Smythe, Dallas, 45

Snowden, Edward, 144

social forces: in capitalism, 10, 106; policy produced by, 53

social media: influence peddling in, 4; targeted ads of, 140; techlash against, 3; user-created profiles in, 139–40. *See also* Facebook

Software Publishers' Association, on information superhighway, 49

Srnicek, Nick, 96

Starr, Paul, 8, 30

Stiglitz, Joseph, 26; on *Framework for Global Electronic Commerce,* 44; on New Democrats, 30; on telecommunication deregulation, 28–29

stock market: dot-com transactions in, 77, 87; DoubleClick's removal from, 138; news media's role in, 78. *See also* capital, risk

Stole, Inger, 131

surveillance, internet: anonymous, 168n46; as integral feature, 72–73; interactive spaces of, 106; shared, 97; third-party, 70; unaccountable, 147; as web default, 113

surveillance, mass: by National Security Agency, 144; targeted persuasion in, 17

surveillance advertising: barriers to, 108; business models of, 3, 4–7, 71; capital accumulation in, 10; civil society challenges to, 115; construction of, 15–16; continuity in, 145; cooperative, 110; creators of, 2; DART software for, 68; to desirable customers, 105; as digital enclosure, 106; in dot-com bubble, 15, 73, 75–76, 78, 92, 98, 113; DoubleClick's, 15, 16, 108, 136–37, 140–41; economic roots of, 2; effect on marginalized communities, 6; exploitation of emotions, 5; first generation of, 16, 55; in global capitalism, 4, 17; improved technologies for, 73; intersecting forces of, 1; legal foundations of, 146; versus legitimate advertising, 70; lobbying by, 6; market forces propelling, 111; measures of development for, 107; origin story of, 1–2; outgrowths of, 4; persuasive power of, 5; platformization in, 16; political economy of, 10–14; political roots of, 2, 7–10, 57; pressure to implement, 144; private sector leadership of, 14; public policy concerning, 8–10, 145–47; public scrutiny of, 129; receding market shares in, 138; regulatory foundations for, 9; rhetoric of precision, 109; social relations of, 102–6; sociotechnical infrastructure for, 16; speculative investment in, 75; structures of privilege in, 105. *See also* advertising; consumer data; internet advertising

TBWA/Chiat/Day agency, dot-com clients of, 80

techlash: against digital networks, 2–4; executives' accounts of, 7–8; against social media, 3

Technology for America's Economic Growth, 26

technology sector: effect of private regulation on, 119; lobbying by, 31; manipulation models of, 8; outpacing of government regulation, 29; political involvement of, 7–10, 25, 30; public opinion on, 2; regulation for, 7–10; relationship with Clinton administration, 27, 31–32; support for New Democrats, 30–32; surveillance models of, 8

Telecommunications Act of 1996, 32, 86

telecommunications industry: deregulation of, 28–29; free market orthodoxy for, 52; lack of competition in, 21; NTIA hearings on (1995), 164n35; political contributions from, 30; reform of, 28

teletext, 34

television, cable, 79

television, interactive (iTV), 21, 35, 109; Time Warner in, 36

television advertising, 13; consumer aversion to, 37; dot-coms', 81; networks' inventory of, 62; online video and, 139

Thiel, Peter, 8

Thrift, Nigel, 79

Time Warner Cable, investment in interactive television, 36

tracking technologies: of advertising networks, 57; DoubleClick's, 101; Google's, 142; necessity for web advertising, 70. *See also* cookies, HTTP; surveillance, internet

trade associations: on Clinton administration, 49; comments on *Framework for Global Electronic Commerce,* 44–45; lobbying of, 16, 48–49, 114,

119, 122–25; on privacy, 119, 122–25, 131

Trump campaign (2016), use of Facebook, 2–3

TRUSTe (privacy seal program), 119

Turow, Joseph, 14; on advertising audience, 35; on consumer profiling, 103, 104; on customer relationships, 94; on internet privacy, 133, 182n47; on web advertisers, 60

24/7 Media: ad serving capacity of, 89; profile cache of, 112

USA Today, on DoubleClick, 127

ValueClick: ad serving capacity of, 89; DoubleClick's stake in, 87, 174n104

Varner, Christine, 132

Veblen, Thorstein, 12

venture capital firms (VCs): advertising expenditures of, 83; dot-com investment, 76–77, 79–80, 83; doubling of, 170n9; influence of, 83

videotext, 34

Violent Crime Control and Law Enforcement Act (1994), 29

Wall Street, driving of internet commerce, 92

Wall Street Journal: on advertising relationships, 108; on CMGI, 85; on dot-coms, 83; on DoubleClick-Abacus merger, 126–27; on internet privacy, 130; on online consumer recognition, 66

Wanamaker, John, 94

Warzel, Charlie, 142

Washington Post: on DoubleClick, 127; on television advertising, 37, 38

web advertising: commitment of resources to, 59–60; cultural barriers to, 58; distribution in, 61; during dot-com bubble, 107, 108–9; early adopters of, 59; economies of scale in,

62; first three years, 57; Google's leadership in, 138; guessing in, 60; interactive media dominance, 93; keyword searching in, 136, 138; loop between consumer actions and, 101; necessity of tracking for, 70; outsourcing to ad networks, 63, 64; personalization in, 65; post-click analysis of, 100–101; purchasing space for, 60; "rich media" experiences of, 65; standardization of, 60; targeted, 3, 17, 57, 68, 89, 95, 100, 137, 138; technological limitations of, 58–59. *See also* internet advertising; World Wide Web

weblining, discrimination in, 104–5

web publishers: communication channels of, 101; online advertising auctions for, 99–100; outsourced ad services to, 97; partnerships of, 98, 100, 108; as terminals of surveillance, 111–12

WebRep (firm), banner ad sales, 61

web technology: amalgamated elements comprising, 63; anonymity in, 7; communication protocols of, 58, 63, 65

Weinberg, Gabriel, 147; contextual advertising model of, 145–46

Wetherell, David, 85, 86

White House Council of Economic Advisors, lobbying of, 44

White House Office of Management and Budget, privacy working group, 55

Williams, Raymond, 10

Wirth, Tim, 24

Wojcicki, Susan, 141–42; on behavior profiling initiative, 143–44

Wolff, Michael, 91

World Wide Web: advertising trade press on, 35; anonymous browsing of, 65; business priorities in, 11; commercial monitoring in, 2; goals of, 7; history of, 166n2; low bandwidth problems, 65; marketing complex and, 13; open protocols of, 58; third-party surveillance on, 70; user recognition capacity, 65–66. *See also* internet; web advertising; web technology

Yahoo: search engine of, 139; use of NetGravity system, 64

YouTube, Google's acquisition of, 139, 140

Zuboff, Shoshanna, 5, 8; on surveillance capitalism, 10, 155n66

Zuckerberg, Mark, 140; congressional testimony of, 3; on regulation, 146–47; wealth of, 7

Zuckerman, Ethan, 82

Zucman, Gabriel, 53

MATTHEW CRAIN is assistant professor of media and communication at Miami University.